PRACTICAL
GUIDELINE
FOR
THE TEACHING
OF
PHYSICAL
EDUCATION

PRACTICAL
GUIDELINE
FOR
THE TEACHING
OF
PHYSICAL
EDUCATION

GERALD S. INSLEY, *Southern Oregon College*

ADDISON-WESLEY PUBLISHING COMPANY
Reading, Massachusetts
Menlo Park, California
London · Don Mills, Ontario

This book is in the
Addison-Wesley Series in Physical Education

Photographs courtesy of Mr. David L. Otto and Mr. William Bayley

To My Family, Harvey, and "Sig"

PREFACE

The purpose of this book is to provide prospective physical educators with basic guidelines and teaching methods that will enable them to function as vital and integral components of both the school and social communities in which they work. The material should lend itself to use within special teaching "Methods" classes, "Student Teaching Seminars," and as an adjunct to "Introduction" and "Principles" courses.

This text represents the culmination of ideas gleaned from formal training, colleagues, observed situations, and past years of teaching experience in the public schools and higher education. Each chapter deals with a particular phase of teaching believed to be critical to the complete function of the physical educator. Physical education occupies a unique position in the school community, but it also has a definite relationship to its fellow subject matter disciplines. Therefore, this material is intended to provide the reader with guidelines which will enable him to better integrate himself into the *complete* institutional function.

Having supervised student teachers for some time, we find that many are searching for information that would extend beyond the technical skills and provide direction in areas that had not previously been discussed to any degree in the available texts. With this thought in mind I turned to my collection of notes, which had been used as a point of departure in certain professional classes, and from these notes this book evolved. My purpose was to disclose various positive and negative educational practices and to offer suggestions that, hopefully, might inspire future physical educators to develop programs that will relegate various undesirable procedures and practices to obsolescence.

South Oregon College   G.S.I.
September, 1972

INTRODUCTION

On entering the teaching profession many beginners believe themselves to be fully qualified to embark on a course of successful pedagogy that is bound to startle the educational world with its efficiency and facility to impart knowledge. It is frequently discovered that there are many facets of the teaching process and school environment that can be gained only through experience. Some teaching methods and principles are successful and others seem to be ineffective and of doubtful value. After schools in several states and at various levels were observed, it was found that students have changed their attitudes and desires considerably; far more rapidly than the education system itself. Youngsters are asking questions and seeking answers as never before in the history of education. Surely similar questions lurked in the minds of students of the past, but they dared not query those in authority. We, in the field of physical education, have possessed many of the answers to these questions for years but have often neglected to effectively demonstrate to our students the relevancy of our offerings to their basic life patterns and needs. Until we as a profession, and as individual teachers, implement a more thorough and meaningful curriculum for our students at *all* levels, we will be looked upon by some with criticism and suspicion.

Those whom we teach today represent the voters and school board members of tomorrow whether we readily accept that fact or not. If funds are to be allocated to physical education in the amounts necessary for the promotion of satisfactory programs, the public must be convinced of the inherent values of the subject. Therefore, a satisfied student customer is the best advertising we can get. Similarly, if students are continually exposed to a meaningless core of irrelevant activity and the drill of many present programs, they will not in later years support that which to them has become "just another gym class."

It is my fervent hope that the professional students who study this text will profit from the readings and be better able to grasp the true meaning of learning *through* physical education. The material has been written in a manner believed to be direct and representative of experience in both public schools and institutions of higher learning. The examples and case studies cited are the result of observations of actual instances derived from personal background as well as from experiences of many friends and associates.

The prospective teacher will find some of the material controversial, perhaps even shocking. It is not our intention to have this text serve as a philosophical "cure-all." We have to provide some basic methods and guidelines whereby a neophyte teacher can more effectively function. It would indeed be gratifying if future teachers would not only use these guidelines, but improve upon them over the years and provide a much broader interest in physical education and athletics.

CONTENTS

xiv   Contents

1
PLANNING
FOR
INSTRUCTION

PLANNING OR PITFALLS

At the conclusion of each chapter in this text the reader will find a number of case studies related to the material discussed. Some of the case studies reflect errors in human judgment while others show evidence of a lack of planning and the decision-making process. The reader will also discover that answers to certain questions which accompany each chapter and/or the case studies will necessitate additional discussion and research. The intent of these questions is to provoke thought and possible alternatives to the problems presented.

THE FUNCTION OF PLANNING

Plans are frequently divided into two categories: single-use plans which are for short-term purposes, and long-range plans which are expected to be used for a protracted period of time. Architectural plans would be a classic example of single-use plans, which once utilized would probably not be used again. Long-range plans would be those related to such things as campus development, curriculum, or other functions which operate on a continuum. They are usually accompanied by policy statements and functional guidelines which assist in the determination of direction, continuity and consistency. Both types of plans should result from carefully made decisions and the only major difference being that of duration.

In the planning of buildings, curriculum, special events, or any other aspect of the physical education program, any and all who are affected by the deliberations should be involved at some stage of this function. Such involvement may be either direct or indirect, but those charged with overseeing the planning should ensure that all parties concerned have had a part in the procedures.

Planning is a time-consuming process and as such cannot readily be confined to the school day. The deliberations over the construction of new facilities, curriculum revision, athletic programs and similar difficult tasks will frequently have to be done after school hours or on weekends. A teacher who believes that he can readily adhere to an eight-to-four, five-day-a-week schedule and adequately fulfill professional responsibilities is sadly mistaken. In fact such an individual is guilty of poor planning in choosing his life's work and should have researched the teaching field prior to entering a college teacher training program.

The true purpose of planning is to promote purposeful and consistent action so that the program runs as smoothly as possible with the least amount of interference with the educational process. No plan is better than those who develop it. Furthermore, a plan is only as good as its underlying assumptions or objectives. If the assumptions and objectives are correct the plan will be beneficial, if the assumptions and objectives are incorrect, the plan will be of little value.

PLANNING AND THE DECISION-MAKING PROCESS

Plans are the result of human thought processes. As the case studies illustrate, some of the thought processes represented were based upon logical and rational premises and others were not. Plans are the result of decisions made either independently or collectively. Therefore the decision-making process should entail a systematic approach. One of the most widely used systems is described as follows:

1. Define or diagnose the problem.
2. Develop one or more possible solutions to the problem.
3. Project and determine the consequences of each possible solution to the problem.
4. Evaluate the consequences in light of which would be the most favorable.
5. Select and implement the proper course of action.

When one is assessing a problem, it is analogous to the physician making a diagnosis. The physician has discovered that problems are usually indicated by certain symptoms. He also realizes that the symptoms may be treated, and perhaps even eliminated, but the problem will persist. For example, a patient may have recurring headaches which are only symptomatic of a more serious malady. The doctor would prescribe medicine to relieve the symptoms but then would run a series of various tests to discover the specific nature of the underlying ailment. He might discover that his patient's difficulty was basically psychological; he was tense and suffered certain anxieties. For such problems the physician could conceivably prescribe a mild tranquilizer or he might refer the patient for psychiatric help. On the other hand, the tests might reveal a brain tumor which would, of course, demand a completely different type of treatment. From this discussion it has become apparent that when *only* the symptoms are treated the problem persists; in order to effect a permanent change the problem or *major obstacle* must be removed.

In the development of alternative solutions to problems, certain obstacles may arise that render the alternative useless. For example, the proposed remodeling of an existing structure may cost more than its replacement. To redesign certain aspects of a curriculum might entail additional staff members which are not available either because of budgetary considerations or uniqueness of the activity and lack of specifically trained personnel. Therefore, many alternatives may have to be considered prior to the selection of the one best approach. Before any idea is discarded, however, it should be thoroughly investigated. Unfortunately many innovative ideas have been discarded in the past without such scrutiny. When alternative solutions are to be selected, it is often wise to "brainstorm" the problem. This involves the contributing of any idea that comes to mind, regardless of how "far out" it may sound. Then all ideas are evaluated and the most plausible are placed under close scrutiny and evaluated for possible adoption.

Decisions that affect any aspect of the physical education program must be made within certain boundaries. Some decisions may be made by the individual teacher and others must be made at the departmental level. Still other decisions must be made by those to whom authority is granted to perform specific tasks such as policy making. If major policy is involved, the matter is usually the concern of the school board. Decisions made by individual teachers are limited by policy and guidelines. These limitations could also apply to decisions made by groups such as departments, which are involved in collective decision-making. Such limitations, for the sake of convenience, could be categorized as policy boundaries.

In addition to policy boundaries other factors may well affect the choice of solution to a problem. Items such as budget, staff training, facilities, interest, student need, public opinion or demand, religious considerations, weather, student socioeconomic background, community politics, and a multitude of other considerations must be taken into account in deliberations concerning problems related to the conduct of a viable physical education program. *No selected course* of action will satisfy *all* of the demands placed upon it. However, the *best* course of action selected is usually the one that, to the greatest extent, meets the criterion against which it is measured.

The final selection of any solution to a problem should always be based upon the assimilation of every known fact, and yet this procedure still does not eliminate all chance of error. The most that can be expected is to reduce the chance of a *serious* error to a minimum. Even after a decision is made, the decision makers must realize that they might have been wrong and that another alternative might have to be selected. No one can accurately measure the success of any decision until it has actually been tested under operating conditions.

PLANNING AND THE PROSPECTIVE TEACHER

learn die
Job

The beginning teacher usually has had virtually no practical experience in planning and decision-making. Students need such experiences if they are to assume their rightful role on entering the teaching profession. Some college students involve themselves in student government and related activities on the nation's campuses, but the vast majority does not find the time for such endeavors due to work schedules, heavy class loads and/or extracurricular activities that are basically directed by others.

One of the frequent criticisms by public school teachers who supervise student teachers is that the supervisee is not able to plan properly. Teacher-training institutions are becoming more aware of this weakness and many are providing experiences for the students to assist in making decisions. Such programs, however, must provide opportunities that entail meaningful decisions and planning, not just cursory suggestions. In this manner, true leadership ability could be discovered early in the student's college career.

Student professional organizations such as physical education majors' clubs, lettermen's clubs, women's recreation associations, and similar enterprizes should be encouraged. It has even been suggested that active participation in such organizations should be mandatory for those who wish to enter the profession as physical educators. If such organizations are to provide practical training in planning and decision-making, a large amount of their work should be done by committees, and the advisor and the officers of the club should ensure an opportunity for all members to participate.

Class projects which involve planning are sometimes used by professors to stimulate student planning. Some professors have even used student steering committees to coordinate class efforts and have, themselves, served in a capacity similar to that of "chairman of the board." Some classes lend themselves to such structure and others do not. Obviously the teacher of such a class must retain control but he can delegate certain aspects of the planning to subordinate committees. Preparing college classes of this kind is very demanding, and considerable effort must be made to coordinate all aspects of the course; it is not merely a matter of "letting every group or committee do its own thing."

Students need field experiences, which involve planning, in public education, prior to student teaching. Teacher's aid programs, student coaching, assignments, administrative aid services, and observational periods should expose the prospective physical educator to direct and indirect involvement in the planning process. All education majors should have the opportunity to observe faculty and school board meetings. These experiences should be compulsory for student teachers and could be arranged for other students through cooperating school districts. Obviously such observations could not take place when administrators or school boards were meeting in executive session to discuss personnel; however, all other school board business is a matter of public record and should be conducted in open sessions, as with city council deliberations. Inasmuch as it would be impossible for most school board meeting rooms to accommodate all of the interested observers, it would be more practical for student observers to visit planning commissions, city councils, county commission meetings, and other similar gatherings. Planning should involve the same procedures whether the planning agency is a school board, a county commission, or the executive board of a corporate enterprise. The subject matter will, of course, vary but the decision-making process should involve the same procedures and principles. Prior to attending various community meetings, students should learn what to look for and how to systematize their observations so that they can later objectively evaluate the procedures they have seen in terms of good and bad practices. This can be done by establishing observational guidelines before the actual visitations are made.

Theoretical situations, such as the case studies in this text, may well serve as points of departure in stimulating students to analyze problems and make decisions. After reading about either positive or negative aspects of teaching and related activities, students should be encouraged to evaluate them and propose plans that would lead to more favorable solutions and meaningful alternatives.

All prospective educators should be exposed either formally or informally to group dynamics. Most teacher-training programs are flexible enough to allow a student to elect a course in group dynamics, and there are enough activities on campus that involve the use of the skills learned in such a course to enable the student to practice and sharpen such skills.

PLANNING AND THE BEGINNING TEACHER

After the graduate has accepted a teaching contract he should immediately begin to plan for the coming year. New teachers should visit the district office and request such items as faculty handbooks, curriculum guides, unit plans, lesson plans, department policy handbooks, and any other pertinent procedural materials. These materials should be carefully read and questions related to them should be asked as early as possible. Such preplanning can assist the new teacher in avoiding many embarrassing moments which could conceivably occur due to his ignorance of policy and/or procedures.

On entering a new school in the fall, a beginning teacher should not hesitate to consult with fellow faculty members whenever the need arises. Moreover, it is always wise to keep one's eyes and ears open, remain amenable to suggestion, and not attempt to reform the entire system of operations even though it is apparent that reform is desirable and perhaps even necessary. The neophyte teacher must realize that his *ideas* will not be readily accepted until *he himself* has been accepted. Many brilliant suggestions have never been implemented simply because they have been "pushed" at the wrong time and often by freshman instructors or administrators.

In faculty or department meetings wherein the decision-making process is used, the beginning teacher should not hesitate to make contributions to the discussion but he should restrain himself until he has something of value to contribute. If the new teacher has ideas that he has gleaned from other districts in which he has worked as a student teacher, he should *never* refer to "the way we did it at Holton Tech." This error is probably committed by transfer teachers to a greater degree than by beginning teachers; nevertheless, it is a poor practice and tends to alienate the contributor from fellow faculty members who are proud of what has been accomplished within their own district.

STANDARD OPERATING PROCEDURE

Standard operating procedure is procedure that is generally prescribed by school or district policy. Such procedure relates to methods of taking attendance, cleaning and maintenance schedules, record keeping, transportation, excuses, dress codes, disciplinary channels, library usage, student governance, faculty duty hours, lunch programs, and many other functions that are a part of the daily operation of the schools. Standard procedures should be reviewed periodically to determine whether or not better methods could be used to expedite the functions for which the procedures were intended. Unfortunately many school districts find that they have been operating in the same manner for years, and when compared with newer districts which have been more innovative, they discover that their methods of operation are completely outmoded. Therefore, standard operating procedure should include a regularly scheduled review session wherein all procedures become subject to examination and necessary revision.

LESSON AND UNIT PLANS

Lesson and unit plans are designed for specific instructional purposes and should be continually updated and improved. Some teachers fall into the trap of regarding these plans as standard operating procedure and the result is a stagnated program. There are many satisfactory forms that can be used for unit and lesson plans but all should include the following items:

1. Objectives
2. Subject matter content
3. Progression and sequence of the content
4. Teaching methods to be used   *or bog down*
5. Timetable
6. Equipment and facilities

Lesson and unit plans should serve as a blueprint for instruction. The architect of such plans must look upon these plans in much the same fashion as one who is designing a building. He must be able to implement the plan himself and he must design it so that it can be interpreted and implemented by someone other than himself should he become ill or otherwise incapacitated.

Unit and lesson plans should be annotated as they are used so that they are more easily revised during evaluation periods. Files of such plans should be maintained not only by individual teachers but by the principal's office as well. This method of filing can render the administration a valuable service when parents or other interested parties call upon the school to determine what type of instruction is taking place. A dual filing system is also a worthwhile precaution against fire or other similar loss.

New units of instruction as well as new courses need to be planned carefully and should not be mere whims of someone's imagination. Such units need to meet certain criteria such as interest, need, practicality, availability of funds, staff support, administrative support, and time considerations. Planning, to be effective, should not be hasty; additional effort in planning is usually compensated for by greater rewards in both teaching and learning.

SAFETY PLANS

It seems to be a human frailty to ignore safety precautions until there is a catastrophe which focuses attention upon them. Many schools hold fire drills and some post charts indicating the proper flow of traffic during such drills. We find that most school fire drills involve the *same* flow of traffic on each occasion. What would happen if this traffic flow was interrupted by an explosion or a fallen beam? Obviously alternative traffic patterns should be developed and practiced. What about the youngster who is caught in the shower room without clothing during a fire or fire drill? What is he or she supposed to do? Should provision be made so that towels in the drying room could be picked up on the way out of the building? What other alternatives might be suggested? To assume that *all* students in a school building will be properly attired for fire drills or actual fires is a false assumption and false assumptions lead to negative planning. Safety plans, as all other plans, should take into consideration every possible contingency and should therefore be undertaken by all who are concerned in the conduct of the program for which the plan was designed.

PERSONAL PLANNING

All human beings have ambitions to rise professionally, in their social groups, financially, in their community, and in the interest of their own self-esteem. To accomplish these objectives a young teacher should begin to plan early in his career. A general plan can be easily devised and more specific plans designed as one progresses toward an ultimate goal.

Beginning teachers are usually confronted by salary schedules that provide for pay increases based upon years of experience and educational advancement. The educator possessed with a true missionary spirit would probably determine that educational advancement and knowledge were ends in themselves and that salary considerations should be of secondary importance. A professional person should, of course, be altruistic but also practical. It costs money to obtain advanced degrees, but if the graduate training results in better teaching it should be rewarded accordingly. It is true that "man cannot survive on bread alone," but neither can the man's family survive on his professional zeal and personal satisfaction gained through teaching. Husbands, wives, and children of teachers need the goods and services that extra financial remuneration can and should provide.

A teacher should plan his or her professional life so that the most efficient service possible is rendered to the students taught. Such plans demand many decisions, both major and minor. As we will see by the case studies in this text, some people are more perceptive planners than others. Not a day passes without some kind of a plan being formulated as to the conduct of one's affairs. Those who plan well and are diligent in gathering and assessing facts correctly are generally those who succeed. Virtually all successes, which are attributed to luck, are nothing more than the results of positive planning and decision-making. Both financial reward and personal satisfaction are the result of one's ability to organize information and select appropriate actions which culminate in some form of personal or professional achievement.

QUESTIONS FOR DISCUSSION

1. What is systematized decision-making? What factors are involved?
2. What is the proof of a good or bad decision?
3. What are single-use and standing plans? Where do such plans fit into the educational system?
4. Why is it necessary to involve more people in planning than just the chief executive of an organization?
5. Should an administrator or executive ever delegate planning to subordinate committees? Why?
6. In your opinion, to what obligation of time should the teacher be committed for planning?
7. When plans are once formulated how often should they be revised?
8. Do you believe that prospective educators (college students majoring in a discipline) should be required to involve themselves in some phase of the planning process? Why or why not?
9. What practical experiences have you as a student had in planning and decision-making?

SUGGESTED RELATED READING

Cotton, Donald B., *Organizing for Company-Wide Planning.* New York: Macmillan Co., 1970. Concept and process.

Ewing, David W., *The Human Side of Planning.* New York: Macmillan, 1969. Tool or tyrant.

Hagman, Harlan, *Administration of American Public Schools.* New York: McGraw-Hill, 1951.

Newman, William H., *Administrative Action,* 2nd ed. Englewood Cliffs, N.J.: Prentice-Hall, 1963.

2
QUALITIES
NECESSARY TO
GOOD TEACHING

FORMAL TRAINING AND GENERAL EDUCATION

The professional preparation of physical educators varies considerably throughout the United States. Each state has certification standards which must be attained by the college and universities serving that state. In addition, most of the colleges and universities have formulated departmental qualifications which are often more stringent than those demanded by the states. Unfortunately, there is little being done nationally to standardize these professional offerings other than the efforts of accrediting organizations such as the National Council for the Accreditation of Teacher Education (NCATE) and the American Association for Health, Physical Education and Recreation (AAHPER) committee on professional preparation. As a result of the efforts of these groups, the preparation of physical educators is in general better than it was in the past, but still leaves much to be desired in certain institutions.

Any educational process worthy of the name should have as its intended purpose the enlightenment of the student. The student's primary goal should be to identify with his environment and therefore lead a more enjoyable and useful life. For these reasons the first two years of college are usually devoted to "general education." In some colleges the general education curriculum is very prescribed; in others, it is more flexible. In any event, the courses taken during the freshman and sophomore years of college can be extremely valuable to the prospective teacher. If a teacher is conversant in many fields, he will find that he can reach many youngsters through the expedient of catering to their interests. He will also discover that his life is enriched by exploring areas that are not particularly germane to his own discipline. My experience has shown that students are usually attracted to those teachers who are knowledgeable in many subject areas and who are well-adjusted individuals.

In the selection of courses offered by professional education departments, the student is required to take coursework in human growth, principles of teaching, a general course in the American public school system, and related education and psychology offerings. Often the student enrolled in these courses sees little relationship between the course content and his particular field. It is at this point that he should be apprized of the fact that his specialty in physical education is only one of the many courses that his future students must pursue, and that his department will be but an integral part of the entire school operation. It should be further emphasized that only through cooperative enterprise can a school function in a progressive, positive, and dynamic manner.

The physical education teacher needs an adequate understanding of the following areas within his chosen field.:

1. Basic principles underlying the "why" of physical education; and what physical education can offer the student in order to realize his own potential, physiologically, psychologically, and sociologically.

2. The scientific bases of human performance which include anatomy, physiology, kinesiology, physiology of exercise, basic physics, and remedial activities for the exceptional child.

3. A selection of professional activities which is comprehensive enough to encompass those which will be taught in the public schools, and demanding enough so that the prospective teacher will have to demonstrate the competency necessary to teach those activities.

4. The proper methodology to be used in the teaching of motor skills. This preparation should include a thorough understanding of the psychology of motor learning.

Teachers spend all of their professional lives working with human beings—pupils, parents, colleagues, and other interested parties. Therefore, it is wise for the prospective teacher to prepare himself by taking coursework in the behavioral sciences. In America we have a true admixture of culture, yet very few college students enrolled in teacher-training programs, courses in social anthropology, or the sociology of race relations. However, they will be confronted daily with problems of cultural origin.

Physical educators and coaches are involved with laws of physics and their relationship to all aspects of human motion and body mechanics. Principles of leverage, force, friction, and momentum are common to every activity. Many physical education students pale at the thought of electing a physics course. This is because they have not been thoroughly oriented to the relationship between what they will teach and what they will need to adequately prepare themselves through cognate courses, which can be scheduled during the freshman and sophomore years of college.

MUTUAL RESPECT FOR YOUR FELLOWMAN

A college president once stated "all that two people actually owe one another is mutual respect." If a person conducts his affairs at all times according to the tenet of mutual respect, life can be much more satisfying. A school community, operating on a cooperative basis in which all factions are pulling together, is a delightful place to work. However, if the students are disrespectful toward the teachers, and the teachers choose to castigate one another, the morale is low and everyone becomes dissatisfied.

Some years ago an observation was made of a high school which was in a complete state of chaos most of the time. The problem arose from constant bickering between the staff members and the administration and between individual staff members of different departments. It was apparent that the principal was autocratic and respected no one's opinion of anything. In turn, staff members became hostile through frustration and began to fight among themselves. After the school situation had degenerated to an extremely low point, the principal resigned and moved to another community. A new man, of more democratic demeanor, has since occupied the principal's office and the school is currently being operated with the cooperation of all department heads who, in turn, consult with their staff members. The administrative change has resulted in a complete reversal of attitude and the entire climate of the school is one of mutual respect and general enthusiasm.

The teacher, or administrator, who places himself in a position of being above reproach and in no need of counsel from others, is generally his own worst enemy. He will discover his position to be much easier if he will learn to trust and utilize the professional competencies of those around him.

All teachers must demonstrate mutual respect if they hope to instill similar attitudes in their pupils. They must work diligently to ensure that when a student is speaking to the teacher or class, he is extended the courtesy of silence on the part of other students. By the same reasoning, the teacher should insist that when *he* has something to say, attention is paid to his remarks. This type of classroom relationship does not just happen and it is not spontaneous after just one or two instances of explanation. Courtesy, as is the case with *all concomitant learning,* must be constantly stressed until it becomes a conditioned response on the part of those concerned.

THE DEMOCRATIC "TAKE CHARGE MAN"

The industrialist, Andrew Carnegie, maintained that he had surrounded himself with brains and thereby achieved the success for which he was credited. Teachers are usually not consulted in hiring those with whom they wish to work. They can, however, draw upon the talents of their colleagues whenever possible. It must be remembered that the teacher, even though utilizing the thoughts of others, must be in complete control of his classes at all times. He cannot rely upon others to do his teaching, he can only glean ideas from people and then implement them in his own way.

The essence of class control is planning. If the time is properly used and the material presented is interesting, discipline becomes a simple thing. The teacher who is well organized is going to have a much more satisfying and productive experience than is the one who functions on a day-to-day basis, "teaching from the top of his head" with no unit or lesson plan to guide him. Taking charge of a class and pushing through to the conclusion of the class period with no time for questions or consideration for individual problems is sometimes misconstrued as taking over in a dictatorial manner. Youngsters need leadership but they need *understanding leadership.* They need to know that a question will receive an answer, not a cutting criticism. This is not to say that the teacher must be a "buddy" to the students or that he should attempt to "identify" with them as one of their peers. On the contrary, youngsters at present have enough friends; they need leaders who can conscientiously guide them. They *don't* need teachers who try to bridge the so-called generation gap by conducting themselves as teenagers. Many young teachers have fallen into this trap and ultimately discover that familiarity does breed contempt. Seeking to discover the latent interests of students through inquiry, conversation, and observation is to be commended. However, one should confine his social activities to his own group, and the group with whom a teacher should associate socially is *not* the student body. Maintaining the proper social distance can be effected very easily by the diplomatic expedient of not becoming involved in the student's social life in the first place.

Once a teacher has compromised his position by placing himself on the same plane with his students, he risks alienation from the role of leadership. Command is lonely, be it on the battlefield or in the classroom. A line of demarcation exists between officers and men, and also between teachers and students. You cannot lead and follow at the same time. A good democratic leader is one who is attuned to the positive needs of his charges, and in order to determine those needs, the teacher needs the confidence and the respect of his students.

Physical education teachers must set standards and adhere to them without playing favorites. They must do everything in their power to ensure that the students can attain the standards. They do this by *teaching*, not by rolling a ball out and playing with the "kids." Teaching is accomplished by explanation, demonstration, example and

No such thing as generation gap.

precept, questioning and answering questions, not by criticism and snide remarks about poor performance. Teachers further gain the confidence of their students by discovering their interests and trying to relate those interests to the subject matter being presented. Lastly, the democratic leader makes a habit of speaking to his students out of class in order to show that he regards them as individuals and human beings worthy of his respect and consideration in the community as well as in the classroom.

DEDICATION TO PURPOSE AND THE MISSIONARY SPIRIT

A great many people have entered the teaching profession over the years. Most of them have been extremely conscientious and have dedicated their lives to the instruction of others. A few, however, have been primarily interested in receiving a monthly paycheck and couldn't care less whether or not a youngster was actually gaining anything positive from their classroom instruction.

What is the purpose of teaching? A rhetorical question to be sure, but one that many a prospective young teacher should ask himself. To begin with, it would be best to identify some of the terms. Teaching, according to the dictionary, is the imparting of knowledge. Learning implies that the student is acquiring some knowledge. Therefore, the teaching-learning relationship involves the teacher who is instilling knowledge, and the learner who is, hopefully, assimilating knowledge. Thus far we have an easily understood situation, but let us investigate further.

The person who has assumed the role of the teacher must actually be imparting some measurable amount of information or skill, otherwise no learning has taken place. On the other hand, the learner should be gaining knowledge from his class experiences or he is just occupying space and wasting his time. In order to impart knowledge a teacher must actively *work* at it. Initially, well-designed unit and lesson plans must be developed by the teacher. These take time and research to be of any value. Unfortunately, not all teachers take the time to thoroughly prepare an individual lesson, much less a complete unit of instruction. Such indolence indicates a complete lack of dedication to the purposes of teaching. If one is to teach, then one must prepare thoroughly or expect nothing more than absolute minimal results.

At times introspection is necessary to clarify a point. Let us assume that the teacher walks into his doctor's office for his annual physical examination. The doctor gives the usual neurological examination and discovers something wrong. He conducts further tests which disclose a small brain tumor that must be removed, so he recommends a competent neurosurgeon in the community. The patient quite naturally assumes that the surgeon has adequately prepared himself for the operation by reading the X-rays, making sure that the operating room personnel has been duly instructed, all equipment is in order, and the facilities are ready. The same type of analogy might be made in reference to an attorney who is preparing for the defense of a man's life who was wrongly accused of murder. The point is, how many times has a teacher gone into a classroom totally unprepared because of a lack of dedication of purpose, and as a result made a complete farce of the instructional period? How many college professors have used the same unrevised notes for the past twenty-five years because of the lack of preparatory dedication? It would be embarrassing to state how many situations have been observed in which a total lack of preparation has been obvious. The result of such negligence is usually a bored instructor and an equally bored class. No teaching has taken place and, therefore, certainly no learning. Had the aforementioned doctor or lawyer been as negligent in their preparations, the death of the patient or client might well have ensued. The result of negligent teaching is ignorance, and surely that is no crime, or is it?

The truly dedicated teacher, possessed of a missionary spirit, is the individual who can divorce himself from all things save his purpose. From the standpoint of the practicality of daily living, such dedication is impossible for the vast majority of teachers. They simply cannot devote *all* of their waking moments to preparing lessons and marking papers. Time should, however, be budgeted so that no lesson is taught without thorough preparation of class notes, equipment, and facilities.

Many teachers can rationalize their lack of planning simply by stating that they are not being paid for overtime and therefore don't expect to work overtime. The obvious answer to this logic is that they should have entered the profession with their eyes open and with the realization that theirs is not an eight-hour-a-day, forty-hour-a-week job. The average work week for a teacher, who adequately prepares his lessons and corrects assignments, would probably be about sixty or more hours, dependent upon his subject discipline.

In order to better acquaint prospective teachers with the realities of the teaching profession, an intern program during at least one entire year of the college training program is highly desirable. Such a program would give the student greater insight into such matters as planning, committee work, grading and evaluation, and the extracurricular calendar that consumes so much of the working teacher's time. This type of program has been implemented in certain colleges and universities and has been very successful. As a substitute for an intern program, many colleges are utilizing field experiences in which the students are assigned to a master teacher and are given exposure to those duties that are specifically related to the "after-school-hours" program. In some instances, those students who are reluctant to undertake these additional duties have withdrawn from the teacher-training program after being exposed to the unseen work of the teaching profession.

The missionary zeal in teaching is something that demands the *second effort.* The teacher occupies a position that does not allow him to give up when confronted by problems. He cannot, in clear conscience, dismiss the slow learner or the recalcitrant with a wave of the hand and then assume that perhaps, later on, the youngster will master fundamental skills by himself. For that matter, the teacher cannot spend his time working with only the highly skilled student. A teacher who relegates the slow learner to the sideline is only succeeding in driving the student from those things which he needs most. Teaching is not easy; it is not glamorous; it is not a highly paid profession; it is difficult but challenging work that requires long hours and derives its greatest satisfaction from seeing students become interested and improve upon the skills being taught.

HONESTY AND INTEGRITY

A high school English teacher often paraphased to her students a passage from Shakespeare: "To thine ownself be true, and as the night must follow the day, thou cannot be false to any man." This expression was usually forthcoming prior to an examination or to the writing of a theme which was assigned as homework. Any teacher reflecting upon those words would do well to follow the example. That particular English teacher returned papers meticulously corrected and none of her pupils objected to homework assignments because they knew that their work was being read and they would profit from the critical analysis of their papers. Care was taken in class to explain why certain mistakes had been made and why those same mistakes, if consistently repeated, could cause embarrassment in the future. Although it was not realized by her students at the time, their teacher was a person of true professional honesty and integrity. However, she was respected for her efforts and the students looked to her for guidance in matters of grammar, sentence structure, and literature.

On analyzing the performance of exceptional teachers, one soon discovers that they have one single factor in common—professional honesty. Some are liked by students and others are disliked, but in most cases, they are respected.

Certain individuals exhibit quite a personal facade and make a grand showing in professional meetings, committee work, and at social gatherings, but neglect their classroom obligations and therefore violate the trust placed in them as teachers. For example, one such individual was highly regarded by many of his associates in the state professional association. He held various offices in many educational organizations and yet joked about "working" three months during the summer and spending the remainder of the year on "winter vacation." This man has since left the teaching profession and probably should never have entered it initially.

Pupils of both elementary and high school age have little difficulty in discerning who is, and who isn't, doing a thorough job of teaching. Moreover, they don't hesitate to advertise that fact to both parents and classmates. Professional integrity does not go unnoticed by the students even though they may never mention it to you personally.

Honesty and integrity extend beyond the classroom into such areas as budget making, community relationships, personnel matters, job seeking, and other facets of personal and professional life. Teaching is not the type of endeavor one leaves behind when he closes his room and goes home in the evening. As a teacher, one must project his profession into all aspects of his community life.

ADAPTABILITY AND A SENSE OF HUMOR

Learning psychologists have found that people learn more rapidly when placed in pleasant surroundings. It is also believed that attention span varies considerably among individual pupils. Therefore, the proper school environment is of paramount importance if children are to profit from their class experiences.

Adaptability has many ramifications for the physical education teacher. He must learn to readily adjust to schedule changes prompted by everything from weather and illness to spontaneous assemblies and other extraneous forces that disrupt his best laid plans. If he is to survive these sometimes frustrating experiences, the teacher must first develop a philosophy that allows him to be flexible in his thinking. He most assuredly should realize that his offerings are important, but he must also realize that the experiences the pupil receives under his tutelage are only a *part* of the total educational endeavor. To this end, the teacher needs a variety of tools with which to work. He needs alternative lesson plans to accommodate such things as inclement weather or lack of facilities. Further he must learn to cooperate with other school departments and agencies in order to ensure as much continuity and as little disruption as possible. He must also realize that he is not being singled out as a target for persecution each time his class is inconvenienced.

Quite often the physical educator finds himself teaching in a gymnasium which is designed as a multipurpose facility. This facility may serve as a combination gymnasium and auditorium, and it may even function as a lunch room during the noon hour. Ideally, the multipurpose facility is not recommended by authorities in the field of physical education. However, for reasons of economy, many such facilities have been constructed. Teachers of the performing arts are just as handicapped by having to use these facilities as are physical educators. These rooms are not usually acoustically treated, and all of the seating is on the same plane and therefore undesirable. Thus, the sharing of facilities, even though frequently done, places a joint hardship upon all parties concerned.

When programs are scheduled in the gymnasium, alternative lesson plans are necessary, and preplanning is a must. The need to adapt to the situation can usually be foreseen by conscientious cooperation with the administration and other interested departments. It must always be remembered that school policy on such matters is the overriding factor in the utilization of facilities, and physical education facilities are not the exclusive province of the department alone.

Most units of instruction lend themselves to the use of alternative lesson plans. Various phases of any activity can be reviewed; audiovisual materials can be presented in lieu of actual practice in the event of inclement weather, and a good teacher can always dwell upon the associated learnings involved with body mechanics and the basic physics inherent in motor skills. Adaptability is something that requires effort and desire on the part of the teacher, but leads to a more satisfactory learning experience on the part of the students if harmonious relationships prevail within the school community.

Tension builds rapidly in class situations. Frequently this tension arises from overconcentration and sometimes from the intense attitude of the instructor. A good teacher senses this tension and will interject some levity in order to relax the class. Such humor might assume the form of a comment on performance (as long as it is not sarcastically directed) or even a tastefully told joke or anecdote related to the lesson being taught. Contrary to the belief of some teachers, humor is not a waste of time. The release from tension or boredom often refreshes the class and stimulates learning. The adage "all work and no play" does contain a certain amount of validity.

Stories have circulated around college campuses for years about the jokes told by certain professors. Many of these jokes are either not funny, or are poorly told. Not everyone has a flair for telling stories and would do better by laughing *with* others rather than trying to provide all of the humor himself.

Sarcasm is mistakenly used by some teachers in the place of humor. They make remarks about a student's efforts that elicit laughter from others in the class and show no regard for the feelings of the youngster toward whom the remarks are directed. Such treatment by a teacher is inexcusable. Before making sarcastic remarks, it would be well to ask yourself whether or not you would appreciate similar treatment. Sarcasm does not endear a teacher to his students and often alienates them completely.

Pupils often make mistakes and are laughed at. Laughing *with* someone is one thing, laughing at someone is quite something else. A good principle to follow is to laugh with the pupil who makes a mistake and then assist him in correcting it. However, if a pupil commits an error and fails to evidence any humor, the teacher should maintain a sober demeanor and proceed with the correction without calling undue attention to the incident. The proper blending of a businesslike approach with a sincere sense of humor and an appreciation of each pupil as an individual, provides a challenging yet pleasant environment in which learning can take place.

The taskmaster who invokes such strict discipline that it instills fear and tension within the students is going to discover that his class gains the reputation of a sweatshop rather than a learning experience. Some teachers argue that theirs is a function of teaching, not running a personality contest. In part this is true. Rules and regulations need to be enforced and safety precautions must be observed. However, the teacher who really has his fingers on the "pulse" of his class is one who continually adjusts to the situation and knows the temperament of each individual pupil. He further realizes just how lenient or how strict he must be with each youngster in order to provide the optimum learning experience and thereby elicit the best performance. He must know when to reprimand and when to praise, and above all, he must constantly evaluate the character of the class in general and personalities of each student therein.

QUESTIONS FOR DISCUSSION

1. What are some of the basic understandings necessary for the professional preparation of good teachers of physical education?

2. Of what value is the general education usually provided for the prospective teacher during his first two years of college?
3. What is entailed in mutual respect for one's fellowman? Why is this of importance?
4. Discuss the differences between autocratic and democratic procedure and how these differences affect the school community.
5. How would you contrast the dedicated teacher as opposed to one who is merely interested in job security and a regular paycheck?
6. How does the professional competence in teaching relate to the public trust of the community?
7. Of what importance is a missionary spirit to the teaching profession?
8. Does honesty and integrity, on the part of a teacher, have any effect upon the learning processes of the student? If so, how?
9. Why must the teacher of physical education learn to adapt to variations in schedule and how can he adjust to these adaptations without completely disrupting his instructional units?
10. Why is sarcasm such a nemesis to the teacher?
11. Of what value is a sense of humor in teaching?

CASE STUDIES

Honesty and integrity

HAGER AND JOHANNES

Mr. Hager had been teaching for a number of years and had quite a reputation throughout the state for his diligent efforts on behalf of his state and local professional organizations. He was well liked in the community and in fact had been active in business prior to entering the teaching profession. Parents liked and respected Mr. Hager and the students were well pleased with his classes during his initial teaching years.

As time passed, Mr. Hager became more and more involved in community affairs and his state professional association. As outside interests began to demand more time and effort, Hager's classes were neglected to the point that they were poorly planned and at times even chaotic. Instead of diligently planning lessons, Hager resorted to using motion pictures to the extent that the students came to refer to his classes as the "daily flick session." Examinations were very cursory and frequently were never handed back to the students. Students began to grumble about the quality of Hager's classes and advised others to stay away from them if at all possible when they made out their schedules for the coming year.

During the preparation for a visitation by a regional accrediting committee, teachers were advised that they should not deviate from their normal instructional methods because the accrediting team wished to observe the school and its attendant activities as they were normally carried on. As per instructions, the faculty conducted their classes in regular fashion and paid no undue attention to the observers who came to visit their rooms. Mr. Hager's classes were exemplary in their conduct and the accrediting team awarded him high marks on his teaching proficiency. It was discovered after the evaluating team left that Mr. Hager had rehearsed his classes for three weeks prior to the regional evaluation. Although he was not formally censured by his colleagues, Mr. Hager soon discovered that his image as a teacher suffered greatly in the eyes of his fellow teachers, but even more so in the eyes of his students. When queried by the principal, Mr. Hager insisted that he wanted to make as favorable an impression on the evaluating team as possible so that the school would be placed in a more favorable light; the principal concurred that this was a fine idea.

Mr. Johannes, a second-year teacher of commercial subjects, was employed at the same school as Mr. Hager. Mr. Johannes had been a member of his professional associations and was an avid supporter of various extracurricular student activities. He was rather quiet in his professional dealings and dedicated to the art of teaching. He spent many an hour after school giving individual assistance to students and was very creative in his classroom methodology.

The evaluating team spent their time in Mr. Johannes' class watching him admininster a test which was normally scheduled for that particular time on his curricular calendar and was to be used for review purposes as well as for partial evaluation for the grading period. One of the evaluators seemed a bit upset that Mr. Johannes was not conducting a lesson at the time of the visitation whereupon Mr. Johannes informed him that he was instructed to maintain his normal schedule of instruction and not deviate from his usual procedures.

During the general discussion meetings which followed the evaluation period, the school administration was informed that the investigating team had discovered that there were two teachers on the staff who deserved special consideration ratings. They openly boasted that Mr. Hager's class was without a doubt the finest that they had seen but were highly critical of Mr. Johannes who spent the entire instructional period administering a test; when in fact they had come to see people perform a teaching function. Mr. Johannes was later called into the principal's office and verbally chastised for creating such a disastrous image of the school in general and the commercial department in particular.

QUESTIONS

1. What is your reaction to the behavior of Hager and Johannes in the matter of their deportment during the regional evaluation? Which do you believe to be right and which was wrong? Why?

MORLUND AND SPANNER

Mr. Morlund had been placed in the position of athletic director at his school and immediately launched into a compaign to let everyone in the institution know that he was not only going to conduct the program in a military manner, but that his judgment was infallible.

During the football season a junior varsity team was dispatched to a community 170 miles distant for a game. After traveling approximately 50 miles, the junior varsity coach noticed that they had just been met on the road by a bus from the opponent school which carried some type of identifying insignia. The recognition was apparently mutual because both busses stopped to inquire as to which was going in the wrong direction. It was discovered that Mr. Morlund had misread the game contract when drafting the schedule and had not rechecked prior to dispatching the team for the contest.

After returning from the game, which was played on a neutral field, the coach, dispatched by Morlund, descended upon his athletic director in righteous wrath because of having been sent to play away from his school when in reality he was to play a home game. Morlund stated that the mistake was not his because the principal, Mr. Spanner, had signed the contract. Mr. Spanner maintained that he was not at fault because he assumed everything to be correct on a contract and therefore signed without reading the print above. Both of these gentlemen then retrenched and said that what they actually had discovered, after thinking about it a while, was that they had been right all along but that the coaches who sent the schedule to the printer had somehow mistaken the site of the game. Neither Morlund nor Spanner would admit making an error even though both were guilty.

QUESTIONS

1. What lessons of administration can be drawn from the discussion of the Morlund and Spanner case? What moral principles are involved?
2. What would have been the most direct and honest explanation of the mistake by Morlund and Spanner?

RUMMAGE AND STEVENS

Mr. Rummage had been principal of his school for many years, and before that a fine teacher and counselor. Mr. Stevens, an excellent biology teacher, approached Mr. Rummage one day and stated that one of his students had taken issue with him over a statement read in a pamphlet in his class which alluded to "Biblical Legend." It seemed that the student was the daughter of a fundamentalist family and had always regarded the Bible as absolute truth, not legend. Mr. Stevens said that he had explained to the student that the reference to "Biblical Legend" was a direct quote from a piece of written work and that she was entitled to interpret it in her own way or choose to ignore it entirely. He did not believe that the child was completely satisfied with his explanation and informed Mr. Rummage that he felt that the father of the girl might call on the school and demand a retraction of the statement.

Mr. Rummage received a phone call in the afternoon from the father of the student in Mr. Stevens' class demanding that he be called on the carpet and reprimanded for what had been said. Mr. Rummage calmly informed the irate parent that he would be happy to arrange a meeting between the father and Mr. Stevens so that the difficulty could be resolved and further offered to sit in on the meeting between the two. The father paused for quite a while and then muttered that a meeting was not necessary but that such nonsense should never occur again or he would see to it that Mr. Stevens was fired. Mr. Rummage thanked the father for his time, hung up the phone, and filed a report of the whole incident with the superintendent's office. Prior to filing the report, Mr. Rummage consulted Mr. Stevens in order to clarify any errors in the report and thereby ensure its accuracy. Both Mr. Stevens and Mr. Rummage signed the report as a true and accurate account of the incident and it was filed accordingly, never to arise as an issue again.

QUESTIONS

1. Do you regard Mr. Rummage as a competent administrator after reading his method of handling the Stevens case? Why or why not?
2. To whom did Mr. Rummage owe his allegiance in this case—the teacher, the parent, or the student? Why?

MISS HEFLEY

Miss Hefley had been on the staff of Eldrige High School for approximately fifteen years. She was the senior member of the physical education department and was highly respected by all of the members of the school community.

As department chairman, Miss Hefley was charged with the responsibility for scheduling the facilities for use by both men and women and approached the task in a most democratic manner. At the conclusion of each school year a meeting of all of the physical education staff members was called so that curriculum problems, as well as those of scheduling, could be discussed and resolved.

Miss Hefley usually chaired the department meetings but always observed the accepted techniques of group discussion and subsequent involvement of all personnel. She solicited suggestions from the men and women alike and had become well known for her ability to incorporate the best thinking of all of the teachers in the program. She had initiated situations wherein classes were exchanged between men and women and in which the special interests of each staff member were exploited. For example, units were taught with women teachers instructing the boys in the concepts of various aspects of girl's sports, and the men teachers would instruct the girls in certain aspects of games such as football and baseball—sports in which girls did not participate but evidenced a strong interest from the standpoint of spectators.

Most of the softball classes for both men and women were taught by males; in turn the archery sections for both sexes were instructed by women. Such cooperation within the department led to a mutual understanding of the problems confronting both men and women.

Miss Hefley was well aware of the complexities of scheduling and the conflicts that arise when attempting to schedule facilities for intramurals, class activities, and interscholastic teams. She had an excellent relationship with the athletic director and coaching staff at Eldrige. She encouraged support of the interscholastic teams through rally squad activities as well as through units in spectator sportsmanship that were taught in the physical education classes. In turn, the men became willing to assist with women's intramurals whenever possible and gained a more thorough knowledge of physical education as an integrated rather than a segregated enterprise.

QUESTIONS

1. Do you believe that Miss Hefley was unique as a female administrator? Would you be willing to work for such a person if you were a male staff member?
2. What were Miss Hefley's strengths? How do you suppose she developed these strengths?

MISS McDONALD

Pierce Junior High school was overcrowded to the point that physical education classes were offered only twice a week; even so the facilities were totally inadequate. The only large facility available to both men and women was an old gymnasium which was not large enough to encompass an official basketball court. Adjacent to the gymnasium was a small utility room that was used for tumbling, wrestling, and weight training. Next to this area was the school cafeteria which also served occasionally as a lecture hall for hygiene classes.

Miss McDonald was a very innovative person who had learned to adapt to almost any situation. She believed strongly in recreational games such as shuffleboard and table tennis which were taught in her classes under rather trying conditions. The shuffleboard courts were painted in a hallway outside the gymnasium and the table tennis players were confined to the cafeteria and "multipurpose" room.

Miss McDonald had approached Mr. Foster, the principal, and requested that the school provide her with enough ping-pong tables for adequate instruction. Mr. Foster listened patiently to Miss McDonald and agreed that her justification of the unit was not only valid from the standpoint of class instruction, but that these tables could be used for noon recreation and other similar circumstances. He stated that the budget was rather meager but that perhaps if they were to buy tables, it might be a good idea to get good ones that would last. Miss McDonald agreed that buying a few quality tables each year would be a fine idea and in the meantime she would improvise.

Two folding portable tables were ordered for Miss McDonald and she immediately placed them into service. However, rather than having youngsters wait in turn to play, the cafeteria tables were placed together for interim use. Adapters for the nets were designed by Miss McDonald because two tables placed together produced a wider surface than that used in regulation table tennis.

The table tennis unit was well taught and the instructor did the best job possible under rather extenuating circumstances. It happened that the daughter of one of the school board members was a student in Miss McDonald's class. The young lady enjoyed ping-pong and mentioned to her father that the equipment was not quite regulation in all aspects. The father attended a class and later indicated to Miss McDonald that he would attempt to find some additional funds to assist her in purchasing equipment.

He then consulted with Mr. Foster who told him of the plan of projected deferred purchase that had been discussed. The board member had been so impressed by Miss McDonald's improvised equipment and her attitude of overcoming adversity that he pursued the matter further with the superintendent who then procured the necessary tables.

QUESTIONS

1. How do you perceive Miss McDonald as a teacher? What alternatives did she have in her situation? Do you believe that she gained more by her actions than she would have by making demands for equipment? Why?
2. After reviewing the cases cited, which of the people involved would you rather have as an employer and why?
3. What are the implications of these cases for the area of human relationships?

SUGGESTED RELATED READING

Bucher, Charles A., *Administration of School and College Health and Physical Education Programs*, 4th ed. St. Louis: C. V. Mosby, 1967.

Griffiths, Daniel E., *Human Relations In School Administration*. New York: Appleton-Century-Crofts, 1956.

Knapp, Maude L., and Francis Todd, *Democratic Leadership in Physical Education*. Millbrae, Calif: National Press, 1952.

Snyder, Raymond A., and Harry A. Scott, *Professional Preparation in Health, Physical Education, and Recreation*. New York: McGraw-Hill, 1954.

Voltmer, Edward F., and Arthur A. Esslinger, *The Organization and Administration of Physical Education*, 4th ed. New York: Appleton-Century-Crofts, 1967.

Ziegler, Earle F., *Administration of Physical Education and Athletics*. Englewood Cliffs, N.J.: Prentice-Hall, 1959. The case method approach.

3
STUDENT APATHY
VS. POSITIVE
CONCEPTUAL TEACHING

APATHETIC TEACHERS BREED APATHETIC STUDENTS *Take held*

Lecturing, explaining, and demonstrating are all tools used by the teacher of physical education. How these tools are used will determine the amount of learning that takes place. Anyone can use a hammer, trowel, or paint brush, but only an artisan can succeed in creating a building that is structurally sound as well as aesthetically pleasing to the eye. In order to create such a building, one must know not only *how* to construct and decorate, but *why* various techniques are of greater value than others.

When lecturing to students about various strategems employed in sports and games, or when enlightening a health class, the physical education teacher has two alternatives. He can easily parrot information in hopes that it will be absorbed and later utilized, or he can adequately prepare his lesson and relate the material to allied fields such as physics, psychology, physiology, sociology, and the humanities. Such teaching efforts then effectively illustrate *why* certain precepts are sound and *why* they are necessary to the task prescribed.

The easiest method of imparting lecture material can be accomplished as well by tape recordings as by a teacher. There are no questions raised, no spontaneous analogies drawn, no use of blackboard or other visual aids; in short, no imagination or creativity. Anyone can refer to notes and speak before a group in an articulate but mechanical fashion and then feel complacent in the belief that the students have been duly impressed and have amassed great knowledge. This same teacher is usually gratified by the fact that his students perform well on tests by regurgitating the information which has been previously provided. However, he is often amazed by the student's lack of insight when it comes to applying the same information to actual practice.

A football coach once explained a play and then interjected, "Don't worry about anyone's assignment except your own." He failed to convey that any particular play is a team effort, and that the overall pattern or concept of the team's performance lends importance to the function carried out by each individual player. When a group comes to understand *why* each player must perform in a given manner for a particular play to succeed, the value of each individual as a team member becomes more apparent.

Frequently students who enrolled in physics classes have been asked to memorize Boyle's Law which stated $P_1 V_1 = P_2 V_2$, or that the volumn of any gas is directly proportional to the pressure exerted on it, provided the heat and amount of gas remain constant. A very creative professor, who had taught basic physics for years, reviewed the gas law by illustrating with a balloon. He simply blew up the balloon, squeezed it, and said "the tighter you squeeze, the smaller it gets, and the minute you release your grip, the larger it gets, provided that you don't release air or change its temperature; so much for Boyle's law." Instantly everyone in the class had a clearer picture of how pressure exerted upon a gas affects the volumn of the gas and why. The gas law was therefore understood not only as theory, but also from the standpoint of practicality.

In applying practical principles of explanation to motor skills, a football coach effectively livened up a blocking session by explaining simple laws of force and leverage to his players. After the players were shown why foot and body placement should be a prescribed to effectively move an opponent, the practice session took on new meaning and learning was perceptibly improved. Too often teachers fail to realize that concepts are an absolute necessity if the student is to attain meaningful comprehension of the lesson being presented. The creative teacher asks himself "why is this true?" He then develops an imaginative method of getting the information to the students in a meaningful way. Conversely, the instructor who expects his students to accept his every word on blind faith, and who does not utilize conceptualized instruction, is one who will rapidly gain the reputation of being dull and uninteresting. This, in turn, leads to the student's complete apathy toward the subject matter being presented.

THE UTILIZATION OF ALL THE SENSES

Dewey's tenet of "learning by doing," is an integral part of physical education. No youngster can master a skill without actually performing it. Teachers can lecture, demonstrate, explain, show film loops, and utilize all other methods of instruction, but the skill does not become meaningful until the student experiences it himself.

Visual aids are of definite assistance to the physical educator in that he can stop a film or video tape at any given point in the performance and thoroughly explain the basic body mechanics and aesthetic considerations. Obviously it is impossible to do this while actively engaged in the demonstration of skills such as gymnastic maneuvers. The use of visual aids, accompanied by explanation, utilizes both the visual and auditory senses simultaneously. Also, in a darkened room, extraneous environmental influences are minimal. The visual aids used should be previewed prior to the instructional period so that the teacher can completely coordinate his explanation with the visual material. The instructor should solicit questions as he proceeds with his presentation and should ask *direct* questions at the conclusion of the showing. When accustomed to the method, pupils become less reluctant to ask questions and are kept alert because they know that they are going to be held responsible for the material at the conclusion of the lesson.

After a lesson has been properly introduced, the actual performance by the pupils begins. This portion of the instructional unit should be prefaced by the statement that beginners usually make mistakes and that some will possibly make more errors than others. Any class needs to be placed at ease with the realization that they are not expected to perform perfectly during their initial attempts.

The tactile sense, or sense of touch, develops into more of a general "feeling" in gross motor skills. We define this sense of relationship with our surroundings as kinesthesia. We can all remember when we could not ride a bicycle, but we cannot readily pinpoint the exact moment when we achieved success in the skill. Even though a skilled rider has not ridden a bicycle for a number of years, he can usually mount the vehicle and ride it with little difficulty. He has therefore developed the kinesthetic "sense" for bicycle riding. This "sense" has thus become a part of the individual's relationship with his present environment. Kinesthesia cannot be developed through observation, it must be attained by actual performance which has been correctly learned.

Physical education teachers have discovered that it is much easier to teach a rank beginner than it is to teach a person who has preconceived notions or incorrect skills. The pupil who has learned to perform incorrectly has developed a kinesthetic sense for an erroneous performance, and therefore feels awkward when he is required to change his style and form. He subsequently feels resentful toward his instructor when a change in form results in poorer performance. In skills such as bowling or golf, the transition from incorrect to correct procedure may initially produce poor scores. When this occurs, the pupil should be informed that this is to be expected and that his scores should improve appreciably as his corrected performance improves and becomes more natural.

The sense of touch also directly relates to the selection of equipment. If a pupil is to learn to play badminton, tennis, or squash, he should be provided with a racket that is suited to him. For this reason, grip size and weight should carefully be considered. In the selection of balls, for example, it would make little sense to attempt to teach basketball-shooting skills to fifth grade boys while using collegiate-sized balls. Their hands are too small to properly grip the ball and, therefore, bad habits can easily be developed. The same rationale should be used when building baskets and backboards for elementary schools. All equipment used in physical education classes must be of a size and weight that enables the pupil to execute the basic skills with efficient and mechanically sound style and form. This type of progression in equipment is just as important as is the sequence and progression in curriculum. It is more expensive to supply adequate and suitable equipment for youngsters in physical education classes, but to do otherwise is false economy.

The sense of smell is not ordinarily associated with the actual performance of motor skills, but it could influence general class conduct in the following manner: When locker rooms are dirty and poorly ventilated, the mere idea of dressing and showering in such a malodorous environment is rather unpleasant. Many girls complain of being subjected to such "sweatboxes" and can scarcely be blamed for their belligerent attitude. Clean, pleasant surroundings should be of basic concern in the planning of any facility and program. Newly painted and well-ventilated locker rooms have improved the attitude and conduct of many students in physical education classes. It should also be mentioned that clean uniforms and sanitary conditions enhance the physical education program in the eyes of the public. Any facility, regardless of its size and condition, can be kept clean. Dirty uniforms and poorly maintained facilities tend to advertise lack of planning or control on the part of the teacher.

The physical educator is generally responsible for the cleanliness of a much larger area than is the classroom teacher. He has his instructional areas to consider, but his supervision also extends to the locker rooms, rest rooms, shower areas, and storage facilities. In all of these areas, neatness and attractively decorated clean facilities will have a positive effect upon the students. When a student sees a well-ordered facility, it usually imparts the concept that the teacher himself is well organized and that discipline must be positive in order to maintain things in such a prescribed manner.

In summary, all of our attitudes are directly affected by the various senses, and teachers must remain cognizant of this at all times. One practical key to use in determining whether or not students are positively motivated by their surroundings is to place yourself in their role. Ask yourself if certain aspects of the instruction or the environment are offensive to you. Often you will find that there are a number of things that you would change if you critically evaluate the total situation. Only through positive change does instruction improve.

Constant dissatisfaction with poor environmental surroundings and programs breeds contempt by teachers and students alike. Unfortunately, positive changes in programs or surroundings involve work, and there are teachers who, rather than expend the additional effort, would rather suffer in silence and content themselves with mediocrity of curriculum and instruction.

Schools that stay abreast of the latest advances in audiovisual education and the psychology of learning are schools that are progressive. Such institutions don't just "happen," people make them happen. People devise programs; therefore, any physical education program that encompasses a profound consideration for all of the sensitivities involved in learning must be designed by an enthusiastic staff. However, an effective staff must be backed by an equally enthusiastic and competent administration and school board which has vigorously convinced the public of the need for adequate facilities, equipment, and programs.

"WHY" AS A BASIS FOR "HOW"

Many of us can remember how we slaved over drills in arithmetic classes in school. We also recall asking ourselves why certain mathematical functions worked as they did. These unanswered questions have remained with some individuals all of their lives. Pupils who are exposed to the modern math are now learning concepts in the elementary grades that only a few years ago were being taught at the college level. As a result, they are gaining insights into the "why" of mathematical function, and the entire mathematical procedure has become meaningful to them.

In a high school civics course, constitutional law was discussed for an entire semester. The teacher did not ask the students to memorize the entire document; instead, each measure was discussed in view of why it was written and how it would affect the conditions of daily living. The students learned a considerable amount of history as they progressed; moreover, they thoroughly understood *why* the various amendments came into being as a result of our changing society. For those pupils, the constitution gained new meaning. They had reviewed the same constitution in the eighth grade and committed everything to memory, including the preamble, but had mastered no conceptual understanding of the laws under which we live. As a result of the instruction by their senior civics teacher, those pupils now have a definite working knowledge of history and government that they might otherwise have never gained. Exposure to this master teacher prompted numerous discussions about him outside of class. Students became interested in the person as well as in his class. They knew what kind of car he drove, what his hobbies were, and they became acquainted with his wife and children. Therefore, teaching methodology had established this fellow as a powerful influence upon the lives of the young people whom he taught. At a recent 25th class reunion, the man's name was foremost in the minds of his former students, while other former teachers were long forgotten.

In physical education we dwell extensively upon body mechanics and kinesiological principles when discussing movement among ourselves. However, we fail to inform our students of the same elements. We are often in such a hurry to illustrate *how* to perform a specific skill that we completely neglect to tell pupils *why* it should be performed in the proper way. By establishing the proper cognitives between the *how* and the *why*, the lesson can be made considerably more interesting and impressive. We can easily demonstrate such principles as a broad vs. a narrow base while executing a headstand or similar movement. We can further demonstrate the effect of the center of gravity in relation to balance and the various progressions of the headstand. Thus, by positioning the youngsters and explaining to them the mechanical *whys* of these positions, an entirely new dimension can be reached.

How many students have asked themselves the following questions: Why must I shoot a right-handed lay-up shot and take off from the left foot? Why should I extend my elbows when doing a handspring? Why should I place my left foot forward and follow through when I pass a football with my right hand? Why should I tuck my head when I perform a front roll? Why must my head be back when I execute a front pullover on a horizontal bar or when I polevault? Why can't I duck my head and protect my face when I am blocking an opposing lineman? Why? Why? Why? Most teachers will attempt to answer these questions when they arise, but few will attempt to introduce a unit or individual lesson by taking the time to instill these basic concepts *before* they become questions. Some teachers of physical education spend so little time on basic skills and concepts that it is a wonder the students learn anything of a substantive nature. In order to play a game, or fully appreciate an athletic contest, the participant or spectator must know precisely what is taking place. It is also axiomatic that the more thorough his knowledge, the greater will be his interest.

A co-ed, attending a college football game, was overheard asking her escort, "Why do they use so many different defensive formations?" The young man was at a loss for an answer. It was obvious that the young lady knew nothing about football and that her escort knew little more, although he claimed to have played in high school. If indeed the boy did play, he probably executed his defensive patterns at the command of his coach and was never told why such patterns were necessary. Many youngsters are exposed to similar treatment; it is no wonder that they begin to feel they have lost their identity as individuals and have assumed the roles of mere numbers.

If, in the learning of any activity, a pupil can grasp the significance of *why* a certain movement must be performed in a given way, or a strategem executed in a prescribed manner, *how* the maneuver is carried out becomes a much less formidable task because it is meaningful.

THE CONCEPTUAL VERSUS THE TRADITIONAL APPROACH TO ACTIVITY MOTIVATION

Teaching concepts involve the development of insight into an individual movement, a complete routine, or an entire game plan. This type of teaching takes imagination, perseverance, and a thorough knowledge of the subject matter. Moreover, conceptual teaching demands a great deal of planning and organization.

The traditional approach to activity motivation seeks nothing other than a simple stimulus-response association, without any insight as to the *why* of the function under consideration. That type of approach is related directly to drill and more drill, or the "practice makes perfect" school of thought. The military establishment has used this traditional approach for centuries and with good reason. In a military operation, the *why* of overall strategy is left to those officers of high rank who are trained in tactics. Time is of the essence in a military engagement and there is no time for explanations relative to the carrying out of orders. Moreover, the less the individual soldier knows about a battle plan, the less he can divulge to an enemy should he be captured. Conversely, in a democratic society, each citizen has the *responsibility* to learn as much as possible about the workings of his community, state, and national government so that he can become a more effective member of the electorate.

Schools in the United States are democratic institutions. This does not imply that students should have a vote in all of the deliberations of the faculty and administration because we should recognize that youngsters do not yet have the experiences and maturity to make many of the decisions that must be made. We, as members of the teaching community, are committed to provide the proper experiences so that our pupils will ultimately mature and gain the wisdom to make their own decisions. Yet, often our traditional approach of command and response does nothing to provide pupils with the insights necessary to adapt to new situations which may well utilize the same components taught in the classroom. For instance, in the games of basketball, field hockey, soccer, volleyball, and speedball, there is one defensive concept which is common. That concept is field or court coverage. This simple concept lies behind every defensive combination that we devise, yet is is seldom thoroughly explained to students. Once this concept is learned, any defense becomes relatively easy to teach because the basis for it has been previously established and the rationale is more easily transferred from one situation to another.

Conceptual learning induces thinking and the use of insight. It motivates youngsters because they are not only *allowed* to think about why a movement or strategem is employed, but they are *encouraged* to analyze and think. Therefore, the pupil becomes an individual and as such has a certain identity that he would not achieve in a system of drill and command. Youngsters need to feel that they are an integral part of something in order to establish a feeling of belonging, and to do this, they need a thorough conceptual understanding of the activities in which they are engaged.

To avoid any misunderstanding, it should be mentioned that drills are a necessary component of instruction. It should further be stated that drills are not a really valuable tool unless the drill *and* the concepts behind it are thoroughly understood by the pupil. It then becomes apparent that some traditional methodology is necessary, but *only* after the basic concepts have been learned and are understood.

CONCEPTUAL APPROACH AND GRADE LEVEL

Concepts, just as any subject matter, must be related to the intelligence of the pupil. A good rule of thumb to use is "the younger the pupil, the less abstract the concept." Concepts are necessary from kindergarten through graduate school, but obviously in order to have meaning, they must be understood. This is not to say that only highly abstract concepts would be acceptable to graduate instruction. On the contrary, quite often a simple analogy will explain quite easily new and strange material to advanced students; however, highly abstract concepts would have little meaning to first graders.

Youngsters in the primary grades are usually quite curious, full of questions, and impressionable. They live in a brand new world and want to become more aware of their surroundings. They are observant and appreciate being shown different things. This is an age when movement education and the kinesthetic concepts thereof should be taught. Demonstrations on the part of the teacher are excellent. These demonstrations should be carried out by students, transferring what has been learned to daily situations where similar movements would apply. When involved in game situations, youngsters should be made aware of the necessary movements as well as the basic physics upon which the movements are founded.

Gadgets are excellent conceptual aids. Simple examples of the arms and legs can be made of dowel rods, articulated by leather "joints." The muscle groups can adequately be shown by using rubberbands connected to cup hooks which have been inserted in the proper areas. This provides a graphic conceptual approach to such things as flexion, extension, adduction, abduction, and reciprocal innervation and its effect upon the antagonist and protagonist muscle groups. Any imaginative teacher could make such aids in an evening and at very little expense. With these aids, the principles of leverage can be taught to even the youngest of pupils who will then have a foundation to later learn more advanced concepts.

As the pupil progresses through school, the presentation of broader and more abstract concepts, along with a more sophisticated terminology, should take place. Elementary school physical educators have found that younger children have a short interest span and that they perform best in games of low organization. In these games of low organization, strategy is held to a minimum but nevertheless is present. Concepts of simple strategy should be explained so that when the pupil, at a later age, is exposed to more complex games, such as basketball, soccer, field hockey, and other team activities, he appreciates the strategy involved in the various offensive and defensive patterns.

Junior and senior high school students should learn not only the team activities and the concepts related to them, but also should begin to master the dual and individual sports that have carry-over value. In the junior high school, the concepts taught should more closely relate to the individual skills. After the skills have been properly learned, court strategy should be strongly emphasized. Many high school tennis and badminton players are well-skilled mechanically but have minimal concepts of court position or shot placement. These individuals often get discouraged when they are defeated by players who have mediocre skills, but they play an intelligent game and therefore make all of their efforts count.

During a college registration, a psychology professor questioned the rationale behind the awarding of only one hour of credit for physical education activity courses that met three hours per week. He then surmised that "perhaps the reason for this is that the activity courses demand no cerebration on the part of the learner." Indeed, if the participant in an activity is moving automatically, with no thought being given to strategy or to the changing situations of field position, ball placement, etc., then perhaps the professor was right. However, if the participant is aware of the strategic concepts of the game, and if he readily adapts to an ever changing situation, a great deal of cerebration must take place and it happens under considerable psychological pressure. Perhaps the professor had been exposed to a physical education program wherein he had never experienced anything other than the command-response and drill type of activity. It is unfortunate, but there are many who have never benefitted from a conceptual approach to physical education and who therefore believe that a minimal amount of thinking is attendant to our subject area.

Each school system should have a sequential, progressive curriculum for all disciplines. When such curricula are designed, the progression and sequence of conceptual values, and their instruction, should be included as an integral component of each unit. For this comprehensive type of curriculum to properly function, periodic staff meetings should be held in order to coordinate the efforts of all concerned and to gain new ideas from one another in how to better implement the conceptual approach. Traditionalists sometimes hate to change their methods of teaching, but many have discovered that conceptual teaching is not only more stimulating to the student, but that it is also more challenging to the teacher. Constant drill is indeed a bore; however, developing the conceptual approach challenges the intellect, stimulates creativity, and gives new dimensions to the teaching process.

QUESTIONS FOR DISCUSSION

1. How does a really creative teacher differ from the sterotyped, humdrum absentminded professor?
2. How would you justify the time taken to teach the *why* of any movement or activity?
3. What kind of visual aids are available and how should they be used in order to be most effective?
4. What is kinesthesia? How does kinesthesia relate to physical education, and why is it important that students understand the meaning of the word?
5. Of what importance to physical education is the sense of touch? Does this feeling have any practical application?

6. How can the environmental conditions of locker and shower rooms affect the physical education program?
7. Of what importance are drills in a program that is conceptually oriented?
8. What personal qualities are necessary in the teacher who is involved with a conceptual physical education program?
9. What is the meaning of progression and sequence in conceptual training? How should progress and sequence be implemented and maintained?
10. Why would a conceptually oriented program mean more work but yet be more satisfying to a teacher than the traditional approach based exclusively on drill?

CASE STUDIES

ROE AND GRISWOLD

Mr. Roe had been an instructor of physical education for approximately five years. He had graduated from a reputable institution and was hired as a gymnastic coach. Roe's gymnastic classes were conducted with positive progression and sequence and his students were very receptive to his instruction. During the school year Mr. Roe offered many units of instruction but never spent much time on lesson plans or other preparation for his classes in activities other than gymnastics. Flag football, basketball, speedball, softball, tennis, badminton, and other units entailed a procedure of taking roll, a quick review of the game, and "tournament" play. Roe's philosophy was that students gained experiences in playing games by their exposure after school hours and that the physical education period should be devoted to recreational pursuits, not the teaching of skills. His one deviation from this philosophy was that gymnastics was a unique activity which could only be taught in a formal class situation.

The youngsters in Mr. Roe's classes constantly complained about having to go to "gym" class and waste their time in activities in which they were not interested. When they asked for help they were told that they should know better and their questions were left unanswered. It became apparent that Roe's students were in the minority in the intramural program and when asked why they did not choose to compete, they often replied that "they were not good enough." Many who did compete constantly complained about rules being enforced about which they knew nothing. Mr. Roe was subsequently relieved of his duties as a physical educator and placed in charge of the study hall.

Mr. Griswold replaced Mr. Roe and for the first year followed the same curriculum as his predecessor. Griswold was very well organized in his planning and classroom demeanor. He used definitive lesson plans, employed many audiovisual aids, and was patient in his teaching of skills. Griswold's students not only learned the basic skills, they also learned court and field strategy, rules and training procedures necessary to the activity being taught. Moreover, the students were presented with the basic concepts underlying the "why" of each lesson and unit, and were given written assignments relative to their classwork. Skills tests and grading procedures were explained to the students and *no* question was ever left unanswered.

Students in Griswold's classes took great pride in their intramural participation and many could be found turning out for the inter-scholastic sports. Griswold kept his students occupied every moment of the class period and discipline problems were practically nonexistent. Students began to ask Mr. Griswold if activities other than those presently in the curriculum could be included and in many instances these requests were granted as circumstances permitted. Students also became interested in establishing clubs which were centered around such activities as badminton, weightlifting, tennis, and gymnastics. All such clubs stemmed from the service course program and were a welcome addition to the extracurricular program of the school.

PERRY AND ENGLE

Weight-training was offered at the junior college in which Mr. Perry was teaching and was a well-attended class. Many students had received prior instruction in high school and entered the class because of the interest previously generated. Mr. Perry's classes were well organized, the individual movements were prescribed for the students, no horseplay was allowed, and all students were kept busy for the duration of each class period. Perry was friendly toward his students and ready to assist them whenever necessary in the proper execution of any exercise.

Safety procedures in Perry's classes were explained at the outset of each term and the students were expected to observe these precautions at all times. During Perry's tenure, no student suffered an accident in class and the equipment was always replaced properly at the conclusion of the class so that the instructional area was in readiness for the next group of students who entered. Perry was liked by his students not only because of his knowledge of weight-training movements, but because he kept progress charts for each student and they knew where they stood at all times in relation to their own improvement and the class as a whole.

Mr. Engle had completed his education as a physical educator later than Mr. Perry and had undertaken a project in conceptual learning as a requirement for a graduate course in the psychology of motor skills. His classes were just as well organized as Perry's and he had learned much from his colleague in the area of equipment maintenance and safety procedures. The instructional methods of both Perry and Engle were similar with the exception of one marked deviation. Mr. Engle was as concerned with the "why" of weight-training as he was with the proper execution of the various movements. He spent a considerable amount of time with his classes explaining the physiological benefits of weight-training and used many visual aids to emphasize his lessons. Furthermore, Engle had constructed some models of lever arms of varying lengths and exposed his students to all of the principles of leverage. He was patient in explaining why individuals of varying somatotype could lift greater or lesser amounts of weight dependent upon the leverage that they were working against.

Engle's classes were assigned outside work in the area of exercise, physiology, and body mechanics and seemingly enjoyed the assignments because they related directly to individual problems and the subject matter which was explained in class. Many were heard to remark that they had never been exposed to this type of instruction and that while it was more demanding, it was also more interesting and worthwhile.

As time passed, Perry became aware of Engle's instructional methods and began to periodically observe Engle's classes. He quietly observed, took notes, and then conferred with Mr. Engle in the privacy of their office. Perry and Engle were the best of friends and both were competent in their instructional field. Perry admitted that he had never seen a conceptual approach in weight-training and was happy to incorporate the information into his own classes. These gentlemen worked together for three years before Engle accepted a position at another institution, and they mutually profited from the experience of one another. Perry has since returned to graduate school and has become extremely interested in the aspects of motor learning which were not a part of his training at the time he was an undergraduate.

QUESTIONS

1. How would you rank Mr. Perry as a physical educator when comparing his performance to others that you have known? What were his positive characteristics?
2. Do you feel that Mr. Engle might have alienated himself from Mr. Perry by employing new methodology and thereby challenging the experience of his

older colleague? If you were in a situation wherein you wished to alter an accepted teaching procedure, how would you proceed?
3. Describe the human relationships that must have existed between these two men that led to such mutual understanding.
4. Which type of instruction would you, as a student, appreciate more—that prescribed by Mr. Perry or that prescribed by Mr. Engle?

MISS WATKINS AND MRS. SHARP

Miss Watkins entered Jackson High School as a beginning teacher. She was added to the staff to supplement the efforts of Mrs. Sharp who had long been plagued by overloaded classes. Mrs. Sharp was very traditional in her approach to all units of instruction and she proceeded to inform Miss Watkins that most students would respond better to command than suggestion. She also believed that such units as dance should be structured and formal, somewhat patterned after classic exercises in ballet.

Mrs. Sharp delegated all of the dance classes to Miss Watkins and also informed her that she would henceforth be responsible for directing the rally squad. Miss Watkins eagerly assumed her duties. However, she was met by groans and sighs on the part of her students when it was announced that dance classes would begin. Many of the students fabricated various excuses and flatly stated that they saw no value in dance at all.

Miss Watkins introduced her instructional unit with an historical background of dance and explained how it had evolved. She alluded to the fact that some forms of dance were highly structured because of the need for precision movement and also how creative dance could be construed as an expression of the "self." It became readily apparent that none of the students had ever been introduced to creative dance and that structured movements were in reality a true expression of the "self" of Mrs. Sharp.

As the dance unit progressed, students were allowed to select their own music and interpret the rhythm in a pattern or patterns developed by themselves. At the conclusion of the unit a recital was held during which virtually every girl enrolled in the classes performed either in groups or singly. Many of the girls later admitted that they felt that they had developed an aesthetic sense that they never before realized they possessed. Even Mrs. Sharp seemed pleased at the outcome of the instruction and did not hesitate to inform everyone that she had "picked" Miss Watkins for the position because of her training in dance.

Miss Watkins incorporated many dance forms into her rally squad activities. Precision movements were practiced diligently and many of these became components of routines which were created by the girls themselves. Parents were pleased, the students were completely satisfied, the coaching staff and athletes were happy with the support they were receiving, and the program was met with many compliments on the part of almost all the teachers on campus.

Miss Watkins moved from Jackson High School after only three years to accept a more lucrative position in another community. She was publicly thanked for her contributions by the superintendent of schools and asked, prior to leaving, to serve on a screening committee to select her own successor. Clearly she had made a lasting contribution to the community as well as to her individual students.

QUESTIONS

1. Why was Miss Watkins approach more acceptable to the dance students than that of Mrs. Sharp?

MRS. HAMBLIN

Social dancing to the seventh graders of Yates Junior High had about as much appeal as a spoonful of Castor Oil. The school was small and the social dance unit was taught by Mrs. Hamblin with very little assistance from the male member of the physical education department.

Mrs. Hamblin was a very patient individual; she was precise in her approach to teaching and was a fair and impartial disciplinarian. She knew that many of her students were shy and also that they lacked social graces so necessary to getting along in our society.

The dance unit was a complete instructional program and was not taught merely as a skill class. The concomitant instruction in how to get along with people at a social gathering was emphasized to nearly as great an extent as were the dance steps themselves. Films on dating and social graces were shown. Exchange of ideas between boys and girls was encouraged and even those excused from actual dance instruction because of religious reasons were invited to enter into such discussions.

It was pointed out that younger people should have the opportunity to acquaint themselves with all types of individuals of varying interests. Such practices as "going steady" and attempts to act in a psuedosophisticated manner were discouraged. Moreover, Mrs. Hamblin was quick to point out *why* certain social graces must be observed in an organized society. Her efforts were seldom wasted on deaf ears as she ensured that good manners were practiced at every opportunity—in the halls and during various school programs as well as at the few dances held at the schools. Many students in later years returned to thank Mrs. Hamblin for the background information provided which had made their lives so much more meaningful.

QUESTIONS

1. Do you believe that Mrs. Hamblin's method of teaching social dance had any greater value than some of the more traditional approaches used? Why?

MISS DENSER

The community of Colton was fortunate to employ Miss Denser as an instructor in the women's department of physical education. She was an outstanding teacher and one who spent a great deal of time not only preparing her classes but also in searching for innovative methods and units of instruction that were relevant to present day conditions.

Miss Denser had spent some time in the armed forces during World War II and during her period of service had developed an interest in personal defense for women. She constantly upgraded her course by employing the most recent techniques and methodology related to the field.

Personal defense had received such compliments from the students that Miss Denser was prevailed upon to teach a class for the mothers of the community. While instructing the first class, Miss Denser realized that her adult students were not as "conditioned" as were her regular pupils, and they were highly desirous of knowing *why* certain movements and training procedures were necessary as well as how to execute the maneuvers. Miss Denser was caught somewhat unaware by the questions but agreed to devote her own time to researching the problem and answering the queries.

Through diligent efforts, the entire unit of instruction was revised so that each training procedure and defensive movement was analyzed in reference to balance, leverage, force, and related components. In addition, the legal implications of what measures one can or cannot employ in personal defense were emphasized. Law enforcement officials and an attorney were called in as guest lecturers for the class and all aspects of the subject were discussed.

As a result of her experiences with the adult class, Miss Denser began to examine all of her curricular offerings in terms of what might constitute more meaningful instruction in the form of better conceptualization. She completely revised her instructional units and once remarked that she had begun to feel a "rebirth" as a teacher. The students seemed to be pleased with the new approach and with subsequent curricular revisions. The entire physical education department began to assume a new and more desirable image in the eyes of both students and faculty.

QUESTIONS

1. What experiences did Miss Denser have that might provide some insight in many classes? Do you believe that her approach was sound?

SUGGESTED RELATED READING

Barrett, Kate Ross, *Exploration: a Method for Teaching Movement.* Madison, Wis.: College Printing and Typing Co., 1965.

Metheny, Eleanor, *Connotations of Movement in Sport and Dance.* Dubuque, Iowa: Wm. C. Brown, 1965.

Mosston, Muska, *Developmental Movement.* Columbus, Ohio: C. E. Merrill Books, 1965.

Mosston, Muska, *Teaching Physical Education From Command to Discovery.* Columbus, Ohio: C. E. Merrill Books, 1966.

Smith, Hope, ed., *Introduction to Human Movement.* Reading, Mass.: Addison-Wesley, 1968.

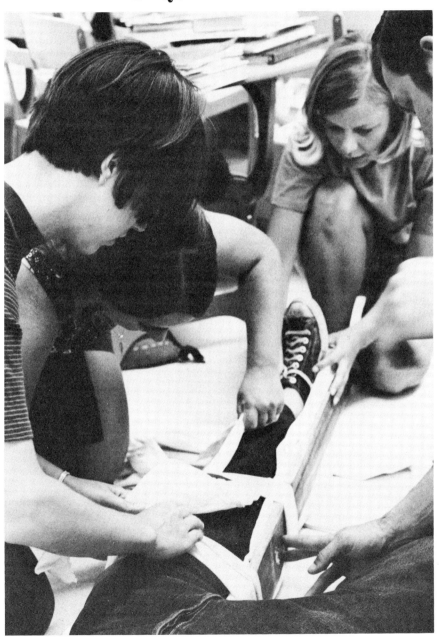

THE MEANING OF PROGRESSION AND SEQUENCE

A definition of progression, as related to curriculum, is a continuous and connected series, as of acts, events, or steps, one logically leading to the next; hence, a sequence. By such a concise definition, we may readily relate to program planning. Such planning entails a meaningful pattern of one skill leading to another in a rational and systematic manner, wherein basic movements are perfected, and in turn lead to more advanced elements of performance. Therefore, progression and sequence in curriculum determination may be analagous to the construction of a building.

An architect plans a building so that its basic form follows the function for which it was designed. Plans are then drafted according to the building code which specifies the materials that may be used in construction. The architect must initiate the plans for the building by designing a suitable foundation that will support the structure as well as the various stresses and strains that will be imposed upon it.

As the contractor reads the blueprints for a well-planned structure, he should discover that the basic elements form a sensible pattern that is well engineered both functionally and aesthetically. If the planning and construction is thorough and the workmanship of good quality, the building will function well for the program for which it was designed. If the initial planning is slipshod and the workmanship poor, the structure will most likely be completely unsuitable.

When considering physical education curriculum, we have only to examine existing programs to find that all too often very little detailed planning has been done. This is especially true of the programs that are offered throughout an entire school district. Frequently the individual schools within a district will have a progressive, sequential curriculum of merit; however, the articulation of programs *between* the schools may be virtually nonexistent. For example, let us assume that each elementary school diligently plans a well-constructed curriculum based upon sound concepts of the progression and sequence of skills. Let us further assume that the junior and senior high schools of the district do likewise. We now have three or more levels of well-planned curriculum. However, if the curriculum planners for the entire district have not worked together so that program articulation between every school level has been thoroughly correlated, there could conceivably be three or more individual curricula, each in conflict with the other. Such planning leads to duplication of effort, lack of staff efficiency, confusion of purpose, and ultimately, disinterested students who are bored with instructional repetition.

PITFALLS OF "THE CART BEFORE THE HORSE"

When proper procedures for curriculum construction are neglected in favor of expedience, chaos results. It is apparent in many schools that the program content is nothing more than a matter of an individual teacher's preference and reflects no cooperative planning at all. Therefore, the activities offered are those most familiar to the teacher and are constant only with his beliefs and bias. As a result, the needs of the students and the full utilization of facilities, personnel, and curriculum possibilities are sacrificed. Ultimately such programs engender the disinterest of the students and the entire community in matters pertaining to physical education.

In describing school curriculum, it can be said that offerings generally fall into the two following categories: (1) The program is completely disjointed and filled with duplication, repetition, and lack of planning. (2) Curriculum is so infinitely detailed and prescribed that it discourages any innovation or flexibility. The two extremes are equally unsatisfactory. Curriculum must be thoroughly planned and it must be progressive and sequential in character; however, it should also provide for a certain degree of flexibility within its instructional units to meet the varied needs of the students served.

To illustrate the point further, a public school district was awarded a large financial grant which was used to develop an extremely comprehensive curriculum in the field of language arts. Meanwhile, the physical education instructors were following a completely spontaneous program of unrelated activities which evidenced no preplanning whatever. Each school in the district had an entirely different curriculum, the content of which was obviously determined on a day-to-day basis. One day was devoted to the "teaching" of a team sport, the next day offered a smattering of tumbling, and the following day might entail a lesson in dancing or badminton. There was no attempt to teach skills and the random selection of activities was abhorrent. Yet this type of curriculum had been in effect in the district for quite a few years. The inconceivable overriding factor was that the administration evidenced a *complete* lack of concern for the course of study in physical education but was extremely interested in a curricular revision for language arts. Much of the administrative apathy toward the physical education program was, unfortunately, a result of the negative attitude of the physical education staff itself.

While observing another school district, we found that the physical education curriculum was so restrictive that supervising teachers were constantly reprimanding staff members for not adhering, line by line, to the daily lesson plans which were published at the district office. The result of this constraint was that the teachers assumed the role of technicians and the students were pushed along regardless of whether or not they had mastered any of the skills related to the instructional unit. This overly regulated system created extreme disinterest on the part of the students and a feeling of utter frustration within the ranks of the teaching staff. The subsequent high rate of teacher replacement was most indicative of a true exercise in curricular futility and the suppression of faculty creativity.

The aforementioned cases serve only to illustrate that incomplete planning, as well as strict adherence to highly definitive plans with no regard to student needs, is a sheer waste of time and a detriment to faculty morale.

WHO DETERMINES CURRICULAR DIRECTION

Reference to something called public relations is often heard in discussions relating school affairs to the community at large. There is not just one public, there are many. These various publics are composed of students, parents, major tax-paying groups and industrial firms, school boards, and other subgroups of interested individuals. All of these people have an equity in curricular direction. For this reason, curriculum determination and direction must involve some representation of the thinking of each of the publics served by the schools. However, lay representation on curriculum committees should never supersede professionally trained personnel.

Curriculum committees should be carefully selected by those individuals charged with the responsibility of curriculum construction and/or reevaluation. This is not a responsibility that should be taken lightly, therefore, certain criteria should be established prior to the selection of committee members. The basic factors in selecting committee members should be considered as follows:

1. Professional training and experience in health and physical education.

2. Ability to think logically and objectively.

3. Familiarity with the school and the school system.

4. A desire to serve as a contributing *member* of the committee, not as its focal point.

5. An inherent interest in the total educational process.

6. Willingness to devote the necessary time and energy to the task.

7. A genuine interest in the welfare of youth.

8. A respect for the democratic process of decision-making.

If the committee is to be representative of the various publics served by the schools, it is apparent that not all members will possess factors (1) and (3) of the preceding criteria. It is nevertheless desirable to include some nonprofessionals in the group. However, leadership of the committee should be assumed by a professionally trained educator. If the committee is to be representative of the various publics, it should include lay personnel, administrators, a board member, and students. Contributions by lay persons and students are valuable but should not be accepted if they contradict the basic precepts and knowledge of trained persons. It is therefore *imperative* that ground rules be established and adhered to in all deliberations for committee function. On some curriculum committees, lay personnel and students are called upon strictly for consultation. In such instances, this limitation of function is specifically stated in the structure of the "ground rules."

The basic principle behind curriculum planning is that all committee members should meet and plan together for the common good of the students for whom the program is designed. In large districts, curriculum committees are more manageable if the members are selected on a representative basis. Their work should be directed by one person whose responsibility is the coordination and control of the entire project. After the curriculum is formulated in rough draft, the assigned committee members can refer to the individual school staffs for suggestions and subsequent revision. Any competent school superintendent, and/or board of education, should request a letter of transmittal from a curriculum committee. In the body of the letter there should be a statement that the committee work has been, in fact, a unified effort and that district wide articulation and staff acceptance have been accomplished.

The assignment of a specific individual within a school district as Coordinator of Physical Education is one in which progression and sequence of curriculum can be initiated. This administrative assignment could comprise only a portion of the duties of the designated person. The coordinator should be provided with released time to perform his functions, and should be charged with the responsibility for periodic curriculum revision for the district. *How* the coordinator functions is as important as the fact that someone has the authority and responsibility to carry out the task. A wise teacher, placed in a coordinating role will usually involve the entire staff in pertinent deliberations and decision-making. If curriculum is to be effective, it must evolve from those who have an equity in the teaching process. Programs then become meaningful because the people directly affected by them have been involved in the planning and can sense a true feeling of personal interest.

FACTORS RELATED TO CURRICULUM DETERMINATION

Curriculum determination must be directly related to the needs of the students. Every aspect of growth and development, plus the attendant factors of pupil interest, motivation, and the psychology of learning must be considered prior to the inclusion of any subject matter. It is only through diligent planning that an acceptable curriculum can be developed. The curriculum must be oriented to the students, facilities, equipment, climate, and faculty personnel. Furthermore, curriculum planners must constantly ask themselves the following questions: What are we now doing? What do we want to do? Who is going to be affected by the program? What are our aims and objectives? How does each unit of instruction logically lead to the next so that the entire pattern is acceptable psychologically, sociologically, and physiologically to the groups being served?

If curriculum is to be placed in its proper perspective, certain aspects of the total school and community environment need to be thoroughly studied prior to the drafting of a course of study. The following factors should be considered by curriculum planners before any additional work is initiated.

1. Survey of the school and community to determine
    a. Location of the institution (geographic and climatic conditions)
    b. Type of institution (elementary, junior high, senior high, or college)
    c. Size of school and/or schools
    d. Personnel (administrative)
    e. Personnel (teaching staff—number of men and women)
    f. Assigned instructional load of teaching staff
    g. Auxiliary personnel (custodians, grounds keepers, equipment cage managers, secretarial, etc.)
    h. Characteristics of the students (age range, sex, maturity, previous experience in physical education)
    i. Equipment (on hand and proposed)
    j. Budget (available and projected)
    k. Facilities—indoor and outdoor (existing and proposed)
    l. Type of community (ethnic groups, culture, types of occupation, financial status in general, agencies influencing

the educational enterprise, attitude of people toward the schools in general, and physical education in particular)

2. Administrative policies
   a. Grading
   b. Academic credit
   c. Time allotment
   d. Excuses (daily and permanent)
   e. Purchase—maintenance and repair
   f. Equipment issuance and accounting
   g. Gym suit services (including laundry and linen)
   h. Classification of students
   i. Size of classes

3. Instructional offerings
   a. Team sports
   b. Rhythmics
   c. Conditioning
   d. Dual and individual sports
   e. Co-educational activities

4. Testing and evaluation procedures
   a. Skills tests
   b. Knowledge tests
   c. Fitness tests
   d. Program evaluation (regularly scheduled)

5. Restricted and adaptives program
   a. Scheduling
   b. Program content

6. Intramurals
   a. Policies and procedures—relation of intramurals to instructional program
   b. Scheduling
   c. Personnel

7. Interscholastic athletic program
   a. Relationship to overall physical education program
   b. Administrative policies and control
   c. Personnel
   d. Scheduling of practice sessions
   e. Program content
   f. Budget and sources of funds

8. Health education program
   a. Relationship to overall physical education program
   b. Personnel
   c. Scheduling
   d. Health services—health instruction—contributions to healthful school living
   e. Physical examinations
   f. School insurance program

9. Community recreational opportunities
   a. Degree of community involvement
   b. Scheduling (time and facilities)
   c. Personnel
   d. Finance (equipment, facilities, and personnel)

10. Library resources
    a. School and departmental holdings
    b. Budget

11. Educational media
    a. Audiovisual aids and equipment
    b. Use of equipment (scheduling)
    c. Personnel
    d. Budget

The above survey of related factors should be followed by comprehensive statements of the school district's philosophy of education and physical education. These statements reflect the collective thinking of all curriculum committee members and the school administration. It is only through a cooperative effort that a viable and complete course of study can emerge as a vehicle based upon the needs of all parties concerned.

Many school districts do not possess a curriculum guide which is available to the teachers and school patrons. Without such a guide, curriculum direction is difficult to determine by those who are experienced, much less by those who are new to the faculty. It might also be noted that school districts who do provide curriculum guides have frequently not provided for regular periods of program assessment and evaluation.

Once a course of study has been formulated and placed into operation, it cannot be forgotten. Curriculum determination is a continual process that demands regular review. If this review is not scheduled on a regular basis, the program will deteriorate and thereby become stale and lifeless. It is only through constant review and revision that any curriculum can survive the rapidly changing pace of the educational process.

QUESTIONS FOR DISCUSSION

1. What is the meaning of *progression and sequence* in curriculum and what is its value?
2. What is the purpose of a curriculum committee and who should be placed on such a committee?
3. What is the purpose of any curriculum? Is this a valid purpose or one that is open to question?
4. What are the steps that should be followed in the preparation of a well-constructed curriculum?
5. Why is a complete survey necessary to the preparation of a well-designed curriculum?
6. From your own observation, do you believe that all schools have made an honest attempt to develop and implement a comprehensive curriculum which has been drafted according to the suggestions set forth in this chapter?
7. As a beginning teacher would you be interested in reading the curriculum guide? What steps would you take if no curriculum guide had ever been constructed?

CASE STUDIES

Metro High School had been in existence for approximately twenty years and had required all sophomores and juniors to take physical education. The units of instruction for boys consisted of flag football, basketball, wrestling, gymnastics, and softball. The women's program consisted of archery, badminton, volleyball, tumbling and softball. These units of instruction were identical for both juniors and seniors and were taught by the same instructors.

Metro High was evaluated by a regional accreditation team, and the administration was informed that the curriculum in physical education would have to be revised in order for the school to receive full accreditation. Suggestions were made as to subject matter content and those suggestions were relayed by the administration to the physical education staff. In turn, the physical education staff chose to ignore the suggestions of the administration and no changes were implemented for the balance of the academic year.

During the summer months Mr. Henry, the principal of Metro, drafted a physical education curriculum for both boys and girls that included more dual and individual activities, thereby increasing the offerings to which the students were exposed. However, the curriculum was again identical for sophomores and juniors with no consideration being given to sequence or progression. The physical education staff returned to school in the fall to discover that a new curriculum had been placed in their mail boxes. This "curriculum" consisted of only one sheet of paper which simply listed what was going to be taught and at what time of the year.

The entire Metro High School physical education staff descended upon the principal's office to demand what had taken place during the summer without their knowledge. Mr. Henry listened patiently to his staff and admitted that he was no expert in the area of physical education curriculum, but was forced to take some sort of token action in view of the fact that his staff had been aware of the problem and had done nothing about it. The chairman of the physical education department then stated that his staff would be happy to construct a new curriculum but they would have to be given released time to do so. Mr. Henry replied that no released time was available and that they should use their preparation periods and conduct meetings after school hours to construct a new curriculum. To this the chairman stated that if no released time was available he believed that they would implement the suggestions made by the principal and let it go at that.

QUESTIONS

1. How would you evaluate the curriculum at Metro High School?
2. How would you categorize the professional attitude of the teachers at Metro High in relation to their obligations?
3. What is your reaction to the manner in which the principal of Metro High handled the matter of curriculum construction for the physical education department?
4. What is your reaction to the matter of released time for curriculum construction?

ELM JUNIOR HIGH

Elm Junior High School was an old school that was inadequate for instructional purposes and was therefore sold to an industrial firm which needed a new site for expansion purposes. The money from the sale of the school, plus funds gained from a bond issue, were used in the construction of a new junior high facility on the edge of town where land was less expensive and the area more conducive to building.

The faculty at Elm was eager and enthusiastic about the prospect of moving into new quarters even though the actual move was not to occur for at least a year. While the construction of the new school was progressing, Mr. Figuth, principal of Elm, decided that the energies of his staff should be channeled into preparing new curricular guides which could be placed into immediate use when the students were moved to their new quarters. All faculty members were called together in a general meeting and it was decided that each department would reconstruct its own curriculum and should therefore formulate a curriculum committee immediately. After receiving the blessing of the district administration, Mr. Figuth consulted with his department chairmen and established a meeting schedule so that faculty with multiple responsibilities could meet with more than one committee without conflict.

Departmental curriculum committees were formed and each consisted of the chairman of the department, faculty members, one student, a parent, and Mr. Figuth who served as an ex-officio member. Complete surveys of the new facility were made and data relative to student and parental interests was gathered. Then, prior to actual curriculum construction, an understanding was reached within each committee that even though all information would be discussed, everything that was desired by all parties could not be included in the final curriculum.

As the months passed, meetings were held and the curriculum was developed. Many friendly arguments took place and even a few heated debates. A rough draft of each department's curriculum was made available for the perusal of all staff members, regardless of discipline, and suggestions were solicited. After the period of time for suggestions had elapsed, the departmental committees met again to finalize their curricula and draft a letter of transmittal to the local school board.

When the new Elm Junior High School opened its doors it was not only the opening of just another new building, it was the birth of a vastly improved educational procedure in which all interested parties had been involved. There were some rough spots in the first year of operation under the new curricula, but as they arose they were noted and later discussed during the spring evaluation prior to the dismissal of school. Minor changes in curriculum have been found necessary from time to time, but this was a continual process and it was decided that complete evaluation for purposes of revision might be needed only at five-year intervals.

QUESTIONS

1. How do you perceive the attitude of Elm Junior High to the matter of curriculum?
2. Was the method of curriculum construction at Elm Junior High in accordance with accepted methods?
3. How would you evaluate Mr. Figuth as a professional administrator?
4. Do you believe that students should be present on curriculum committees? If so, why? If not, why?
5. How often do you believe that curriculum should be revised either in part or totally?
6. What is the professional obligation of the physical educator in matters of curriculum construction? Should department chairmen take the initiative in curriculum construction and revision or should they await a directive from the administration?

MISS PEREZ

Miss Perez was a specialist in elementary physical education and had taught in the Farnsworth School system for only two years before she began to realize that the curriculum throughout the district was not as well articulated as it should be. She discussed the matter with the women physical educators at both the junior and senior high schools, who in turn decided to initiate a curriculum study in the interest of improving the course of study.

Movement education was a new facet of instruction to all of the Farnsworth physical educators except Miss Perez. She planned diligently so that the expression of her views would be well presented and logical. Her basic plan was to orient the basic elementary program toward movement education in the hope that students would then be better prepared for learning individual skills necessary to the sports and games taught in the junior and senior high schools. The women instructors were enthusiastic about the new approach, but the men maintained strongly that they believed the present curriculum, which involved the teaching of game techniques and individual skills in the elementary grades, would be of greater advantage to them, especially in the interest of the interscholastic program. The women however agreed to restructure the elementary curriculum and give the new system a three-year trial period.

Miss Perez reorganized the curriculum for the elementary school girls and the results of her teaching became very apparent after only two years. The students in the upper elementary grades who entered the seventh grade were far superior in their performance than those of preceding years. After the third year of operation the women physical educators within the district agreed that they believed the new elementary curricular concept should be adopted permanently. The men in the district were not impressed with the results claimed by the women and insisted that the curriculum for elementary boys not be changed.

QUESTIONS

1. Why do you suppose the men in the Farnsworth schools were against changing the elementary curriculum?

MISS ROARK AND MISS HILL

Miss Roark and Miss Hill taught at the same high school and occupied one office in the women's gymnasium. Miss Roark was a young and vivacious teacher who strongly believed in structuring curriculum around student interests as well as student needs. Miss Hill was a very capable teacher but was very conservative in her views on curriculum and did not believe that any student was mature enough to have a voice in deliberations regarding curricular matters.

In discussing curriculum construction at a departmental meeting Miss Roark mentioned that she thought it would be an excellent idea to survey the students as to their interests and restructure the curriculum accordingly, at least in part. Miss Hill replied that she had spent five years in professional training and therefore believed that she was much more aware of what the students needed than they were. After discussing the situation for some time, Miss Roark proposed that since each teacher was working with a different grade level it might be in order to alter the curriculum for her classes to satisfy student interest, leave Miss Hill's curriculum as it was, and then compare the responses of the students at the end of the year.

Miss Roark administered an interest survey to all of her students and spent the summer restructuring her curriculum so that she included some of the more desired units and at the same time did not duplicate what was being taught by Miss Hill. The students who took part in the interest survey were not told what it was for and not all of their requests were incorporated for obvious reasons.

The following year both Miss Hill and Miss Roark worked hard to do the best job possible teaching the units of instruction in their respective curricula. Student performance, attitudes, excuse rates, complaints, compliments, etc., were charted to see whether or not reaction was more favorable to the one course of study than to the other. The single factor which emerged was that the incidence of excuses in Miss Roark's classes was at an all time low. There were no significant differences in the other items being investigated.

QUESTIONS

1. Do you think that Miss Hill and Miss Roark conducted a fair evaluation of comparative courses of study? Why or why not? What other techniques might they have better used?

SUGGESTED RELATED READING

Cowell, Charles Clarence, and Helen W. Hazelton, *Curriculum Designs in Physical Education.* Englewood Cliffs, N.J.: Prentice-Hall, 1963.

Irwin, Leslie William, *The Curriculum in Health and Physical Education*, 2nd ed. St. Louis: C. V. Mosby, 1951.

La Porte, William Ralph et al. *The Physical Education Curriculum: A National Program*, 5th ed. rev. Los Angeles: University of Southern California Press, 1951.

Nixon, John E., and Anne E. Jewett, *A Physical Education Curriculum.* New York: Ronald Press, 1964.

Willgoose, Carl E., *The Curriculum in Physical Education.* Englewood Cliffs, N.J.: Prentice-Hall, 1969.

SELECTED PSYCHOLOGICAL, PHYSIOLOGICAL, AND SOCIOLOGICAL CONSIDERATIONS

STRESS AND THE RELEASE OF STRESS THROUGH ACTIVITY

Our modern society presents man with many problems which result in psychological stress. The working man or woman is deeply concerned with various aspects of a chosen business or profession; the retired individual is painfully aware of the economic implications of living on a fixed income; and youngsters are justifiably worried about their future. The result of these concerns is psychological stress which often precipitates organic maladies such as ulcers, headache, fatigue, and assorted anxieties.

Mental hospitals are filled with people who have suffered from nervous breakdown due to extended periods of stress. We frequently refer to ulcers as the businessman's occupational disease. Many executives, even though engaged in sedentary pursuits, suffer from chronic fatigue. Oddly enough, the same complaints are seldom voiced by those who are actively engaged in jobs that demand heavy physical labor. Michael (1957) reviewed studies related to the effects of exercise upon the adrenal glands and the autonomic nervous system. The evidence thus produced supported the contention that repeated exercise effects the stress adaption mechanism in the following ways: Adrenocortical activity operating in conjunction with the autonomic nervous system is involved in the body's adjustment to stress. Adjustment is complemented by a reduction in the time necessary to elicit a response to stress and thereby lessens the duration of the adjustment phase of the body's reaction to stress. Adaption to exercise produces a certain degree of insulation against emotional stress. Increased adrenal activity, resulting from repeated exercise, seems to cause an increased reserve of steroids available to consider stress. A lack of activity reduces ability to withstand stress.

Stress seems to be an additive entity that can best be offset by personal involvement in an activity which is completely divorced from that which brings about feelings of tension. Moreover, vigorous physical exercise has been shown to be of greater value in releasing tension than have sedentary pursuits such as reading, woodworking, painting, or crafts. It is rather difficult to be engrossed in a game of handball or tennis, perspire freely, and at the same time be seriously concerned about other problems.

Stress mounts as tension increases toward a point of crisis. The student who faces comprehensive examinations may show little evidence of stress as he initially prepares for his tests. As the examination time draws near, tension mounts and unless the pattern of study and mental anguish is interrupted, the student may begin to display both psychological and physiological symptoms which are detrimental to health. No student should ever place himself on a schedule that does not allow for recreational pursuits.

Since the lay public is generally not informed of the goals and objectives of physical education, many people overlook the contributions that our profession can make to the field of mental hygiene. When we speak of fitness, we should address ourselves to the concept of *total fitness*, not just physical fitness. If we hope to gain the public's confidence in relation to our place in education, we can make a worthy contribution by instilling the *whys*, or concepts, of physical activity as it relates to stress and the release of emotional tension.

One innovative physical educator we observed not only *explained* stress to her students but actively involved them in an instructional unit in which these concepts were used. She used two rather interesting approaches to the problem in order to impress upon the students that (1) people could not really concentrate upon a game situation and at the same time concentrate upon another subject, and (2) that activity could provide for release from an otherwise intolerable stress situation.

The students were given a rather complex problem which involved computing the budgetary requirements for a volleyball team which was to take a hypothetical trip to a distant state for a tournament. The students were told that they were to compute the cost of meals, lodging, and transportation for the trip, but while they were engaged in the mental calculations they were to play doubles in badminton and try to concentrate upon both the game and the proposed problem. After the badminton matches the students were to immediately jot down on paper the figures that they had calculated for the hypothetical trip. At the conclusion of the class period the girls readily admitted that they found it difficult, and in many cases impossible, to move on the badminton court, keep track of their scores, and at the same time devote any thought to the problem of the volleyball trip.

In the second experimental session the girls were placed in a room and told to remain immobile while listening to a high-pitched shrill sound which had been recorded on tape. The noise was deafening and all of the girls evidenced symptoms of anxiety. After ten minutes, which seemed like eternity, the record was turned off and further instructions were given. The girls were provided with shuttlecocks and badminton rackets and told that they would be subjected to the same recorded sound but that they should hit the shuttlecocks back and forth and try to concentrate upon the activity rather than the sound. After another ten minutes had passed the record was turned off and the girls were asked which period had caused them the greatest discomfort. All were in agreement that the exposure to the shrieking noise without benefit of any activity release had been the most uncomfortable. In addition, the girls were very emphatic in their belief that the experiments had been far more meaningful than had the lecture material by itself. Thus the concept of stress was introduced to the class and reinforced by the actual presentation of relevant material.

Many people have *accidentally* stumbled upon the values of activity as it relates to stress, but not enough have had a *formal* exposure accompanied by the introductory material which was presented in the previous discussion. Physical educators spend many hours of college preparation studying the psychological affects of activity and should definitely incorporate this knowledge into their teaching procedures. Lecture is not enough to convince young minds of today; most of our present generation of students have a "show me" attitude. They are receptive but are not willing to accept everything told them as absolute. Such an attitude presents a worthy challenge to the creative teacher who is willing to accept it in the interest of improving both teaching methodology and the knowledge of his pupils.

PERSPIRATION AND INSPIRATION

People usually engage in activities in which they enjoy success. All individuals cannot be expected to succeed in every activity nor should their teachers be discouraged when some students fail to excel. The primary function of any teacher is to encourage the student to reach his own individual potential, be it low, moderate, or high.

If curriculum is constructed only in relationship to the desires and interests of the teacher, it will not meet the psychological needs of the students. Too many physical education programs offer a number of team games, prefaced by calisthenics, and a few lifetime sports (carry-over activities). In some instances the teaching of skills is sacrificed for competitive play, and rules and strategy are not emphasized. To further compound the problem the course content is repeated each year. The net result is often boredom and ensuant disciplinary trouble. The carry-over-value from such programs is virtually nil as compared to the benefits of a comprehensive and dynamic curriculum.

Human beings are rather perceptive; they fail to react positively to situations in which they see little or no value. No thinking individual would place his savings in a bank that does not pay interest; similarly the concept of gain must be apparent prior to any investment, be it in terms of money, time, or energy. Physical educators owe it to their students as well as to themselves to construct programs that inspire rather than dull their interests.

MOTIVATION

Tests are often used as a means of determining pupil progress for the purpose of grading. The use of tests as a motivational stimulant also has definite value. Progress charts are desirable aids for many activities as are skills tests, fitness tests, pulse-ratio tests, and short non-graded knowledge batteries. If a student can actually see evidence of his own progress he will usually put forth additional effort. It is advisable however for the teacher to emphasize that each student is an individual and that all will not progress at the same rate due to such individual differences. Unless youngsters are apprised of their individuality they may easily be discouraged upon comparing their progress with that of another student. Teachers should constantly be aware of what their actions are doing to students, therefore, individual progress charts frequently are more valuable than comparative class charts.

Progress charts which are used to motivate team activities should be conspicuously placed so that all teams have an opportunity to see where they stand in relationship to each other. Such charts are group oriented and therefore do not indicate individual performances. Project charts, either individual or group, take time to construct but have been found to be well worth the effort by providing a substantial motivational force. Individual charts such as those used in weight-training and similar units can be printed commercially. Larger single-use charts and graphs usually have to be designed by the individual teacher. Inasmuch as most physical educators do not have a great number of papers to grade, construction of such aids does not involve any more time than is generally consumed by those teaching in the other disciplines.

Girls are sometimes motivated by ego involvement, in much the same manner as male "body builders." No young lady has any desire to be obese or to have a less than desirable figure. Teachers cannot merely tell their girls about figure control, they must be motivated by measurements, personal progress charts, and encouragement from their fellow students as well as their teachers. They must also understand the basic physiology which underlies figure control in order to gain additional incentive to better themselves.

One of the finest motivators available today is the video-tape recorder. A multitude of uses for these machines has been discovered by teachers. A student can never really understand how his performance or appearance compares to that of another unless he can actually see himself in action. Many students on first seeing their own performances, have been heard to exclaim, "Why, I didn't realize that I looked like that." In many cases poor performers readily perceive mistakes that they have been told about time after time but have been unable to conceptualize.

A good way to compare a good performance with a lesser one is to place a video-taped performance and a loop film projection side by side. The expert performance on the loop film can then readily be compared to the student's performance on the television screen. Such a procedure also has the advantage of comparing the student with an impersonal example rather than with a classmate. Another value accrued from video-tape recordings is that they tend to silence the braggart who has closed his mind to criticism.

Video-tape recorders are initially expensive, but the tape is reusable and therefore not as costly as film. The machines are not difficult to operate and some recent advances in the electronic industry indicate that such units will be available with casettes which will not only be less expensive but offer even greater ease of operation.

Motivation can be either extrinsic or intrinsic. Extrinsic motivation is characterized by that which is imposed from without such as a command, the offering of an award, or other stimulus that elicits a particular response. Intrinsic motivation is usually that which arises from within an individual and could be called desire. Frequently extrinsic motivation such as a film loop of an outstanding performance or a motion picture depicting the life of an exemplary individual will promote intrinsic motivation on the part of a student to perform at the level which has just been perceived as a result of the visual aid. Pregame pep talks are extrinsic motivators but also act as stimulators which are designed to elicit better athletic performance.

The teacher must be a practicing psychologist and must know the characteristics of his students as they relate to different types of motivation. A reprimand may elicit a positive response from one youngster or a negative response from another. Therefore it is the obligation of every teacher to get to know his students and their reactions to various stimuli. Such knowledge comes through associations and experience in working with youngsters. Success is the best motivator there is and teachers should always strive to ensure some degree of success for each and every student, even though the amount of success may vary considerably. Success must also be reinforced if the child is to strive for greater expectancies. A word of praise at the right time can frequently do wonders for a child's ego, especially when it comes from a teacher whose opinion is highly respected.

Praise and punishment are both motivators and should be used very judiciously. Youngsters can spot a "phony" without difficulty and are usually very much aware of occasions wherein either punishment or praise is unwarranted. Both punishment and praise must be administered in an atmosphere of honesty and sincerity. Above all, the teacher must have feeling and compassion for his students, regardless of whether he is using praise *or* punishment as a motivator. A teacher should feel elated when praise is given but also some degree of remorse upon having to administer punishment. It is only human to occasionally mix anger with remorse, but anger alone should *never* be the sole excuse for motivating a youngster by reprimand or punishment.

Motivational aids of any kind may be used to stimulate better performance and/or behavior. However, the intrinsic psychological drive of "wanting to do better," and striving toward perfection is the ultimate in the learning process of any student. Whether the motivation to learn is extrinsic, intrinsic, or a combination of indefinite proportion is really not important. What is important is that the motivation used should stimulate a real eagerness to absorb knowledge and perform to one's full capability.

MAN AS A BIOLOGICAL MACHINE

Man has changed appreciably over the years in his habits, attitudes, and even in appearance. He has made rapid technological advances and enjoys a much higher standard of living than ever before. He has invented numerous creature comforts for himself due to his technology, and his life expectancy is greater than at any period in history. However, the fact remains that man himself is still an intricate biological machine whose basic systems are precisely like those of his ancestors who lived centuries ago.

We often hear the trite phrase, "exercise is good for you." The immediate question arises as to "why?" Logically we would assume that if bones react to muscular activity by increasing in size with subsequent strengthening, then perhaps other organs might adapt in a similar manner. If the assumption is true, it would follow that physical activity could be the primary key to the growth and maintenance of the basic body systems.

As man has increased his technology, so has he increased his capacity to lighten his physical work load. In our modern society man has devised mechanical means to move from one geographic location to another as well as to move within the confines of buildings. In addition, we have further decreased our apparent need for muscular activity by manufacturing various power tools and household gadgets to perform tasks which previously required muscular force. In short, we now live in a society that contributes to an extremely sedentary form of living.

The tragedy of our present mode of life is that the systems of the body have been found to thrive on physical activity and to atrophy with inactivity.

We have eliminated many of the physical demands placed on the bones and skeletal muscles. Also we have no further need for such ancient practices as pursuing wild game, or related protracted activity which is so essential to the maintenance of the cardiorespiratory system. It has long been recognized that the growth of the bones and muscles, and the maintenance of the cardiorespiratory and other vital systems are dependent to a great degree upon physical activity.

For example, the heart can be compared to a wonderfully efficient small pump. It regularly forces 5 to 6 quarts of blood around the body at least 1500 times per day for a total of about 1800 to 2200 gallons every 24 hours. Such an amount of blood would equal 60 to 70 times the amount of water used by one automatic washing machine performing a single complete cycle of operation. No one would conceive of using a washing machine 60 or 70 times a day without expecting to pay for maintenance of some kind. Yet few people realize that the heart is not only subjected to extremely heavier work loads, but it beats on endlessly throughout a human lifetime without much concern for maintenance on the part of its owner.

Obviously if the cardiorespiratory system is to be improved and maintained, the type of activity prescribed for such maintenance must be of a specific type which will place heavy demands upon the cells for oxygen. This type of aerobic exercise, which involves continual movement of the body over a protracted period of time, is not necessarily a part of our normal daily living pattern; it must be effected through the teaching of physical education in the formative years so that positive habits and attitudes will carry over into the postgraduation period and into later life. The human body cares little about the nature of aerobic activity and will react positively to all kinds. It is the duty of the physical educator to introduce such skills as jogging, swimming, cycling, tennis, and handball. It is also incumbent upon the profession to instill the participant with the physiological concepts underlying the *necessity* of such activities in the interest of systemic maintenance. Many physical educators are presently teaching in innovative programs where the lifetime sports are emphasized; however, such programs should always couple the *how* with the *why*.

WEIGHT CONTROL

For years a dispute has existed regarding the role of exercise in weight control. Certain nutritionists and physiologists have contended that exercise expends so few calories that it can hardly assist in the maintenance of desirable weight and that an increase in appetite due to activity will negate or at least hinder any attempt to lose weight. In contrast to this belief, the National Research Council (1953) found that men engaged in hard labor may consume as much as 6000 calories a day without gaining weight. The Council further stated that an obese individual expends a greater number of calories proportionately than does the person whose weight is considered normal for his body structure. Such is the case because the overweight person requires greater energy to move his body and therefore burns more of the fatty reserves than does his smaller counterpart who is engaged in identical activity. It also appears that inactivity precedes, and seems to be more the cause than the result, of obesity. While experimenting with animals it was found that those who were overweight ate more, and through inactivity stored the extra calories as fat instead of burning them up by being more active (Mayer, 1953).

SOCIALIZATION THROUGH ACTIVITY

The protest cry of "relevancy" is currently being heard throughout the land in relation to education in general, and to specific course offerings in particular. Such protestations are not without some justification. For years physical educators have paid lip service to the fact that socialization is a process that can be adequately met through active participation in sports and games, yet not enough teachers have seized upon the opportunity to capitalize upon the obvious laboratory of human interaction offered by the court and field.

Man's technological advancement has been extremely rapid; however, his ability to get along with his fellows has lagged miserably. In most segments of society one can discern a certain amount of dissension, racialism, distrust, social jealousy, and even contempt. Much of this has undoubtedly been precipitated by the current population explosion and our failure to cope with social problems at the rate that they have arisen. In the classroom sociologists concern themselves with explaining problems which bring about social unrest and also poses solutions to these problems. In classroom situations the atmosphere is artificial and is not charged with the emotional aspects which are attendant to actual life situations. In real life such hypothetical issues are stripped to the bare bones of temperament and the subsequent flow of adrenaline brought about by the excitement of the moment. In physical education classes the teacher deals with situations that truly meet the children at a level at which they live. The youngster who involves himself in any sport—individual, dual, or team—will eventually undergo every manifestation of human behavior which accompanies competitive endeavor. Competitors will relate to moments of joy, sadness, anger, disgust, dispair, humility, fear, courage, and anguish. They have the opportunity to learn to control their emotions or to let them run rampant. They may also gain respect for authority or learn to detest it. In short, the student who is actively engaged with his or her peers in physical education classes and athletic contests is placed in a microcosm of society in which the teacher or coach may exert a powerful positive or negative influence upon habits and attitudes that might carry over into the world at large.

MOTOR ABILITY AND RACIAL INTERACTION

Motor ability knows no ethnic boundaries. This fact is evidenced by outstanding performances from all of the various national groups represented in the Olympic Games. In certain track and field events, such as the sprints, dominance by black athletes has become apparent. In contrast, the weight events such as the shot, discus, and hammer throws are characteristically won by athletes of Caucasian descent. There has not been enough research accomplished in the area of ethnic differences and motor skill to determine whether heredity or environment is the primary factor in skill performance by the various groups. It has been postulated that in such sports as swimming, golf, and tennis, both socioeconomic background and the opportunity to compete may be valid reasons why such activities are championed by a predominance of Caucasians. Once the opportunity for competition has been presented, many tennis players, for example, Ashe, may rise from the ranks of minority groups; the same could occur in the sports of swimming and golf. After all, at present one does not see many Indians, Blacks, or Chicanos competing with the country club set which spawned the popularity of such activities. The only opportunity many of these people would have to compete in swimming, golf, and tennis would be through public school physical education classes and interscholastic sports programs.

If socialization is a process to be seriously sought through physical education, it is going to have to be effected by broadening the curricular offerings in the lifetime sports. It is well for us to point with pride to the racial interaction that takes place in team sports and to refer to the school athletic field as a place wherein no color line is drawn. However, we should be just as concerned about what happens to our students after they leave school and socially interact in the future. If our classes are to serve as a laboratory for life then it seems only logical that we must be inclusive rather than exclusive and provide *every* student with the opportunity to drink from the cup that exposes them to *all* facets of the nectar of "the good life." It is no wonder that some athletes of minority groups feel exploited when they discover that they have been encouraged in, and exposed to, only those activities in which they could excel for the benefit of the paying public. Many of these youngsters discover, on leaving school, that certain avenues are not open to them any longer and that schoolboy friendships with other ethnic groups dissolve because they are no longer in the proper social setting to play golf, swim, or engage in a tennis match now and then. They may not have had the opportunity to learn these skills in school because of being scheduled in an "athletic period" rather than in a regular physical education class or they may be merely the victims of an abbreviated curriculum. In any event, we must begin to accommodate these youngsters to a greater degree and provide for them the things they need to lead a full and productive recreational life after their school days are over. The physical education curriculum must be constructed to meet the needs of *all* children and should provide them with experiences needed to function on an equal footing with any social group. How refreshing it would be if the idealism of youth could pierce the callous social barriers of later years. It certainly never will until we provide the vehicle whereby people may learn to interact in youth and carry their enthusiasm for mutual friendly competitive activity into private life. If we as physical educators are to answer the cry for relevancy, then we must involve ourselves in more action and innovation and less discourse.

SOCIALIZATION—POSITIVE OR NEGATIVE

If socialization is to be positive, participants must learn to follow as well as to lead. Players must have a thorough understanding of rules and be willing to abide by them and also to enforce them. Many times youngsters become emotionally embroiled in arguments simply because of misunderstandings regarding proper procedure. Fights break out, insults are hurled, and chaos becomes the order of the day. More often than not, these unnecessary problems arise from ignorance. They not only develop on the playing field, but occur with great regularity among spectators who have little understanding of the intricacies of the rules of the contests they are witnessing.

If a student is to involve himself in a contest, he must have a complete knowledge of all aspects of the activity. One of the finest ways to learn something is to be placed in a position of having to teach it. Therefore, students should all have an opportunity to officiate, organize teams, and develop strategies that demand a working knowledge of the game. These factors take time; they must be well-planned and appropriately scheduled within the unit of instruction. Obviously, some written work is required and the thinking processes must be utilized. Moreover, if the teacher is going to teach skills and involve the students in actively leading as well as participating, short units will not accomplish the task. Exposure to this type of class interaction must begin early and progressively increase with the grade level of the child. There is nothing sacred about three or four week units in the secondary schools, and if an activity is worthwhile, it should be approached from all aspects. It is far better to teach six units a year correctly than to teach twelve in a haphazard manner. When an automobile is mired in a hole, no progress is made regardless of how many revolutions the wheels make until they finally reach solid ground. The same is true of education. Unless some learning ground is gained the instruction has been less than worthless because it has taken time from something of value. Objectives don't just happen; they must be fervently sought after with dogged determination.

The athletic program of a school is an area charged with emotion, both on the part of the students and townspeople alike. Nothing is quite so disgusting as to watch two groups of spectators fighting after an athletic contest, and yet it happens with increasing regularity. Much of the antagonism of spectators is spawned by ignorance and the lack of common courtesy compounded by the lack of respect for superior performance by the opposing player or team. Whose job is it to help eradicate these prejudices and erase this ignorance? The coaches and physical educators, of course!

Those charged with the responsibility of teaching and/or coaching cannot shirk the obligation of indoctrinating their students with the game knowledge and conduct becoming a good spectator. Neither can those who assume the authority for game management divorce themselves from the fact that they cannot condone irresponsible behavior on the part of any individual or group of partisan fans. When one individual exhibits poor sportsmanship, it sometimes becomes infectious and an entire crowd may misbehave. If students are regarded as potential spectators and are taught proper manners in their formative years, hopefully some carry-over will result. These manners are best taught by example and precept on the part of both teacher and coach.

Teachers and coaches are looked upon as leaders. A coach, in particular, is subject to the scrutiny of any crowd and as he reacts so will many members of his following. If teachers and coaches want positive social interaction as a result of their efforts, they must conduct themselves in an exemplary manner. If they fail to do so, they have only themselves to thank if their athletes and followers misbehave. At times, a teacher or coach is sorely tempted to react to an unsavory decision by an emotional outburst, but he is most assuredly helping no one, least of all himself. He should be mature enough to control his emotions. As President Truman said, "If you can't stand the heat, stay out of the kitchen."

At the present time it is not uncommon to hear four letter utterances by all age groups of both sexes, especially those who are involved in the heat of competition. The person who has to resort to such language is doing nothing more than enunciating his poor command of the language. He could be much more descriptive with a bit of creative grammar and would thereby illustrate intelligence rather than boorishness. Finally, the language of the gutter has no place in friendly competition and, in fact, may create serious problems when taken in the wrong vein by those who hear it. Speech habits can be corrected. It is certainly the duty of the teacher or coach to discourage the use of four letter epithets whenever or wherever he or she hears them. It is even less becoming to the teacher or coach to personally use these words. Some prospective teachers might not think that the use of inferior language is of any importance. However, discipline is a problem that entails many considerations, and social interaction of a positive nature is indeed a form of discipline.

RECOGNITION OF STUDENTS OF VARYING ABILITIES

It is one thing to preach tolerance and quite another to practice it in a classroom situation. It would be utter hypocracy to vocally allude to the matter of "concern for the individual" and then ignore the individual differences which occur in the classroom or on the field. It takes time to group youngsters and to encourage those who are having trouble learning skills and assist them in overcoming their problems. It is also gratifying to perceive the smile of appreciation on the face of a student who realizes that the teacher really cares about him and is trying his level best to help. Often all that is needed is a word of encouragement, a pat on the back, or a brief period of individual instruction to improve the performance of a given student. By the same token, the student who is making a nuisance of himself and is distracting those who wish to learn should also be given individual attention to straighten him out so that he ceases to be a distracting influence on the remainder of the class. Students appreciate individual attention, be it in the form of help to themselves, or in the form of ensuring that they will not be bothered by others who are interfering with their progress. Help is usually most beneficial if administered individually, and discipline should be handled in a similar manner. It is quite disconcerting to a student to be taken into partnership in a situation over which he has no control. Group control of both positive and negative factors has a place, but the "shotgun" approach should never replace individual assistance.

Every human being fervently desires individual identity. It is human nature to want to belong to a group, but all of us want to be individuals within the group. Moreover, people are desirous of recognition for positive performance. The conscientious teacher should always dwell upon the positive aspects of any performer, however slight the positive aspect may be. He should play down poor performance and seize upon every opportunity to compliment those features of progress that he perceives. As the ego of the individual develops, so does his self-confidence and subsequently his performance. It may be only a minute improvement, but the student must be encouraged if he is to be motivated to greater heights.

By being positive, the teacher will set an example for the students to follow. Negativism is rampant in the world today and can only be counteracted by educating youngsters to think more in terms of a positive outlook. If these virtues are learned in school, many youngsters will carry a positive attitude toward others into their private lives and, hopefully, a more favorable social climate will ensue. Negativism breeds contempt and positivism breeds friendship and cooperation. This is not to say that *no* negative aspects of performance or social attitude should be called to the attention of the student. On the contrary, these negative attitudes need to be brought to the surface, but should always be counteracted by alluding to the positive characteristics of the individual and the relatively greater importance of such attributes.

Many students become unruly because they are poor performers. As a result, they become disenchanted with their classwork and may, in fact, become serious disciplinary problems. The perceptive teacher must always point up the fact that individual differences do exist and for a variety of reasons. Kinesiologically some students can never perform certain stunts and skills as well as others because of various principles of leverage which mitigate against them. Somatotype leads to good performances in certain activities for some and to poor performances for others. As the type of activity changes, the relationship of body type to performance also is altered. Students must be made aware of all differences which affect performance negatively or positively. Through these understandings they will then be able to better adjust accordingly and learn to accept the fact that in some skills they will excel and in others they will not. As physical educators we understand these things because we have had the training to do so. The student does not necessarily understand, and until we educate him in these particulars he will remain clouded in ignorance and most assuredly this ignorance can lead to his becoming an antisocial animal because of a compensatory attitude directed toward attracting attention to himself.

SOCIALIZATION THROUGH CO-EDUCATION

Boys and girls must learn to get along well together in the elementary grades and the opportunity for co-educational activities should extend throughout the school years. Frequently, curricula have been constructed in which the kindergarten, primary, and early elementary years present an opportunity for co-educational pursuits; and then, because of game-oriented programs, the boys and girls are isolated during the later years of elementary education. Later, the junior high curriculum offers rhythm units of co-educational nature and the process of reacquainting boys and girls must begin anew. It would be much wiser to preserve some co-educational continuity throughout the entire school program from kindergarten through the senior year of high school. In this way, shyness which develops during the years of isolation inherent in some programs would not develop to such an extent, and the students would learn to appreciate the relative abilities of the opposite sex. Interaction and mutual respect would increase, and a much more harmonious relationship would develop as a result. Obviously, each sex has certain limitations in regard to various activities because of interest as well as physiological, psychological, and anatomical considerations. However, a balance of activities can be maintained wherein certain units of instruction, especially in co-recreational activities, can be included in the curriculum. These co-educational opportunities should definitely include those carry-over activities in which people can participate as adults. Therefore, it is imperative that co-educational activities be emphasized in the schools if they are to be of any value later on in life. Many family ties are strained and indeed dissolved because of the lack of common interests and recreational pursuits on the part of the marriage partners.

It should be emphasized that just because physical educators are aware of the anatomical, physiological, and psychological differences between the sexes, it does not follow that the students are equally aware. These differences which lead to variations in performance should be explained so that a mutual appreciation of the relative capabilities of each group will be understood. This is a topic which, in and of itself, can stimulate a lively discussion and positive social interaction of a co-educational nature. Concepts will be gained which may reach beyond the boundaries of the physical education class and truly assist in the founding of worthwhile understandings which would otherwise be lost.

Co-educational offerings demand a great deal of cooperative planning by the teachers involved and the social interchange must therefore originate within the staff. Frequently, the male and female members of the physical education staff themselves are not too amenable to proper social interaction, and as a result their programs tend to isolate youngsters even more. One reason that this has happened is that separate departments of physical education for men and women have long been a part of the college and university scene as well as the secondary schools. Certainly the men and women of higher education have special interests, but the overriding fact remains that we who train teachers must learn to cooperate and interact before we can expect the same of our students.

Acceptable social interaction, both between and within groups, must be a major objective of physical education if we are to seize upon the unique opportunity we have of educating youngsters in a truly viable environment. To do less is to invite justifiable criticism from every quarter and to abdicate the responsibility entrusted to us by the people we serve. We can train well-skilled performers by the dozens who can execute their various maneuvers with perfection. However, if we fail in our mission to assist our students in the process of learning how to properly conduct themselves as functional members of a complex society, we should indeed stand convicted of gross malfeasance.

QUESTIONS FOR DISCUSSION

1. How can physical education activities best relate to the problem of stress in our society?
2. What could a physical education department do to assist adults in offsetting stress? What type of programs could be implemented for this purpose?
3. What types of practical experimentation, other than the examples presented in this chapter, could be implemented within a physical education class that would illustrate stress and the alleviation of stress?
4. What is the importance of motivation in the learning process?
5. What is the difference between intrinsic and extrinsic motivation? Why are these factors important to the teacher?

6. How many people do you suppose could actually explain clearly why exercise is good for a person? What can the physical educator do to contribute to a thorough knowledge of the "why" of various forms of physical activity?
7. Do you feel that knowledge in exercise physiology could be understood by elementary school youngsters? How would it have to be presented in order to be effective? Is this the job of the health instructor or the physical educator?
8. Why does physical education present a better laboratory for socialization than an academic classroom situation?
9. Why are lifetime sports so necessary to the socialization process?
10. What are some of the duties and obligations of the teacher of physical education in regard to the socialization process?
11. Of what importance to the socialization process is co-education? Why should age groups be encompassed by co-education?

BIBLIOGRAPHY

1. Food and Nutrition Board. "Recommended Dietary Allowances." Washington, D.C.: National Research Council Publication 302, 1953.
2. Mayer, J. "Decreased Activity and Energy Balance in Hereditary Diabetes Syndrome of Mice." *Science* 117, 504 (1953).
3. Mayer, J. "Genetic, Traumatic and Environmental Factors in the Etiology of Obesity." *Physiol. Rev.* 33, 472 (1953).
4. Michael, E. D. "Stress Adaptation Through Exercise." *Res. Q. Am. Ass. Hlth. Phys. Educ.* 28:1 (1957).

CASE STUDIES

MR. MALLORY

Mr. Mallory resigned his position as a high school physical education teacher and returned to the university to pursue graduate work in his discipline which hopefully would lead to an advanced degree. Mallory's funds were limited; he therefore planned his year in residence carefully so that he could take as much coursework as possible to avoid the expense of additional summer sessions. There were no restrictions placed on the hours of credit for which graduate students could enroll, and Mallory carried a heavy overload each term.

During the last two weeks of the winter term, Mallory noticed that he was getting rather nervous and irritable and that he seemed to suffer from indigestion after almost every meal. He became despondent about his health and decided that he should have a complete physical examination to determine the cause of his illness and hopefully to effect a cure. He consulted a physician who listened to his complaints, advised X-rays of the gastrointestinal tract, and then reported that nothing could be found that would indicate any serious problem.

Mallory then sought the services of another physician and informed him that he believed the first doctor to be incompetent and therefore requested another complete physical examination. The second physician listened patiently and talked with Mr. Mallory at length about his study schedule, past medical history, family life, and related circumstances and then advised him to return the following day for a prescription.

Unknown to Mallory was the fact that his physician, Doctor Girard, had quite a number of graduate students under his care and was completely familiar with the rigors of graduate studies. Furthermore, Girard was a man who exercised daily and found that activity was a release from his own personal pressures and problems.

Mallory was told by Doctor Girard that his basic problem arose from the exhaustive schedule that he was trying to maintain and that he was going to prescribe one hour a day of vigorous activity as a method of alleviating the difficulty. Mallory was surprised by the diagnosis and somewhat chagrined that he as a physical educator had not had the presence of mind to arrive at a similar conclusion prior to consulting a physician. Doctor Girard reassured Mallory by informing him that his schedule was so demanding he had probably not had much time to consider anything other than the fact that he did not feel well and that his symptoms could have easily been those of something far more serious.

Mr. Mallory set aside an hour a day in which he began to jog, play some handball, and swim. He alternated his activity to provide variety and maintained his schedule with the same devotion that he applied to his graduate studies. After a brief period of time Mallory noticed that he was feeling much better, his appetite had returned, and he had no further need of being selective about which foods he ate. He became more confident in his work and by the end of the spring term he could look back upon his year of graduate work as one of high accomplishment, both psychologically and physiologically. Mallory completed his advanced degree requirements and has never since failed to utilize his daily exercise period.

QUESTIONS

1. What symptoms did Mr. Mallory have that seem indicative of many people who are placed in stressful conditions? Do any of these symptoms sound like those described by Selye?

2. What technique was used by Dr. Girard in assisting Mallory that was not used by his first physician? Does this have any implications for physical education?
3. Wherein during the discussion of the Mallory case did the subject show his intelligence and where did he demonstrate his ignorance as an educated physical educator?

MR. NEY

Mr. Ney was the superintendent of a rather large school district and as such was continually involved with committee work, conferences, and administrative detail. He was somewhat distant from his teachers, many of whom came to regard him as a self-centered individual who probably had no concept of mixing with others socially. Ney's attitude was discussed in faculty groups and it was finally decided that perhaps his habit of remaining aloof was not entirely of his own making. No one had ever approached Mr. Ney about the possibility of involving himself with faculty recreation projects and therefore a delegate, who happened to be the high school golf coach, was asked to invite Ney to participate in a twilight golf tournament.

Mr. Ney apparently was quite flattered by being asked to participate in the tournament, but admitted that his knowledge of golf was negligible and therefore indicated that he should perhaps decline the invitation. He was told that none of the players in the tournament were accomplished golfers and finally he condescended to play. The golf coach arranged for a few private lessons for Mr. Ney so that he might be reassured, and it was discovered that the man had considerable undisclosed talent.

Ney cautiously entered the golf tournament and became quite proficient as a player. He entered into the friendly banter that accompanied the informal play and seemingly enjoyed the outings immensely. After a few weeks of play had transpired, many of the faculty members who participated forgot their reservations about Mr. Ney's social prowess and began to ask him to attend other functions which centered about their lives. Ney found that he was asked to participate in a faculty volleyball tournament and also to become a member of a district-wide poker club which met periodically. He had to decline some of the invitations he received due to professional commitments, but did so reluctantly, rather than willingly as he had done before.

As a result of his participation in faculty activities and social events, Mr. Ney endeared himself to many teachers within the district. He became known as a man and a human being rather than an inanimate administrative figurehead. He discovered that people became more willing to work with him on school committees and accepted him as a colleague in the truest sense of the word.

QUESTIONS

1. Do you believe that the faculty members had any business interfering with Mr. Ney's private life by asking him to participate in the golf tournament? If so, why? If not, why?
2. What really changed Mr. Ney as a human being? Was it the activity itself or the companionship involved?
3. What are the implications of the Ney case for those who are sincerely interested in improving relations between faculty and administration? Do you regard this as a sincere way of solving a problem in human relations or merely as a political ploy?

GEORGE LENTZ

George Lentz was a sophomore in high school and had recently transferred to Millvale from a community that was extremely small and had offered a school curriculum which did not include any physical education. George had been a rather sickly child and was obviously overprotected by his mother who refused to believe that physical activity of any kind could be other than detrimental to her son. However, since physical education was required, George was enrolled in class despite his mother's objections.

Mr. Herring, the boy's physical education instructor at Millvale, was a rather large blustering fellow who had absolutely no sympathy for those that could not adequately perform motor skills and furthermore refused to "waste his time on them." At the time of George's entry into physical education, a unit in gymnastics was being offered. George performed miserably while attempting even the simplest of stunts and thereby engendered the wrath of his teacher who ridiculed him constantly. After a few days in class George was reduced to tears each time he was told that he had to perform a stunt and was never offered any positive suggestions or assistance; his every effort met only with further criticism.

George Lentz had entered Millvale as a shy, retiring boy, but had never been a trouble maker and had maintained good grades. After two or three months at Millvale George's personality changed completely. He became sullen, his grades fell, and he began to miss school with great frequency. When he was called into the principal's office to explain his behavior George refused to offer any excuse other than to say that he hated Millvale and wanted to go "home."

George's father had a good job in Millvale and did not want to leave the community. His mother was active in quite a few women's organizations in town and she also did not wish to move to another community despite the pleadings of her son. As time passed, George became more and more truant and finally dropped out of school altogether and took a job in a service station.

QUESTIONS

1. What tactics should George Lentz's physical education teacher have used instead of those which he employed? Why?
2. Can you cite cases similar to the George Lentz affair which might shed light on the change in George's behavior?
3. If you had been the administrator who was confronted by George's difficulty what steps would you have taken to rectify the situation?
4. As a result of reading the Lentz case, how would you handle transfer students who entered your classes? What steps would you take to ensure the success of such a student?
5. Do you feel that any single teacher could have caused George to drop out of school? If so, why? If not, why?

MISS OSBORN

Miss Osborn had resigned her position as a public school physical educator after deciding that she would prefer to return to graduate school, complete the doctorate, and hopefully gain placement in a college or university. She had been accepted for graduate study at a reputable institution and subsequently withdrew her state retirement funds to defray her school and living expenses.

Fall quarter progressed nicely and Miss Osborn made good grades, enjoyed her studies, and made many new acquaintances. She returned home for the Christmas vacation only to discover that her mother was suffering from an incurable illness. Miss Osborn was struggling between the compulsion to remain home and that of returning to graduate school to complete her year of residence which was mandatory for acceptance into the doctoral program. She was assured that there was really nothing that she could do at home that would be beneficial to her mother or family and therefore should return to her studies.

Miss Osborn's class load during the winter term of school was exceptionally heavy and she had virtually no time for any recreational pursuits. Her mind was continually occupied by not only her academic work but by constant worry about her mother's health. As the term progressed Miss Osborn began to get nervous, suffered from sleepless nights and acute stomach cramps. She dismissed the symptoms as nothing other than the classic "graduate student's syndrome"; however, the symptoms increased in intensity until Miss Osborn began to realize that her work habits had been interfered with, and she therefore sought medical advice.

The physician consulted by Miss Osborn was a gentleman who was not only an excellent diagnostician but one who was quite proficient as a psychologist as well. He listened patiently to Miss Osborn's complaints and then gave her a complete physical examination. He spent a considerable amount of time discussing family problems, financial difficulties, and the fact that Miss Osborn was carrying an extremely heavy class load which compounded her other concerns. After the physical examination and other relevant data had been completed the doctor asked Miss Osborn to return to his office the following day for the results.

On her return, the doctor informed Miss Osborn that he could find absolutely nothing with her physically but did state that in his professional opinion her nervous condition had precipitated the symptoms that she had described. Miss Osborn was then told that she was going to have to set aside a period of time each day for strenuous physical activity in the interest of relieving nervous tension; she was then asked what she preferred to do. Miss Osborn settled upon a jogging routine as her most practicable physical outlet since she could schedule routine jogging at her convenience without having to seek out a game partner or group with which to work. The physician agreed that this was a logical solution but also prescribed a mild tranquilizer which he believed to be necessary. Miss Osborn did not welcome the use of a drug but reluctantly decided to try it in the interest of getting some well-needed rest. After following her exercise routine diligently for less than two weeks Miss Osborn began to feel much better, so much in fact that she asked the Doctor to relieve her of the tranquilizer; he agreed.

Miss Osborn continued with her graduate studies and successfully completed her degree requirements. She frequently mentioned the fact that as a physical educator she was somewhat chagrined by the fact that she had not realized what her own problem had been initially and had to be advised by someone from another profession. She has since conscientiously budgeted recreational time for herself to cope with the everyday frustrations of her position as a college professor.

QUESTIONS

1. Do you feel that Miss Osborn was typical of many cases of nervous frustration found in this country?
2. Should Miss Osborn have taken it upon herself to attempt to diagnose her own problem or did she follow a logical course of action? If so, why? If not, why?
3. Can you cite cases you have known which are similar to that of Miss Osborn?

MRS. MCDANIEL

Mrs. McDaniel was a person who had never participated in much vigorous activity because she completely misunderstood the values of such participation. After reaching maturity, Mrs. McDaniel became rather obese and constantly worried about her appearance. As a result of her concern, Mrs. McDaniel tried one diet after another only to discover that none of the dietary measures reduced her weight appreciably; she therefore became disenchanted with the idea of weight reduction.

During a conversation with a member of the physical education department, Mrs. McDaniel mentioned that she would like to reduce and wondered if exercise perhaps would help. Miss Nero of the physical education department patiently explained the theory of calorie intake and expenditure to Mrs. McDaniel and offered her assistance in solving the problem of weight reduction.

Mrs. McDaniel was placed on a diet by her physician and an exercise routine was prescribed by Miss Nero. The activity could be undertaken in the confines of her home inasmuch as Mrs. McDaniel was averse to being seen in public while exercising. The bulk of the program was related to endurance by utilizing the bench-stepping technique which is employed in the administration of the Harvard Step Test. Mrs. McDaniel progressed nicely not only in the length of time she spent in the bench-stepping, but also in the height of the bench which was used. She further combined her endurance efforts with both stretching and strengthening exercises to ensure proper muscle tone. After staying on her diet and exercise routine for some months Mrs. McDaniel lost over forty pounds and was delighted with the results that she had achieved.

Not only was Mrs. McDaniel impressed with the amount of weight she had lost, but also even more intrigued by the fact that she now possessed an entirely new outlook on life and new confidence in herself as a person.

QUESTIONS

1. Why do you suppose Mrs. McDaniel consulted with a professional physical educator instead of drawing upon personal experience?
2. What psychological benefits do you suppose Mrs. McDaniel gained from her experiences?

DR. STRATTON

Dr. Stratton, of the department of physical education at State College, was very much aware of the problems many women have in childbirth. She had been asked many questions in and out of class about natural delivery. Therefore she decided to assist a few young wives with various types of prenatal exercises which were designed to better prepare them for normal and natural childbirth.

Dr. Stratton gathered information from books, periodicals, and physicians relative to the types of exercise suggested for prospective mothers and began to help her students in establishing exercise routines. She assisted only those who had the approval of their physicians and insisted that they work as a team.

As the news circulated about Dr. Stratton's interest in prescribing prenatal exercises, her clientele grew. It seemed that each term a few more expectant mothers called to ask for advice and none were ever turned away. Dr. Stratton was meticulous in her endeavor and began to accept her voluntary duties as part of her regular job routine.

After receiving many birth announcements and the verbal appreciation of her clients, Dr. Stratton remarked more than once that she imagined she was possibly one of "the greatest associate mothers of all time." Perhaps the most satisfaction gained by Dr. Stratton was the fact that many of the former "pupils" were passing the information regarding prenatal exercises on to their friends.

QUESTIONS

1. Do you believe that a service such as that rendered by Dr. Stratton would have a place in girls' high school physical education classes? What precautions would have to be taken in order to teach a unit on prenatal exercises?
2. What outside sources could be called upon in order to better present a unit on prenatal exercise? Would such a unit have any benefit for boys' physical education classes? Why or why not?
3. It is apparent that the people involved in the cases presented were older persons. Do you think that this had any affect upon their desire for activity?

4. As a result of reading these cases, do you feel it incumbent upon physical educators to expand their responsibility beyond that of merely teaching their classes?

5. Why do you suppose that the people cited in all of the preceding cases were so ignorant of the values of physical activity and why were they not able to initiate exercise programs of their own without consulting people in the profession? What does this tell us about our teaching of the past?

MR. MARSYK AND MR. EAGEN

John Marsyk and Fred Eagen were college freshmen who had enrolled in a junior college which was located in a rural environment quite distant from their home community of Chicago. Both boys were city born and reared and they did not relate well to their fellow students who for the most part were from farms and ranches. They were good students but took no active part in the social life of the college and chose to remain by themselves.

Both Marsyk and Eagen were avid weightlifters and had been accomplished high school athletes. Neither lad seemed interested in competing on the intramural teams and frequently offered excuses of one type or another when asked why they did not choose to participate. Marsyk had brought his own set of weights from home and the boys worked out in the basement of the house that they were renting and therefore did not avail themselves of the college weight room.

Mr. Danner, the director of men's physical education, tried to enlist Marsyk and Eagen in the intramural program but they politely declined. It became apparent to Danner that perhaps the two boys would like to compete in some form of group activity but were reluctant to do so because their background was so different that they had not really been accepted as peers. Danner knew that Marsyk and Eagen were skilled in weightlifting and approached them with the idea of initiating a weightlifting club. He promised to handle the publicity and to assist with any organizational details if they were at all interested in such a venture. Marsyk and Eagen reluctantly condescended to appear at an organizational meeting of the club to demonstrate basic lifts and explain some of the tenets of competitive weightlifting.

Danner publicized the meeting widely through the school newspaper and daily bulletins. The attendance at the first meeting was comparatively small but enthusiasm grew rapidly when the demonstrations and explanations were given. Many questions were asked of Marsyk and Eagen relative to how long they had been lifting, what dietary procedures they followed, and how much each could lift while performing any one of the competitive movements. The questions were answered and discussion followed during which both Marsyk and Eagen became eagerly involved. At the conclusion of the meeting all of the participants adjourned to the student center to further engage in friendly discussion. It was at this point that a common purpose was reached among all of the boys and they began to accept the two "foreigners" into their group.

As a result of their initial contact with fellow students, Marsyk and Eagen consented to become involved in the intramural program and both became respected for their talents on the court and field. Within a short time the two lads were invited to many social functions and their athletic prowess became known campuswide. The two boys continued their education until they received their associate's degrees and subsequently transferred to four-year schools within the state. Each elected to attend a different institution but both left the junior college with many friends who transferred with them.

QUESTIONS

1. What do you think of the manner in which Mr. Danner handled the Marsyk and Eagen case? What other approaches might have been taken to involve these two lads in the total program?
2. Do you think that Marsyk and Eagen would have received as much individual attention in a large university as they did at the smaller junior college? If not, why?
3. What lessons in social integration are to be learned from such cases as that of Marsyk and Eagen?

ROXY WELLS

Roxy Wells had played junior high school football for two years and had been quite successful as a guard. He was quick, intelligent, and played his position well. During the winter of his ninth-grade year Wells fell backward against a concrete floor during a physical education class and was knocked unconscious. He recovered readily but suffered a rather severe concussion as a result of the blow. Later in the year Wells suffered another concussion and his physician advised against his involvement in any type of contact sport.

When the football season began the following year, Wells asked the coach if he could come out for the team and he was informed that his physician had advised against it. He begged to play and finally the coach agreed to discuss the matter with Wells' parents and physician. The physician stated that he did not believe Wells should play football but his father pointed out that his son's friends were all competing and that he might be damaged psychologically if he did not get to play in some capacity, even if only a minor role.

The high school coach, who had watched Wells play junior high football, remembered that the boy was a slightly better than average punter and that he had managed to kick a few extra points. He stated that he had always wanted a specialist for punting and place-kicking and that perhaps with a properly padded headgear the lad might be able to fill the position. The physician agreed that the chance for injury in the specialist's role would be negligible but stated that he would have to withdraw his permission to play if Wells suffered only one additional concussion.

An extra large headgear was purchased for Wells and it was thoroughly padded with additional layers of foam rubber. The boy practiced his punting and place-kicking until he became extremely proficient as a specialist. He was contented to sit on the bench until his talents were needed and he was highly respected by his teammates. During the course of the season Wells kicked off, punted, and kicked numerous extra points. He felt that he truly had discovered his niche and possibly was of more value as a specialist than he would have been as a guard. He played out his high school career as a kicking specialist. He enjoyed his role and apparently found great satisfaction in performing a function in which he excelled.

QUESTIONS

1. Do you believe that the Wells case was handled in an appropriate manner? Would you as a football coach be willing to assume the responsibility demonstrated in this case? If so, why? If not, why?
2. Do you believe that psychological damage can be of greater importance than psysiological damage? Why?
3. In a case such as that involving Wells, what steps would you have to take prior to granting the request made by the boy?

KURT NUGENT

Kurt Nugent was a bright and friendly youngster whose legs had been severely damaged by poliomyelitis. He wore braces and walked with two short crutches to support himself. Kurt did not want to be excused from regular physical education classes but discovered that there were many activities in which he could not take part. He learned to perform simple tumbling stunts and worked on the horizontal bar whenever he could. During class units in wrestling Kurt would wrestle his opponents from a mat position. During such matches Nugent's opponent's legs were strapped together so that the match became relatively equal. An adaptives program was formulated for the boy so that he could work by himself during the time instructional units were offered in which he could not possibly take part.

Everyone liked Kurt because he was not only a good student but also cheerful at all times and never felt sorry for himself. He often requested permission to race anyone available, if the person would consent to race while walking on their hands. Kurt had developed a high degree of proficiency in balancing and walking on his hands and was never defeated. The coaching staff was so impressed with the lad's performance that Kurt was encouraged to exhibit his hand-balancing talents during the halftime activities at basketball games and gymnastic meets.

MISS COREY AND MISS ELLIOT

Miss Corey was a strong proponent of co-educational physical education activities. She worked diligently with the male instructors to develop not only co-educational activities in the regularly scheduled classes, but in the intramural program as well. Youngsters were encouraged to play volleyball, mixed doubles in badminton and tennis, and participate on mixed bowling teams. Miss Corey also worked diligently to coordinate co-educational activities throughout the entire school district and was quite successful in her efforts.

When Miss Corey retired she was replaced by Miss Elliot who was a competent teacher but totally unfamiliar with co-educational activities to the extent that they had previously been used. She immediately decided to redesign the girl's physical education curriculum and thereby eliminate all co-educational activities other than badminton. The administration consented to the wishes of Miss Elliot and she was allowed to revamp the program.

During the first year of Miss Elliot's teaching career a storm of protest arose regarding the course changes which had been implemented. Students protested to the principal and superintendent, and many parents complained vociferously about the lack of co-educational activities. With a great deal of reluctance Miss Elliot was forced to alter her curriculum at midyear and return to that which had previously been employed. She completed the first year of her contract and then resigned to seek placement elsewhere.

QUESTIONS

1. How would you compare Miss Corey and Miss Elliot as teachers who were really aware of human needs?
2. Do you believe that Miss Elliot acted impulsively? Why?
3. Do you believe that any professional ethics were violated by Miss Elliot's actions regarding curricular changes? Why?
4. Do you believe that the cases herein were basically sociological or psychological? If they were examples of only one or the other, how would you separate the two?
5. Do sociological problems have psychological origins? If so, why? If not, why?
6. Do you believe that the professional preparation of Miss Corey and Miss Elliot might have affected their attitudes toward co-educational activities? Why?

SUGGESTED RELATED READING

Cureton, Thomas Kirk, *Physical Fitness and Dynamic Health.* New York: Dial Press, 1965.

Cureton, Thomas Kirk, *The Physiological Effects of Exercise Programs on Adults.* Springfield, Ill.: C. C. Thomas, 1969.

Davis, Elwood C., Gene Gogan and Wayne McKinney, *Biophysical Values of Muscular Activity.* Dubuque, Iowa: Wm. C. Brown Co., 1961. Has implications for research.

Jokl, Ernst, *Heart and Sport.* Springfield, Ill.: C. C. Thomas, 1964.

Jokl, Ernst, *The Clinical Physiology of Physical Fitness and Rehabilitation.* Springfield, Ill.: C. C. Thomas, 1958.

Sage, George H., *Sport and American Society: Selected Readings.* Reading, Mass.: Addison-Wesley, 1970.

Steinhaus, Arthur H., *Toward an Understanding of Health and Physical Education.* Dubuque, Iowa: Wm. C. Brown, 1963.

Williams, Jesse F., *The Principles of Physical Education.* Eighth Edition. Philadelphia: Saunders, 1964.

The young people of this nation are crying for positive adult leadership. They desire to have direction applied to their lives by rational guidance from those who have profited from the lessons of experience and prior training. Furthermore, students need discipline and direction as a matter of personal security in an insecure world.

To lead is one thing and to drive is quite another. As someone once observed, it is much easier to pull a piece of thread in a straight line than to push it. Autocratic dictatorial approaches to leadership often succeed in doing nothing more than to alienate the student from the authority figure. What they are really searching for is the type of leadership involved in participatory democracy where possible. Obviously, students who are rational realize that decisions have to be made and policy enacted which sometimes may run contrary to their wishes. However, if they are given the opportunity to be heard and to raise questions which are answered logically rather than emotionally, most are then willing to comply. True, there are some radical elements which are not content with any decision made by other than their own group. These individuals are continually voicing demands for participation but would deny the same rights to others. Theirs is generally a minority voice and their actions are usually tantamount to a group temper tantrum. Unfortunately, in policy deliberations the poorest wheel on the cart makes the most noise and therefore receives the grease.

A perceptive leader is quick to recognize the difference between demands made by a group of rabble-rousers, and cogent questions which are raised by people who are sincerely concerned. It is only when these vital and relevant questions are received by deaf ears, and are not considered in the determination of policy, that the radical minority gains a foothold. Students of this day and age are continually questioning the "why" of the establishment and are often frustrated because they receive no logical answers.

The dynamic leader will involve students whenever and wherever he can. Through the lengthy deliberations and investigations inherent in the decision-making process, the involved student begins at an early age to appreciate the fact that democratic procedure is time-consuming and that policy of any consequence is not easily determined. In fact, many students begin to shy away from asking to assist in the management function once they get a taste of its less attractive features. Colleges and universities are discovering that many committees who have included student membership find that the students absent themselves frequently—some because they have discovered the committee process to be downright boring, and others because they feel a definite lack of experience and training necessary to the deliberations at hand. Many youngsters involved for the first time in governance find to their dismay that it is far easier to complain about decisions that have been made which control their lives than it is to *make* the decisions which in turn affect the lives of their peers. Also, very few discover that they have the true qualities of leadership necessary to initiate worthwhile actions and carry them out. After proper exposure to the mechanics of democratic leadership, many youngsters will excuse themselves to the role of following the policies laid down by others. However, until they have had the opportunity to encounter the obstacles of leadership first hand, students will continue to rebel against even duly constituted authority.

We live in a democratic society and are committed to the teaching of the democratic process. What better way to illustrate the benefits and complications of participation than in the schools of this country. We have at our disposal the greatest laboratory for human interaction that the world has ever seen, and we had better take advantage of the opportunity to involve the majority of rational youngsters before those who are disposed to anarchy leave our schools in utter chaos.

A democratic representative republic such as our own entrusts certain duties and responsibilities to various groups which have been established by law. These groups are charged with the responsibility to govern, but are not endowed with the power of enacting dictatorial edicts which function at the expense of the governed. Each of our duly constituted bodies of authority is subject to the scrutiny as well as the wishes of those of the electorate, and by statute must not exceed its prescribed authority. Therefore there should be a provision for review of any policy, ordinance, regulation, or rule which seems to be operating to the detriment of those governed rather than for their mutual benefit. It should herein be *emphasized* however that *any review* of policy, regulations or other similar edict *must* be accomplished through orderly prescribed channels, and that riot, violent demonstration, and vandalism will not be countenanced under *any* conditions.

STUDENTS NEED LEADERS NOT "BUDDIES"

Our youngsters have all the "buddies" they need within the ranks of their peer group. They do not require this type of companionship from their teachers, not do they expect it. What they really expect is counsel from an understanding adult who is charged with the responsibility of leadership and is willing to assume such a role by virtue of his training, experience, and position. Teachers should be friendly toward students, but at the same time they must realize that they have assumed, at least to a partial degree, the role of the parents while the student is in their charge. In such a role, guidance, direction, and control are all functions that must supersede any other relationship with the student that the teacher may envision. Helping the student, directly or indirectly, in the attainment of his goals and aspirations is the duty of all educators. However, identifying with students by affectations, such as dress, moral and social conduct peculiar to student groups, hair styles, teenage jargon, badgering of administrators, and other similar stunts, is not only ridiculous, it is dishonest. The student often resents such actions as an infringement upon his individuality and an encroachment upon his group. Social distance between students and educators is a must if discipline is to be maintained. No one person can equitably play a dual role and hope to justify either one. The professional must make a choice. Either he assumes all of the responsibilities and obligations pertinent to his chosen occupation, or he should seek some other form of endeavor. He cannot lead and simultaneously be led by the student group. If he attempts to do so, he can do no better than to fail miserably at both tasks. The teacher who is respected by his students is one who executes his duties with responsibility and integrity. He is professionally oriented, prepares himself well for his teaching, counseling and advising, and *earns* respect by virtue of his excellence rather than by running a personality contest with his colleagues.

Students who seek advice and assistance should receive such attention because that is the reason for which teachers are employed. Educators should be ready to eradicate ignorance and render help whenever and wherever possible. They must, however, approach each individual situation with a clearly professional attitude governed by logic and sound problem-solving techniques, not by emotion and subsequent reaction founded upon rumor, hearsay, and supposition. Unfortunately, there are many young men and women attracted to the teaching profession who see their position as an opportunity to assist the oppressed (students) in their struggle against the establishment. They are not as interested in imparting their subject matter as they are in utilizing the educational system as a vehicle for social reform and the purveyance of their particular philosophy. This they attempt by relating and sympathizing with the students in whatever the cause, and ignoring the primary functions for which they were employed. Many go to great lengths to be seen at student gatherings in an effort to be identified as "one of the group." Then when a decision has to be made which places the teacher in a position of having to discipline one of his "buddies," he may well discover that his situation is virtually untenable. He is condemned regardless of which alternative he may select. The neophyte teacher must pursue his profession with dedication and abide by the ethics governing that profession. If he so chooses, he will ultimately discover that he has entered the most satisfying and challenging enterprise possible. He will further find that the only road to self satisfaction, professional fulfillment, and the earned respect of his students is the pathway of diligence, dedication, perseverance, honesty, and professional integrity. This is not an easy road, but it is the only one for the sincere professional physical educator.

ORGANIZATION—THE KEYWORD TO SUCCESS

Planning and organizing are those elements which capitalize upon the full use of class time in the interest of instruction. Students come to class with the expectation that the teacher knows what he is doing and that the instructional period will be profitable for them. Haphazard planning, or no planning at all, generally yields poor results in the matter of discipline as well as in teaching. Motivation and interest cannot be maintained for any period of time when the instructor, through his own laziness or negligence, absents himself and leaves youngsters to their own devices. At the beginning of any unit, the teacher should outline the unit for the students by apprising them of all aspects of the instruction that they are about to receive. This method of unit orientation should immediately convey to the student what is personally expected of him, what instructional material he is going to be exposed to, and why the factors being taught are of importance. Thus, with the instructional stage set, the teacher can go about his business with full knowledge that his students know what to expect. After the presentation of the unit outline, daily explanation becomes valuable in the matter of class control. The instructional time should be fully utilized on the daily lesson plan and no periods of indecision or makeshift instruction should take place unless something completely unavoidable arises, such as an abbreviated period due to an unannounced assembly or other interference that was not previously scheduled.

There is an old saying in the navy that "a busy ship is a happy ship." The basic psychology underlying this adage is that when people are gainfully occupied they have little time for other activities, especially those which might be of a disruptive nature. Youngsters in class react in much the same fashion as sailors. If they are busily engaged in their activities, they have little time to annoy their neighbors or otherwise interfere with the class. If they are unsure of what they are supposed to be doing and become bored, they will seek alternatives that may not be conducive to good conduct.

In organizing instructional units, the interest span of the age group involved must be considered. In general, the younger the child the shorter the interest span. Therefore, the conscientious planner should gauge the length of any particular facet of instruction to the age level which he is teaching. There are no hard and fast rules to follow in the establishment of time blocks, much of which is related to the type of instuction and often to the level of intelligence of those being taught. What to use in a particular drill, and for how long, comes with experience. It can be said however that those things which apply to the planning of lessons for secondary students will not necessarily function well in the instruction of elementary school pupils. Between these age extremes there will be variations in time usage as it relates to interest span.

An adequate amount of equipment is an absolute necessity for good lesson planning, time usage, and student interest. Nothing creates boredom as rapidly as having to stand in line "awaiting one's turn" to shoot a basketball, serve a volleyball, strike a tether ball, serve a badminton bird, or execute a tumbling stunt. Obviously class size is also of primary importance. A large class is much more difficult to control than a small one. The only remedy for large classes, when they are unavoidable, is to work with squads or groups within the class. The primary objective is to obtain the maximal amount of activity from each youngster during the instructional time scheduled.

Discipline cannot be maintained and skills will not effectively be taught without adequate numbers of balls, bats, nets, mats, rackets, or whatever equipment is necessary in a particular instance. No classroom teacher would think of functioning in a positive manner by providing only one textbook for each ten or fifteen students, yet physical educators are asked to do this constantly. It should be mentioned, however, that some equipment shortage is due to the apparent laziness and laxity of individual teachers and is not necessarily the result of administrative penny-pinching. Some people have been used to the "stand in line and wait" concept for so long that they have not taken the time or energy to question it and alter their programs or equipment budgets to counteract the problem. On the other hand, some administrators have ordered adequate equipment and have later discovered that it was not being used. Skills were not being taught after perhaps one or two days and only one or two balls were used for the entire period of so called "free play." Naturally, a perceptive administrator would be reluctant to spend taxpayers money for items which are not used. The new teacher following in the footsteps of a lazy person will have to convince the administration of his intent before he asks that his budgetary requests be granted. Human beings are rather hesitant to be "stung" more than once and, unfortunately, guilt by association is a difficult force to overcome.

The boredom of students is readily perceived in many classes. Those who are bored usually become the troublemakers. It has been suggested that those who aspire to the teaching of physical education observe public school classes in order to determine some of the things that transpire. It would be advisable for the observer to identify *one individual child* and closely watch him for the entire period of instruction to determine just how much activity, or instruction, he actually receives. It is also interesting to observe what the youngster does with his time during the period in which he is *not* actively involved. Such an evaluation can be very revealing as to the true origin of disciplinary difficulties.

Frequently the physical educator is confronted by inclement weather during the period in which he is teaching a unit out-of-doors. Often such periods are filled by having the students come into the gymnasium or other indoor facility and play some irrelevant game or otherwise occupy their time with something that is not relevant to the unit. There is no excuse for not having an alternative lesson plan which could be utilized when the regular instruction is interrupted by schedule problems, inclement weather, shortened periods, or other factors. These alternative plans might focus on strategy, rules, concepts of specific movements, physiological considerations, or a multitude of other factors directly related to that which is being taught. To excuse a class, establish a study hall, or just sit around aimlessly is inexcusable and is a classic example of poor planning and organization. Moreover, when the students perceive that the teacher really doesn't care, they won't care either and will generally find something to occupy their time, usually something detrimental and annoying.

Students want to learn, but they must be motivated by direct action and they must find the instructional period active and stimulating. They must be kept busy, occupied with something new and of interest, and thus be able to understand the reasons for developing skills to the highest level possible for their capability. They must be encouraged and assisted. If they are not kept alive, stimulated, encouraged, and given individual help, they will become disenchanted with the course and seek alternatives for the release of their energies.

The teacher who spends little time teaching skills, institutes a "tournament" before the students have even learned the game, and then stands on the sidelines rationalizing his own laziness and inefficiency is indeed to be pitied. Furthermore, oftimes the youngsters get unruly and the teacher cannot understand why. As a result he shouts, threatens, and cajoles to restore order and then blames all of the trouble on the students. A thorough bit of introspection would reveal that many of the discipline problems arise as a result of teacher inefficiency and lack of planning, not solely because of recalcitrant students. Boredom and insecurity are two of the foremost catalysts necessary to the precipitation of disciplinary problems and these problems can only be prevented by proper and efficient planning and use of instructional time.

STUDENTS MUST KNOW WHERE THEY STAND

The phrase "ignorance of the law is no excuse" is a trite expression that bears investigation. No student can be expected to possess knowledge of school or departmental policy and rules or regulations unless he has had access to them. The knowledge of such policies must be provided by the institution and teachers therein. It is also helpful, in fact it should be mandatory, to have the parents apprised of regulatory procedures so they can assist in ensuring that these policies are observed by their offsprings.

Student handbooks often cite general school regulations rather than those specifically related to a particular department or function. The teachers within specific departments and the directors of the various school activities should therefore undertake the orientation of those students who are subject to their direct control. Physical education departments have a varied number of functions ranging from the service courses to the intramural and interscholastic athletic programs. Within these varied enterprises there is a definite need for regulation and control. These controls encompass such things as safety, equipment care and accounting, consideration for physical education lockers, uniforms laundry, cleanliness, pre- and postclass behavior, fire drills, first aid and emergency procedures in case of extreme injury, and many other related areas of concern. As a result, the department of health, physical education, and athletics must enlighten the students as to their duties and obligations and the policies which affect and control these functions. Some departments have discovered that policy handbooks are one ready source of information for the student. These handbooks are given to students and are explained in detail so as to avoid misunderstanding wherever possible. In some instances these handbooks are sent home to the parents in an effort to establish better public relations. Prior to the writing of any handbook *all* policies should be reviewed, and in no instance should any regulation be included which is not rationally defensible. As previously mentioned, many of these policies may have been drafted with the cooperation of students as well as teachers and coaches. If such is the case, it is wise to include in the handbook an introductory paragraph explaining the manner by which the policies were conceived. It should further be stated that *all* such policies have the blessing of the school board which governs the school district, and this sanction should be implicit in the opening statement of the handbook. Knowledge is security because it provides the individual with the information which should govern his actions. Many a youngster has made an "honest mistake" simply because he was not properly informed. Certainly it is the responsibility of each student to inform himself whenever and wherever possible. However, the job of providing the information and/or sources of information still remains the responsibility of the school and its teachers. It is fallacious indeed to assume that each and every student will become the knowledgeable individual that the school would desire unless a concerted effort is made to impart that knowledge. Even with open communication and the ready availability of material, there will remain those who through lack of concern or sheer obstinancy will remain ignorant of the regulations at hand. The teacher should continually strive to reach each and every student, but in all practicality it is doubtful that he will be able to do so. Nevertheless, he should never cease in his efforts regarding policy orientation.

Specific detailed information related to the care and responsibility for equipment, training procedures, and other obligations pertinent to activities, such as interscholastic football, basketball, and other sports, may not necessarily be included in a departmental policy handbook. It might be more satisfactory for the coaches of the particular sport in question to handle these problems and provide handouts for the players and parents. One excellent method of dispensing information and ensuring that it is read by both athletes and parents is to include a form which states that "we the undersigned have read and fully understand the above statements, and we hereby agree to abide by the policies and regulations stated herein." Included should be a plea by the coach that any questions regarding the information be directed to him for explanation. The student athlete and the parent should then sign the form and return it to the coach for filing and future reference if necessary.

Such forms are easily drafted and duplicated, and are generally appreciated by the parents who so often feel that they are not being considered in deliberations which directly affect the lives of their sons or daughters. This system also places a moral obligation upon athletes and parents alike to live up to the stipulations which they have signed and have thus agreed to. Similar forms might be drafted by directors of intramurals, DGWS activities, and other extracurricular events. In the interest of positive public relations it is always a good idea to include practice schedule times and other pertinent data which is of definite interest to mothers who are involved in meal planning and other family considerations.

SOLVE YOUR OWN DISCIPLINARY PROBLEMS

Nothing is quite as disconcerting to school principals as having a steady stream of disciplinary problems pouring into his office in the form of students sent from class for punishment. Such students quickly learn that certain teachers are unwilling or unable to cope with disciplinary problems and they readily take advantage of the opportunity to cause trouble at every opportunity.

The beginning teacher will discover that his experienced colleagues who are well prepared, demand quality work, are reasonable in their consideration of individual assistance, and adequately orient the students as to what is expected of them, have few significant discipline problems. The true professional who is interested in the causation of difficulties with students, and who makes a sincere effort to counsel such youngsters, will find his life much easier. He must be friendly but firm and logical in his approach to problems and he must not procrastinate, but must act immediately. He should be certain of the facts of the individual case and not drag in the innocent bystander as a partner to the "crime."

In many instances the troublemaker is a youngster who is just trying to draw attention to himself and is really not malicious in his intent. Often just talking with him and being a good listener will alleviate the situation. By taking some time, either before or after school, and working with those who are inclined to be disciplinary problems, the teacher may solve his difficulties before they arise. One must learn early in his career that all students desire identification and that some are more disposed to seek it in a negative rather than a positive manner.

The teacher must learn to *anticipate* trouble and he must be willing to stop it before it reaches any degree of consequence. Much of this can be accomplished by discussing the ground rules for proper conduct and the rationale upon which they are founded before the classes get underway. The instructor must take the necessary time to explain such concepts as mutual respect, safety, care and maintenance of equipment and facilities, proper behavioral patterns, and other related factors. He must also realize that he will probably have to reiterate his position, and sometimes rather forcefully, as the year progresses. If there is horseplay in the dressing room, talking while roll is being taken, instructions being given, etc., the teacher cannot countenance these things and must undertake procedures to ensure that such interference will cease. The offenders should be reprimanded *directly* wherein possible and the "shotgun" approach, whereby everyone is considered guilty, should not be used unless the chatter or horseplay is very general. General misconduct should not arise if the teacher initiates proper control in the first place and does not allow the poor behavior of a few to develop and infect the demeanor of the entire class.

Sound discipline, as is true of any other facet of education, does not "just happen," it is a continual process that must be obtained through diligent supervision by each and every teacher. It is an approach that demands constant thought and adjustment, not arbitrary decision based on emotion. The process of discipline should be periodically evaluated so that inadequacies can be eliminated and it should be remembered that most discipline cases are individual rather than collective.

Most students, when approached in a friendly but firm manner, will respond favorably. The tone of voice should be relatively normal, in fact some have discovered that a very precise but relatively quiet delivery is most satisfactory. It has also been found that if the teacher places himself in a closer physical proximity to the student than is usual during the course of normal conversation, the student will be more attentive. When admonishing a student on the court or field, the teacher should not try to attract the undue attention of others and should enunciate clearly and express himself in succinct terms. Under *no* circumstances should a teacher ever resort to emotional outbursts colored by the use of profanity. This approach serves no worthwhile purpose and tends to place the teacher on the same social plane as the recalcitrant. In fact, a derisive and inflammatory response on the part of the teacher may be just the type of confrontation that the student desires. Once the teacher has lost his professional poise and dignity, he often finds that his troubles are compounded rather than resolved.

A certain segment of any student body may be classified as incorrigible. These individuals are few in number and are usually persons who have some deeply rooted psychological problem. If such individuals are encountered, and cannot be reached by reasonable discourse, they should be referred to the administration for professional help. When such persons are allowed to constantly disrupt classes, the teacher is guilty of rendering an injustice to the rest of the class by robbing them of instructional time to handle the problems of one youngster. Ideally these problem children should be placed in the care of those who have the specialized training necessary to cope with their outbursts and psychological difficulties and the administration should be obliged to remove them from the situation in which they are causing trouble. These extreme cases are very few and the American public is going to have to realize sooner or later that provisions will have to be made for their care. The public schools are not equipped to handle psychotics and should therefore not be expected to do so. Such is not the case in most instances, however, and eliminating the psychotic child from the public schools is often difficult if not impossible. Many are allowed to continue school until they are either old enough to be dismissed under state law or "graduate." The result is nothing short of chaos for those classes who have to accommodate these people and the incorrigible student suffers even more because he never receives the qualified help he should get if he were properly cared for.

In dealing with disciplinary problems, the teacher must acquire all of the background information available relative to the students who are causing problems. There is no substitute for enlisting the cooperation of counsellors, fellow teachers, and the administration. Many times a pattern of behavior can be established by consulting various individuals. If there is a definite pattern, often the problem will lend itself to a solution by group process. Should the physical education teacher discover that no difficulty has arisen in any class other than his own, he might have to evaluate the situation in light of the peculiarities of his situation and make his assessements accordingly.

Beginning teachers can profit from observing those who are more experienced. Time in service does not necessarily imply that the person is truly competent, but it is a good point of departure. The neophyte should ask to visit classrooms of those who are successful professionals and who are noted for having few disciplinary problems. They may find that personality is a key factor or that personality combined with sound concepts and good planning is of primary importance. It should be noted, however, that certain methods will work for some people and not for others. This is, or course, due to the many facets of human characteristics that are possessed by certain individuals and cannot, or for that matter should not, be emulated because personal style is difficult if not impossible to copy. There are basic concepts and elements of timing in the conduct of proper disciplinary procedures that can readily be adopted from others and favorably utilized. The beginning teacher should never hesitate to consult with his colleagues and profit from their experiences. He may also discover, due to his more recent training in certain aspects of psychology, that he may have information the older teachers would welcome in return for their counsel.

POSITIVE MEASURES OF DISCIPLINARY ACTION

Physical education is rather unique in that there is a good deal of preclass activity such as dressing, taking care of both street clothing and physical education uniforms, making sure that lockers are secure, and readying equipment for the instructional period. Some students dress more rapidly than others, appear on the court or field earlier than their classmates, and are eager to become actively engaged in some form of activity. At times the activity outlets are less than acceptable. Some teachers require that all students dress and then remain seated in the locker room until roll is called before moving to the instructional area. Other teachers plan various drills pertinent to the activity being taught and allow the youngsters to move to the instructional area to pursue these drills until a whistle is blown signifying that roll call is about to be taken. It should be understood by all early arrivals that they may take part in preclass drills only as long as they behave themselves. If they misbehave, they lose the privilege and then must sit quietly on the sidelines until roll is taken. Such preclass activity takes time and also demands supervision, and it is not a good idea unless supervision is available in the locker room *and* on the field or in the gymnasium. In a one teacher operation where no supervision is available for preclass drills, it is better for the teacher to detain the students in the locker room. If he does dismiss the youngsters to a play area which is un-supervised and an accident occurs, he would be liable for negligence. Regardless of a teacher's philosophy relative to the utilization of in-structional time, he must always be in control of his pupils and ob-viously cannot be in two places simultaneously.

The matter of roll-taking seems insignificant, but efficiency in the preclass period provides for a greater amount of instructional time. One of the better methods of dispensing with roll calls is to have numbers painted on the baseboard of the gymnasium, placed on a fence, or suitable area on playing fields so that each student may line up on his assigned number. The teacher may then quickly record the numbers which are not "covered."

As soon as the preinstructional duties, announcements, etc., are dispensed with, the teacher should give instructions regarding what he expects of the youngsters for the balance of the period. These instructions should be concise and businesslike and any questions the students may have should be answered. Equipment should be ready for use and no unnecessary delay should take place. The instruction should be initiated at the point it was discontinued on the previous day. At the conclusion of the class period, the youngsters should be dismissed in time to shower, dress, and move to their next class. If clean towels are to be issued, they should be handed out in an orderly fashion and absolutely no "horseplay" should be allowed in the shower and locker rooms. The physical education teacher's duties with one particular class are not over when the youngsters leave the instructional area. Control must be maintained from the time the students arrive from their previous class until they leave for the next. Leaving a class unsupervised for *any* reason is an invitation to disaster. Negligence of duty is only one consideration; poor disciplinary habits on the part of students are often created by the laxity of the teacher.

Every teacher of physical education classes will at some time be confronted by the nondresser. Some of these problems result from the inability of the student to purchase the proper uniform, some are excused for medical reasons, and some just don't care whether they receive a passing grade or not. A contingency fund and/or a supply of clean uniforms should be kept on hand for those who are either poor or perhaps have forgotten their clothing. In the latter instance, the grade for the day might be lowered after the first time that clothes are loaned; this prevents bad habits from developing regarding responsibility for one's belongings.

The child who cannot afford proper attire is really confronted with two problems: (1) he has no clothing and must ask for permission to use a school uniform, and (2) he has probably been using "hand-me-downs" for his daily wear at home and is therefore resentful of them. If a contingency fund is available to purchase new clothing for indigent students, some provision should be made whereby the student can "earn" what is given to him. The job does not have to be too demanding, but should be significant enough so that the youngster doesn't feel that he is getting something for nothing. By working for his clothes, the student can gracefully avoid the stigma of accepting charity and may therefore maintain his pride. Some youngsters come from families that have been on welfare for so long that they have lost all sense of pride and will not work when the opportunity presents itself. They should be given a uniform to wear, but it should be a clean *used* one unless they choose to work for a new one. Let the student make the choice and don't influence him unnecessarily.

Uniforms should be kept clean and if they are not the student should be marked down accordingly. If he used the excuse that "mother didn't do the laundry this week," provide him with a bucket, soap, and hot water and let him wash his own clothes. In all probability, he is looking for an excuse not to dress, or he forgot to take his clothing home to be washed. By the time a student is in the seventh grade, he should be responsible for taking care of his things and should not have to depend solely upon others.

The chronic nondresser who *refuses* to dress can only be marked down for nonparticipation if there has been a uniform made available to him by the school for this purpose. The teacher can talk to the student, try to reason with him, and explore every avenue of approach. However if everything fails, the problem will have to be referred to the administration. You cannot sacrifice your instructional time and energies for one student at the expense of all the others no matter how strongly you may feel about the case. The teacher must do all he can, within reason, to resolve his own problems and the problems of students, but he is being most unfair if he sacrifices the welfare of the entire group for that of the very few. The idealism evidenced by many young teachers is indeed virtuous, but it does need to be tempered by elements of practicality.

One of the most salient features of sound disciplinary procedure is that of treating every student fairly and equitably. Play no favorites and show no animosity toward anyone. Do not let personalities interfere with sound judgment and be willing to investigate all sides of a question prior to rendering a decision as to punishment. When students discover that you are indeed a friendly yet fair-minded and professional person, many of the difficulties attendant to disciplinary problems will vanish.

School policy may well dictate the manner in which many disciplinary problems are resolved. All teachers should be aware of these policies and conduct themselves accordingly. It would be rather embarrassing to discover that what you have done was a direct contradiction to the guidelines under which the school is functioning and would place you in an untenable position with your colleagues. If there are no policies governing some of the unique aspects of your discipline, such as dress regulations, excuses, locker room etiquette, and other pertinent matters, sit down with your administrator and try to initiate action whereby these policies can be devised and implemented. Frequently no policy is made until a problem occurs and then it is resolved in an arbitrary and often misguided manner.

Each and every problem that results in disciplinary action is somewhat unique and should be treated individually. Policy should state those features of what is to be expected in the way of student conduct but cannot cover every contingency that arises. Therefore, blanket punishment should not be enforced. To list, in rank order, infractions and subsequent punishment would be ridiculous. The only generalization that can therefore be made is that all encounters should be managed in a mature, deliberate, and unemotional way and should not bring discredit to the professional posture of the teacher involved. The most vital keys to good discipline are planning, policy, perseverence, and a businesslike professional demeanor.

QUESTIONS FOR DISCUSSION

1. Of what relationship is good planning to sound discipline?
2. Why must a teacher divorce himself from the daily social lives of his students?
3. How could you conceivably involve students in the formulation of policy which governs their classroom behavior?
4. Should students be involved in *all* policy-making decisions? If so, why? If not, why?
5. All infractions of regulations should be punished in the same manner! React to this statement.
6. What is the relationship of equipment, boredom, and disciplinary problems?
7. Why should you not send all of your disciplinary problems to the "office"?
8. If you were an administrator and a constant flow of "troublemakers" poured into your office from one teacher, what would you think and how would you react?
9. What is your obligation in the supervision of your classes in physical education? When does it begin and when does it end?
10. Why must all teachers remain cognizant of policies governing disciplinary measures?

CASE STUDIES

MR. WILSON

Mr. Wilson had been hired on a one-year appointment to replace a teacher on leave. He was told that if a vacancy occurred during the year in his field he might be retained permanently. Both Wilson and his wife seemed to enjoy the community and its environs and were readily accepted by the other teachers and their families.

In conjunction with his regular teaching assignment, Mr. Wilson was asked to sponsor the "Blue Jackets," a male pep club that had been formed on campus the previous year. The club was active in supporting the various high school athletic teams and also engaged in some service work for the school, such as parking cars for musicals, plays, and open-houses. The leadership of the group consisted of boys whose parents were influential in the community and were given to showing off on occasion by making demands of school officials and individual teachers.

As the year progressed, the social outings of the "Blue Jackets" became known for their rowdiness and Mr. Wilson was questioned by the superintendent and principal about the rumors they had heard. Wilson replied that he hadn't noticed any misbehavior of consequence and surmised that perhaps other students were circulating rumors only because of their jealousy. Inasmuch as no evidence was available to the contrary, Wilson's remarks were accepted by the school administration and nothing further was mentioned.

Late in the spring, the "Blue Jackets" scheduled their annual picnic. The outing was held at a nearby lake and the necessary preparations were made for a gala picnic wherein each club member was to bring his date and invite another couple. The picnic was scheduled for a Saturday evening to accommodate as many people as possible; however, the only faculty member invited was Mr. Wilson, the sponsor.

Rumors began to fly throughout the community on Monday morning about the orgy that the "Blue Jackets" held the previous Saturday night. Angry parents contacted both the principal and superintendent regarding the drunken condition their boys were in when they returned from the picnic, and a local beer distributor reported that Mr. Wilson entered his establishment in the early Sunday morning hours to purchase some beer. He emphasized that Mr. Wilson's purchase would not have caused him any alarm except that Wilson was accompanied by a few boys of doubtful age who seemed a bit inebriated.

The Superintendent rushed immediately to Mr. Wilson's classroom to seek information about the calls he had been receiving. He openly asked Wilson if the rumors about the conduct at the picnic were true and Wilson replied that most of them were. When asked why he had allowed such actions to transpire, Wilson retorted "the boys were having such a good time that he hated to dampen their activities in view of the fact that school was almost out and they needed a break in their routine for therapeutic reasons." Wilson was fired on the spot and a substitute teacher was engaged to fill his position for the balance of the term.

QUESTIONS

1. How would you have reacted to Mr. Wilson's antics had you been in the place of the superintendent?

2. What would you think of a colleague who conducted himself as did Mr. Wilson?
3. Would you want Mr. Wilson teaching your children? If so, why? If not, why?

MR. VECK

Coach Veck had coached high school basketball for approximately four seasons with only mediocre success. The teams were well coached but lacked height and substitute strength on the bench. His offensive and defensive patterns were well executed but his boys were simply overcome by the significantly great height of their opponents.

During his last season as coach at Frederick High, Veck was blessed with three tall and exceptionally well-skilled players whose parents had recently moved into the community. He worked diligently with his players and his team showed consistant progress as the season wore on. Two of the three new players were caught violating curfew regulations and were warned in the presence of their teammates that an additional violation of training procedures would lead to their dismissal from the squad.

The night before the state tournament was to begin, a dance was held at Frederick High School's gymnasium in celebration of a successful basketball season and as a sendoff for the team which was to play the following evening. Coach Veck told his boys that they could attend the dance but should be home no later than ten o'clock. At midnight the dance was closing and Veck went to his office to pick up some paperwork that he had forgotten. As he entered the gymnasium he noticed his two problem players leaving the building. They appeared rather shocked at seeing their coach but spoke to him as they walked by. Veck said nothing to them but went directly to his office and scratched their names from the traveling squad.

As tournament play progressed, the Frederick team moved ahead in the standings by virtue of its hustle and accurate shooting. They were finally defeated in the consolation game and as Veck left the locker room he could hear many comments in the crowd about how well Frederick might have done had their coach not been so "bullheaded" by leaving his two best players at home.

QUESTIONS

1. Do you think that Coach Veck was fair or unfair in his handling of the two boys who violated the team curfew?
2. If Veck had not acted as he did, what might have resulted in the future?

3. If you had seen the boys violating curfew but had no witnesses, what would you do?

MR. LUNDQUIST

Mr. Lundquist was a young, energetic physical education teacher who worked hard and had developed an outstanding program for his high school. He was personable but also a good disciplinarian who was understood by the students. His policies regarding student conduct had been explained patiently to all youngsters and he had incorporated many of their suggestions into his safety code. Lundquist was always firm but fair and had a facility for fitting punishment to any infraction that had been committed.

A panic bar had come loose from one of the main doors to the gymnasium and had been reported to the custodian by Mr. Lundquist. The bar had been placed on the floor by the door awaiting repair but was picked up by one of the students and thrown into the creek that flowed past the building. Lundquist saw the student throw the panic bar and asked him to report to his office after school. When the student arrived at Lundquist's office he was handed a heavy steel wrecking bar and told to throw it into the creek and then retrieve it. This process was repeated 50 times one evening and 50 times the next. At the conclusion of each session the student was visibly tired from his efforts but never once uttered a word of protest.

QUESTION

1. How would you psychologically evaluate Mr. Lundquist's disciplinary solution?

MR. CARROL

Coach Carrol was an excellent physical educator and coach. He was well organized in his classes and meticulous in his handling of equipment. He maintained an accurate card file of all equipment that had been issued, marked all gear with the date of purchase, and kept a running inventory of everything that he had on hand for his classes as well as for his football team.

At the outset of every football season a letter was sent to all parents to inform them of their son's responsibilities in regard to training as well as the care and maintenance of his football uniform and pads. Each parent signed the letter and thereby indicated that he approved of the stated policies. The letter was then returned to Coach Carrol who filed it. Only *after* the letter was returned did the coaching staff issue equipment to an athlete.

After the team had practiced for two weeks a clinic was held, and all parents were invited to preview the types of play that could be expected during the coming season. All boys were dressed in their game uniforms, with the exception of shoes, and plays and explanations were executed in the gymnasium. Coach Carrol solicited questions from the audience after all the offensive and defensive maneuvers had been thoroughly explained by the coaching staff. At the conclusion of the question and answer session the parents and coaches gathered for a social hour and discussed problems that were common to both.

Coach Carrol and his staff fervently believed that every boy on their team should learn to take care of his own equipment and they effectively communicated this information to all parents. They also requested that at the conclusion of each season players return game and practice suits in the same condition of cleanliness as issued. They were successful in achieving two objectives by this request. Their players were imbued with the concept of responsibility and also considerable amount of money was saved in laundry bills. Due to the efforts of Mr. Carrol and his staff, a rather small budget provided adequate equipment of superior quality and also endeared the coaches to the administration and school board.

QUESTIONS

1. Do you regard Mr. Carrol's efforts as worthwhile? What else might he have done in the area of organization and public relations?
2. Do you think that Carrol was correct in asking the team members to do their own laundry? Why?
3. What educational objectives were fulfilled by the actions of Carrol and his staff?
4. What obligations does a coach have other than the performance of his actual duties on the field?

MISS GLENN AND MISS VANCE

Miss Glenn and Miss Vance had been teaching physical education at Proctor High School for approximately three years. Both women were well educated and highly recommended when they were employed. Miss Glenn was one who observed a certain amount of social distance from her pupils and was meticulous in her instruction. Miss Vance was a well-skilled individual but believed that teachers needed to be more closely related to their students than when she had attended school.

Miss Glenn and Miss Vance were charged with the responsibility of taking various girls' teams on athletic trips to other communities. Many of the girls preferred to ride with Miss Vance because, as they stated, "she is really cool." Miss Glenn insisted on regular hours for her student athletes, observed a strict training schedule, and disciplined the youngsters who did not abide by the rules. These rules, incidently, were initially established by a committee composed of both faculty and students. Miss Vance believed that students should control their own behavior and therefore established no guidelines for conduct or training procedures.

Miss Vance became ill during the winter, and Miss Glenn was asked to escort the girls' basketball team to a neighboring town. Miss Glenn agreed to accompany the girls to the game but was somewhat upset to discover, upon arriving at the motel in the community where they were to play, that the manager did not want to register the Proctor team. When asked why he was reluctant to accept the girls, the manager informed Miss Glenn that the last time Proctor girls had stayed in his establishment they had been unruly, a few had apparently been drunk, and the women's coach refused to do anything about it because she maintained that one of the benefits of such a trip was "to let the girls blow off a little steam."

Miss Glenn called the girls together in the presence of the motel manager and informed them of the problem. She then told them that should the manager condescend to allow them to stay, they would have to abide by certain rules of conduct and maintain specified hours. The girls agreed to do as Miss Glenn requested and were then housed by the motel manager. After leaving the manager's office Miss Glenn called a meeting of all the girls in her room and proceeded to inform them of exactly what was expected in the matter of behavior. Two of the girls maintained that they did not believe they should have to conform to a code of conduct which had never been utilized under the direction of Miss Vance. Miss Glenn informed the girls that they were now in her charge and would either have to conform or be sent home immediately on a commercial bus.

On her return Miss Glenn informed Miss Vance of the problem she had encountered. Miss Vance in turn blamed the motel manager for being "square," and stated that in the future she would not seek reservations at his establishment. Miss Glenn countered that unless Miss Vance altered her method of handling women athletes on trips she would have to report the entire matter to the principal of the school.

Subsequently the matter was reported and Miss Vance was asked to resign or have her contract terminated after the conclusion of the current school year.

QUESTIONS

1. How would you evaluate the professional ethics of Miss Glenn and Miss Vance? Which of the two individuals would you like to pattern yourself after and why?
2. Do you think that Miss Glenn had any right to tell Miss Vance that she would report the case to the principal? Why or why not?

SUGGESTED RELATED READING

Ackerly, Robert L., *The Reasonable Exercise of Authority.* Washington, D.C.: National Association of Secondary School Principals, 1969.

Daughtrey, Greyson, and John B. Woods, *Physical Education Programs, Organization and Administration.* Philadelphia: W. B. Saunders, 1971.

Holmes, George, ed., *Student Protest and The Law.* Ann Arbor, Mich.: Institute of Continuing Legal Education, 1969.

Larson, Knute G., and Melvin R. Karpas, *Effective Secondary School Discipline.* Englewood Cliffs, N.J.: Prentice-Hall, 1966.

Phillips, Ewing Lakin, *Discipline, Achievement and Mental Health.* Englewood Cliffs, N.J.: Prentice-Hall, 1960. A teachers guide to wholesome action.

7
SPORTS COUNSELING
AND
STUDENT SUCCESS

SQUARE PEGS DON'T FIT ROUND HOLES

Hero worship by the male is perhaps as old as mankind and seems to be a facet of human behavior that is present in virtually every society. Boys of the past worshipped their elders who were warriors, outstanding statesmen, musicians, and possibly in many other revered positions to which the young man would aspire. In our present society in the United States we have been inundated with telecasts of various sporting events ranging from football games to auto racing. The growth of professional athletics in this country since World War II has been phenomenal and the televised exposure of both amateur and professional athletes has indeed brought these personalities into every American home. With the pictures of athletes appearing in the news media, billboards, and even on cereal boxes, it is no wonder that many young men desire to emulate those who are receiving such national notoriety. Furthermore, even the boy of elementary school age often can quote salary figures received by the professional athlete, and this factor alone is a strong motivator to one who is already interested in competitive athletics.

Parents naturally want their youngsters to succeed and this desire is not confined to fathers alone. Some of the most avid fans in the Little League ball parks are well-meaning mothers who just "know" that this son is the greatest thing that will ever happen to baseball. Parents however are often not objective in the evaluation of their own children and guide them into activities in which they have little chance for success. Many fathers who were unsuccessful in athletics channel their sons into competition in an attempt to compensate for their own inadequacies on the playing field. This type of guidance frequently results in frustration for the child and parent alike and is usually founded upon emotion rather than logic. The question then arises as to whom should provide guidance in athletics, the coach or the parents? A sound approach would be to involve all parties concerned, including the youngster, if the welfare of the potential athlete is to be seriously considered.

The physical educator and/or coach who has an adequate background in the basic sciences and the psychology of motor learning should make every effort to counsel parents as well as student athletes in matters relating to success in athletics. Boys and girls differ significantly from other members of their sex in such factors as body type (somatotype), endurance, gross body size, strength, height, agility, speed, power, and coordination. They also differ, and just as significantly, in interest and motivation. Placing a boy or girl in a competitive situation in which he or she is consistently embarrassed by his/her performance will succeed in doing nothing more than driving the youngster away from athletics completely. The late Dean Cromwell, track coach at the University of Southern California for many years, once observed that there was some event in track and field in which every normal boy could enjoy success. He did not state that a boy would become outstanding however, but that he would enjoy some success in competition. Cromwell's observation could be expanded into the entire field of athletics in that a broad program should include enough offerings for everyone to discover something of interest in which he or she could enjoy a degree of success. It is indeed unfortunate that many youngsters, because of limited physical education and sports programs, never have the opportunity to explore those areas which they might enjoy.

The youngster must explore various activities in order to discover his preference, but should not be forced into high pressure competition before he is ready. The child should be *encouraged* to attempt a number of athletic feats and should not be ridiculed for poor performance. Children should not be subjected to situations in which they have no interest however, and even worse, to situations of which they are deeply afraid. The fearful youngster must be led gradually into a strange environment, not shoved and taunted until he becomes a nervous wreck and participates only because of adult pressure. Many parents, and teachers as well, are ignorant of the psychological and physiological implications of certain activities and therefore should seek advice from those who do have the necessary expertise in these matters.

Every coach in the public schools would do well to initiate his particular sport by hosting a preseason clinic for all parents and prospective athletes. Coaches who have held these clinics find them to be of inestimable value educationally and also discovered that they present a fine opportunity to advance the program of public relations. The general format of such clinics is to explain all the ramifications of the game or activity in terms of personnel types, training procedures, equipment, medical considerations, educational values, and time usage. In the discussion of personnel, it should be explained clearly *why* certain types of individuals enjoy more success in the particular activity under discussion than do others. The discussion should bring forth the best information available from the related disciplines of psychology, anatomy and physiology, kinesiology, and the sociology of sports. At the conclusion of the discussion a question and answer session should be conducted. During this period a clarification of any point of confusion can be made. Somewhere in the discussion it is imperative to explain that the school offers other athletic activities and that these activities also possess certain unique characteristics which should be investigated by interested parents and student athletes.

During the course of a sport season when a youngster decides for any reason to leave the team, he deserves the consideration of being counseled by the supervising coach. He may have valid reasons for his decision to leave and should not be ridiculed for his position. He should be informed that there are other activities available to him and should be encouraged to participate in those which seem more suitable for his particular talents and physical characteristics. The duty of *any* coach is to assist the youngster, boy or girl, in discovering and developing latent talent, and it makes no difference whether the counseling coach is responsible for football, track, baseball, swimming, tennis, golf, soccer, field hockey, or any other sport. Personnel in the athletic department should work in harmony and in the best interest of *all* of the students, whether those students will benefit from your particular sport or not. The matter of working together as a coaching team should apply to men and women equally. There is no reason why a male coach should not encourage female students to take part in the women's program, and the women in turn should reciprocate.

PHYSIQUE AND ABILITY—NATURE VERSUS NURTURE

There are three basic body types (somatotypes) found among humans: the endomorph, mesomorph, and ectomorph. The endomorph is characterized by having rather large hips, relatively narrow shoulders, and often inclined toward obesity. The mesomorph is the mid-type or athletic physique with broad shoulders, very muscular, and slender in both waist and hips. The ectomorph is a linear individual who is tall and slender and usually categorized as an aesthetic type. The basic somatotype, according to Sheldon (1940, 1942), does not change throughout life to any measurable degree and therefore people should learn to live with that which they were endowed by heredity. The somatotype of most individuals is a composite rather than an absolute of one or the other; however one of the types is usually dominant. Hence, a person could possess some degree of mesomorphy and perhaps a greater degree of endomorphy. He would not fit into a singular category, but would exhibit the traits of both. By the same logic, an individual could tend toward mesomorphy to a slight degree, but because of a greater amount of linearity than in the classic athletic physique, be categorized as a mesoectomorph. Most people can reflect momentarily and recall individuals who would be classified readily into one complete category or the other, but these definite types are in the minority.

The physique of an individual often determines to an extent the activities in which he or she will be interested. The ectomorphic person would undoubtedly be more interested in basketball than football or hockey. The endomorphic individual would probably prefer interior-line play to that of a halfback, and surely would enjoy more success. The mesomorph would possibly shy away from distance running in favor of the sprints or selected field events and would make a better quarterback than lineman. For those who are knowledgeable of the sport, it would be difficult indeed to imagine a classic ectomorphic individual mounting the platform to give a demonstration in competitive weightlifting. Obviously he would not have the physical equipment conducive to success in that particular sport.

The preceding discussion illustrates the fact that various body types do exist and that physical educators and coaches would be wise to assess a youngster's chances for success in a particular sport, or in a certain position on a team, before they assign their personnel. Furthermore, they should advise the youngsters about activities in which they might best expect to succeed. Any potential athlete, regardless of body type, should be allowed to compete for any position or team of his choice, but his selection should be made only *after* he has all of the available facts. Endomorphs are not characterized by speed, endurance, agility, or great strength in relation to body size. Mesomorphs are not usually identified by large gross body measurements but are often relatively fast, well coordinated, agile, strong in relation to body size, and sometimes aggressive. The ectomorph is generally weaker than the other two types, has less endurance in many instances, and is not as agile or speedy as his mid-type counterpart. It can be determined that the athlete who is readily identified with the extremes of his particular body type does have some limiting physical traits. Fortunately, most youngsters have a composite of endomesomorphy or mesoectomorphy. Therefore, they find less difficulty adapting to the problem than would be the case otherwise.

Weight-training is widely used as a method to increase strength among athletes and nonathletes alike. The muscles of *any* of the individual body types or combinations previously mentioned will respond to progressive resistance, and therefore strength can be increased markedly. However, the ectomorph has greater difficulty in lifting heavy weights than does the mesomorph or endomorph due to the mechanical leverage which works against him as a result of his relatively long extremeties. When youngsters are competing against one another in class, the long-limbed, slender youngster may find that he is at an extreme disadvantage. His concern can be relieved to a great degree if his instructor explains the various kinesiological implications attendant to weight-training. This explanation should be included during the *introduction* of the unit. Teachers frequently ignore the very factors that not only impart meaning to a unit of instruction, but which also alleviate embarrassment and misunderstanding among the students.

One of the primary functions of the teacher or coach is to fully explain all of the ramifications of any activity in which the students are to engage. These ramifications include the physiological, anatomical, psychological and sociological; all should be thoroughly discussed and emphasized. Cursory treatment of any of these factors would constitute an injustice toward the participants who are entitled to learn any activity in depth, not just the fundamental skills and basic strategy.

Some general examples of activities as they relate to body type may serve to provide the reader with basic guidelines, but are *not* intended to include *all* of the variations that the practitioner may encounter in an actual teaching situation.

1. *Basketball.* Generally preferred by the ectomorph or ectomesomorph because of the advantage provided by height and reach. This activity might also be enjoyed by others of a less linear type, but probably with not as much success at a high level of organization as is found in interscholastic competition.

2. *Football.* Interior linemen are usually of the endomesomorphic configuration and enjoy success because of the large gross body size and the superior weight advantage. Offensive ends should possess some degree of ectomorphy that will provide them with height which is an advantage to any potential pass receiver. Backs usually conform to the mesomorphic body type and enjoy success because they are agile, fast, and make good downfield blockers because of their coordination and compact physique.

3. *Track and Field.* Quality distance runners are usually a combination of mesomorphic and ectomorphic types with the mid-type being recessive. Such individuals have a relatively long stride, good endurance, and a reserve of strength.

Sprinters are generally found to possess both mesomorphy and ectomorphy with the mid-type being dominant, and sometimes to a very pronounced degree, as is the case with Bob Hays and other championship sprinters. They have tremendous explosive power, which is so necessary at the start of any short race, and are able to carry through without having to rely to a marked degree on a long stride and endurance.

Weight men are usually large and strong and come from the ranks of those manifesting traits of mesoendomorphy in both greater and lesser degrees. Shotputters and discus throwers are generally larger and stronger than are other field event participants, and the discus throwers often exhibit a greater amount of linearity than hammer throwers or shotputters. Those who throw the javelin also conform to a great extent to the physiognomy of the discus throwers.

Successful high jumpers display a pronounced tendency toward ectomorphy as do many triple jumpers. The obvious reason being that these events demand extreme leg length in order to overcome height in the one instance and height and distance in the other. If the height of the bar, or the distance into the triple jumping pit, was measured relative to body size and individual height, the ectomorph might not fare any better than the mesomorph. However, the height and distance are absolutes and do not consider physique in relationship to performance.

Pole vaulters usually come from the ranks of the mesomorph due to the requirements for speed and strength of the upper body. Therefore the athlete who has good speed, adequate strength in the arms and shoulder girdle, and relatively less weight in the legs, should enjoy success in this event.

Long jumpers often come from the same ranks as the sprinters and are therefore of the same relative body type. They depend upon velocity or speed as much as upon spring.

High hurdlers are usually more linear than are sprinters, and low and intermediate hurdlers may well come from the ranks of those who have the characteristics of the sprinter. The high hurdler does have to overcome a more formidable obstacle, therefore, he should have greater leg length, a characteristic of ectomorphy.

4. *Racket Sports.* The racket sports, with the exception of squash, demand both height and endurance as requisites to successful performance. This is true because of the relationship of height to the net and endurance to the characteristics of the game. A good short tennis player, for example, would probably be somewhat more successful if he were taller and could impart a greater angle to his shots.

5. *Gymnastics.* Gymnasts are generally short and mesomorphic in configuration because their activities usually operate against a combination of leverage and gravity. From the standpoint of basic kinesiological considerations, the tall linear individual or the heavy person has more physical obstacles to overcome than does the mesomorph; therefore, the endomorph or ectomorph would probably not enjoy much success in gymnastics.

6. *Recreational Sports.* Bowlers, golfers, archers, fly fishermen, and marksmen come in all shapes and sizes and perform relatively well. To be highly definitive in these areas would be difficult and would

probably also be fallacious because the physical requirements of these activities are not as closely related to the pertinent skills of the activity as in the case of those sports previously mentioned.

7. *Swimmers and Divers.* Swimmers approximate the same physical characteristics as attributed to track personnel, and divers to gymnasts. Swimming events approximate those of track and field in both sprinting and distance races. Diving is a sport that is actually a gymnastic activity and therefore would demand the same kinesiological and anatomical considerations.

The preceding suggestions should be considered only as *general* guidelines and not *absolutes.* There are exceptions to every rule and these exceptions can be found when contemplating the relative performance of personnel in any athletic activity. The teacher and coach cannot rule out the factors of desire and determination, and must therefore consider the psychology as well as the anatomy of the aspirant. The prime reason for identifying body types with some of the various activities is merely intended to reinforce the concept that each and every youngster should be thoroughly acquainted with the traits which may hinder or enhance his chances to achieve success in any activity he may wish to pursue. If he understands these concepts and still insists upon competing in some sport where his chances for success are slim, he at least has been extended the courtesy of knowing the benefits and limitations imposed upon him by his body type.

Heredity decrees many things for the human being, and among these is body type. This does not imply that improvement cannot be made. His basic somatotype cannot be appreciably altered, but he can improve his performance through a rigorous training program and thereby attain a greater level of satisfaction.

Progressive weight-training programs can enhance the performance of both male and female athletes by developing greater strength of the entire body and specific areas such as arms, shoulder girdle, legs, and trunk. Such programs should be tailored to the needs of the individual and the physiological concepts of muscular development must be an integral component, both from the consideration of knowledge and motivation. Progressive weight-training is hard work if it is to be of value, and the student must thoroughly understand the physiological rationale upon which this activity is founded. Furthermore, if it is to be of maximum value, the weight-training program should include materials related to diet and rest. Many weight trainers do not acquaint their students with all aspects of the program and as a result overlook many of the benefits. A complete training program should be a balanced one and not slanted toward strength development alone but should also include endurance activities, such as running.

Many of our athletic activities, especially contact sports and track field events, demand both size and strength. These attributes can only be developed to the hereditary limits unless certain alterations of the body chemistry are initiated. The use of *anabolic steroids* has come into being in the athletic world in recent years and deserves consideration here. The use of *steroids* in athletic programs should *not* be condoned by any coach, teacher, or administrator. These substances enable the body to gain huge amounts of weight and are purported thereby to increase strength. However, little research has been done in relation to human consumption of steroids, and the lasting side effects of such chemicals might well be as disastrous to the endocrine system as LSD is to the brain. Certain difficulties attendant to the use of steroids have been reported, among which is partial sterility. Until concentrated research indicates otherwise, steroids should definitely be classified as an ergogenic aid that has no place in the school program of physical education and athletics. To administer steroids or even advocate their use by athletes is unethical and cannot be countenanced. They have no more place in the schools than benzedrine, methedrine, or any other drug used to alter human behavior and performance. It is possible that in the future physiologists and biochemists may discover that certain steroid derivitives are harmless and might be prescribed in some instances. However, such conjecture does not alter the fact that even if such drugs are prescribed it will be done by those from the medical profession, not from physical education and athletics.

Performances of athletes have improved tremendously over the years and these improvements can be attributed to many factors. The medical care of youngsters is better; many are not as adversely affected by diseases as in the past; training procedures are superior to previous methods; equipment is of higher quality, and coaches and teachers are being trained by better qualified personnel. In addition, research and its findings have contributed greatly to both physical education and athletics. The research instrumentation is now available which should enable investigators to delve even deeper into the problems of human performance and should afford the opportunity for future athletic performance to be even more outstanding than ever before.

If physical educators and coaches are to obtain the most "mileage" from their students, they must exert themselves to a greater degree in terms of understanding the findings of research, engage in research which is relevant to public school youngsters, and impart *all* of the presently available knowledge to their students and athletes. Many coaches and teachers do not even subscribe to the periodicals available which would assist both them and their students in the matter of sports counseling and human performance. Some make a thorough study of strategy and technique and ignore the implications of personnel qualifications, both physiologically and psychologically. Any quality physical education class or athletic program must first realize that its obligation is to *people*, namely the participants. A complete understanding of students and athletes as human beings, and not as mere chattel, is the essence of a justifiable program.

Nature has endowed us all with certain attributes and limitations which we often fail to understand. Until students and athletes understand their limitations and also understand the procedures whereby they can extend these limitations by training procedures and skill development, they will never attain their full potential. The student cannot entirely overcome certain hereditary factors, but he can, through knowledge and practice, improve upon his performance. It therefore is the duty of the teacher or coach to counsel the student, encourage him, and provide him with the best knowledge available which will spur him to success in his chosen field of physical activity.

EGO INVOLVEMENT AND ATHLETICS

The term ego, as used psychologically, means "self." Ego involvement in athletics simply means the projection of the "self" into the environment of activity. Certain athletes become so centered in self-interest that they ignore principles that are beneficial to the concept of the "team" or that group which is constituted for the purpose of exerting itself as a unified force. Naturally each individual should desire certain personal benefits from his involvement in team play. However, no member of a team of any kind, either in a physical education class or on the athletic field, has the right to place his own interests above those of his teammates. During the preschool years youngsters rarely have the opportunity to participate in team activities. As a result, many students have a difficult time adjusting to the team concept and may rebel at the idea of self-sacrifice and discipline which prohibits them from "doing their own thing" while being the member of a team.

In our present society many individuals are clamoring for the right to assume individuality that is inconsistent with the best interests of that society. People are defying laws and regulations that were designed to insure the safety and welfare of others and are openly questioning the right of any group to set standards of discipline and conduct. Coaches and teachers are not exempt from attacks by radical organizations and individuals in the matter of classroom discipline, team conduct, dress codes, grading procedures, or general deportment.

The coach of any team must have the authority to establish logical rules and regulations which govern the conduct and appearance of his particular athletes. These regulations have been arbitrarily written and enforced in some instances, and in others they have evolved as a result of the deliberations of coaches and players working together for the good of the team. The latter approach to policy implementation is probably the better of the two in that collective thinking has taken place and the regulations were initiated from within. In any event, after the regulations have been drafted they should be explained to the players along with the rationale upon which they were founded.

One of the greatest educational benefits resulting from athletics is self-discipline and identification with a group. This was recently brought forth rather forcibly in an article which appeared in the *Journal of Health, Physical Education, and Recreation* for May, 1970. It would be advisable for all coaches, teachers, and administrators to read the report by Dr. Briggs and heed his message. Identification with a group is an ideal sought by most youngsters and it is certainly more beneficial for a youngster to be identified with an athletic team than a street gang.

The self-centered athlete must be made to realize that his contribution is of no greater importance than that of his teammates. He may perform a key function, such as quarterback, but he should understand that he could not perform his function without the support of his fellow players. Any quarterback who gets the "big head" can easily be returned to reality by having the offensive lineman allow the defense to pour through and stifle his efforts. Similar situations can be established for the other team sports in the interest of deflating over-inflated egos.

The press can often contribute to the ego involvement of a key player and can also dampen the enthusiasm of those who occupy a lesser role. Sports stories should be checked by the coach to ensure that there is some "balance" of reporting and that a few key players do not receive all of the publicity at the expense of others. Sports reporters often do not understand the effect that their stories have upon youngsters because they are totally unfamiliar with the psychology of athletics. Coaches and teachers are also guilty of building the egos of some individuals at the expense of others because they too have become rather "heady" or want to identify with the superior athlete or student. It is only human nature to desire association with a select group or individual, but this is a luxury the the coach or teacher can ill afford.

The matter of lengthy hair and similar facial adornment has

recently become a problem for physical educators and coaches. In some sports, such as football and lacrosse in which a helmet is worn, it is physiologically unsound for the athlete to wear long hair. His head is encased in a plastic, foam-lined container which provides a minimum of ventilation. Hair, when added to the artificial insulation, causes a buildup and entrapment of body heat which has no means of escape. This excess heat can precipitate hyperthermia and thus lessen the physiological effectiveness of the entire human organism. Aside from the previous consideration, skin rash, acne, and other problems are exaggerated by excess facial hair and therefore it is questionable whether excess hair should be condoned.

In sports other than those in which excess body heat is a problem, excess hair may not be a handicap unless it is of a length that impedes the vision or otherwise interferes with the efficiency of the player. In swimming, heat is not a problem, but the hair does exert a pulling or dragging force upon the body, thereby decreasing the speed of the swimmer. In fact, some swimmers have shaved their heads and bodies completely to decrease drag.

When considering the implementation of team regulations, the individual or group charged with the responsibility for drafting such regulations must first direct their attention to what is beneficial to the team as a whole. This is implicit in the team concept and without such considerations, the team as a unit would have no value at all. The members of any team must be taught to realize that certain personal sacrifices have to be made, within reason, for the sake of the entire enterprise. If the aspiring athlete is unwilling to sacrifice his hair, beard, or any other affectation which might jeopardize the team, he should not participate. Individual differences must be respected to a degree, but even in society at large the individual must learn to sacrifice certain things in the interest of all concerned. If this were not so, then logically people could refuse to pay taxes or observe speed laws, burglarize people's homes, and defy the authority of those for whom they work. To state, on the one hand, that everyone should be free to follow his own inclinations, while advocating, on the other hand, that people must learn to work together defies common sense. There must be give and take, and people must learn to live within the confines of a society that is democratically ordered to benefit all; the same rationale should apply to the conduct of the affairs of the team.

The athlete who is placed in the role of a substitute player frequently becomes discouraged and sometimes quits. His is a rather lonely role in that he receives little or no publicity either on or off the field and frequently regards himself as somewhat unnecessary. The youngster in class who is often not selected by his teammates is similarly left with a feeling of uselessness. In the classroom or physical education class, the teacher should ensure that all students participate regularly regardless of ability. Many times the coach cannot field his poorer players in a highly competitive situation without placing the team effort in jeopardy. He must therefore give his substitutes every consideration possible during practice and endeavor to instill in these players the idea that without their help the team effort would cease to exist. No five basketball players or eleven football players can sharpen their skills without another group to practice with. The coach has to communicate the fact that the word *team* is inclusive of all members, not just those who share the spotlight at game time. This situation is analagous to one in our country's space program. The astronauts may get all of the publicity, but such publicity is possible only through the hard work of many thousands of people who work diligently behind the scene. If the less talented athlete receives some recognition periodically, his life becomes more meaningful; he can proudly and justifiably say that he is indeed a valuable member of a team and therefore feel that his personal contribution is worthwhile.

CHARACTER OR CHARACTERS

A rather trite expression often attributed to athletics is that they develop character. The term *character* usually implies a positive position of worth. If a coach is conscientious and truly concerned with the personal development of his athletes, he can develop character. If, however, he is primarily interested in winning at any cost and chooses to ignore rules, ethics and common courtesy, he will develop *characters*—individuals whose personal attributes are less than socially acceptable. It takes hard work and a great deal of planning to instill genuine leadership in boys and to impart the idea of winning gracefully while learning to accept defeat objectively. Many lessons can be taught by athletics and the coach often provides the example which his boys follow. If the coach offers excuses for defeat ranging from blaming officials to sarcastic remarks about his players, the boys can hardly be blamed for following suit. A healthy rivalry between schools is a wholesome experience for all students involved, athletes and spectators alike. However, a rivalry which includes such things as directing inflammatory remarks toward the opponents, castigating officials, wrecking dressing rooms, and throwing objects at the opponent's bus, should not be tolerated. Behavior in athletics, as in any other endeavor, is a learned experience. Frequently poor game management is responsible for crowd conduct that leads to riots. Game management should always include some form of law enforcement which can deal with riotous fans. The conduct of players is the responsibility of the coach. Any lad who uses his fists on an opponent, calls him names, shouts at officials, or otherwise displays himself in an unsatisfactory manner should be barred from further competition until he learns to behave himself. The same could be said of the coach who behaves in a manner unbecoming to friendly competition. Such deleterious actions by either players or coaches only serve to work a hardship upon the team as a whole. Penalties are called, tempers flare, fights are precipitated, and the image of the school suffers irreparable damage.

Occasionally removing an outstanding player from a game for reasons of misconduct may result in victory for the opposing team. However, in the event that poor conduct is condoned by a coach, the administration should call it to his attention immediately and caution him against allowing it to happen again. Youngsters look to adults for leadership and will certainly have little or no respect for one who not only condones but also encourages poor sportsmanship. In any game or contest, there is more than just the score at stake. The entire life of a student might be affected by being allowed to conduct himself in a disparaging manner time after time. His actions might also affect the demeanor of the entire team; at the very least his teammates become his partners whether they desire to or not.

Strategy, training procedures, skills, and game techniques have been taught by coaches for years. Personal player conduct and game etiquette are areas that have been glossed over by many and completely ignored by some. Acceptable conduct on the playing field and in the dressing room is not the only form of behavior that should be emphasized. Good manners in eating establishments, hotels, on the street, and among fellow players also need to be stressed. When a team or a portion of a team acts in an unbecoming manner in the community or on the road, it reflects upon the entire school or home town as the case may be. There is no excuse for unacceptable behavior; however, some youngsters have never been disciplined at home and therefore don't know how to conduct themselves properly in the first place. The coach or teacher cannot assume a thing regarding the behavior of a youngster until he sees that student for himself. Poor manners do not always indicate a poor socioeconomic background. Some of the finest and best behaved boys and girls come from poor families, and some of the worst come from the most affluent background. Athletes of both sexes and all ages need to know what is expected of them in the way of behavior. If they are unsure of how they are to conduct themselves away from home, they should be told. The teacher or coach should never evade the issue by hoping that students will not get into trouble. Those who are charged with the responsibility for supervising groups of athletes, students on field trips, musicians, debate teams, or any other contingent of youngsters, cannot afford to shirk any portion of their duties which pertain to the welfare and behavior of their students. They must prepare the group prior to their departure, supervise them adequately while they are away from the school, and make sure that the youngsters have a way home after they return from the trip. To do otherwise is inexcusable and invites trouble and criticism from colleagues, parents, and administrators and conceivably could lead to curtailment of some of the valuable activities and experiences that some youngsters find available only through their school program.

QUESTIONS FOR DISCUSSION

1. What are some of the factors that have brought athletics into such prominence in our culture?
2. What role, good or bad, might parents play in encouraging a youngster to take part in athletics?
3. What are three basic body types and how might they influence a student athlete's chances for success in any particular sport?
4. What are some of the public relations programs that might be used by a coach or teacher to better inform the various publics about the athletic program?
5. Why should body type be considered when evaluating a student's chances for success in the following activities: football, gymnastics, basketball, sprinting, shotput, discus, diving and swimming?
6. Why would body type be of less importance in some of the recreational skills than in specific activities such as contact sports?
7. Why is it important for the prospective athlete to be aware of his body type and limitations? When should he be provided with this information?
8. Should a youngster be barred from competitive activity in which he is obviously very limited by body type? If so, why? If not, why?
9. Of what importance is ego involvement in athletics? Can this factor be considered an asset or a liability to performance? If so, why? If not, why?
10. Is conduct on school-sponsored trips of any importance? Can it affect the entire school program adversely or positively, and how?

CASE STUDIES

BOB SMITH

Bob Smith was a basketball player of great promise and only a sophomore at La Mont High School. He was 6' 5" tall and weighed approximately 220 pounds. He was agile, functioned well under the backboards, and was extremely accurate in his shooting ability. As a junior, Smith was selected to be on the all-district tournament team and received many phone calls and letters from college coaches who wished to interview him at the conclusion of his senior year.

Prior to the football season of Smith's senior year he was called into the office of the La Mont athletic director. The athletic director and football coach advised him that it would be to his advantage to play both football and basketball during his final school year, although he had never played football before in his career. He was told there was a policy whereby it was mandatory for all basketball players to play football whether they played under actual game conditions or not. The rationale behind the policy was that football provided a valuable training experience for the game of basketball. Smith did not desire to play football and felt that he was being pressured into something against his wishes and stated that he would like to discuss the matter with his basketball coach.

Harry Sanders, the basketball coach, sympathized with Smith's antipathy toward football, but felt in no position to overrule policy which had been handed down by the athletic director. He further explained that perhaps it would be best for Bob to turn out for football "to keep everyone happy," and that a body of Smith's size really didn't have to worry about being injured.

Smith was positioned as a defensive tackle and because of his natural ability faired amazingly well despite his lack of experience. He reluctantly decided to play to the best of his ability and managed to give a representative accounting of himself on the field. Many times Smith was knocked from his feet mainly because he did not possess a thorough mastery of his position but suffered no serious injury during the early games.

Midway through the season La Mont played a neighboring high school which was leading the conference. This team was blessed with large and experienced senior lads who had played together since the seventh grade. The boys were fast, tough, and well skilled in their assignments. Bob Smith was called on to replace the first-string defensive tackle who had been hurt on the previous play. He entered the game and performed well until caught off balance during a power play late in the third quarter. Not being adequately experienced in fending blockers off with his hands and arms, Smith let himself get doubleteamed by two offensive linemen and was then "finished" by a blocking back who was moving at full speed at the time of the impact. Smith untangled himself from the players after the whistle had been blown and when attempting to stand discovered that his left knee would not support him. Smith was carried from the field and a medical examination revealed that the semilunar cartilages and the cruciate ligaments of the left knee were damaged and would require immediate surgery.

During surgery it was discovered that the medial collateral ligament was partially torn, in addition to the other injuries. Therefore the repair of the knee was even more difficult than originally planned and the recovery time longer. Smith was not able to play basketball during his senior year. However he was offered a basketball scholarship, based upon his previous performance at a major state university. One stipulation made by the college coach was indeed a disconcerting factor—the athletic grant was to be made after the preseason practices were concluded. The coach told Smith that he could not really justify a grant unless he knew that the boy's knee would survive the rigors of practice. Smith did not last through the probationary period because of knee problems and was forced to drop from the basketball squad thereby losing any financial aid he might otherwise have had.

QUESTIONS

1. How would you evaluate the actions of the athletic director and football coach in the Smith case? How would you evaluate the reaction of the basketball coach?
2. What lessons are to be learned from the Smith case?

BILL REICHART

Bill Reichart attended a high school with teams in football, basketball, baseball, track, tennis and golf. Bill was a small boy who had a high degree of motor skill but was interested only in track. He was not fast enough for the sprints and did not have either the physique or the stamina to become a distance runner. After attempting most of the field events, Bill discovered that despite his diminutive size he could perform well in the high jump due to the great spring in his legs. He was slightly above average when compared to most prep school high jumpers, and was satisfied with second and third places but worked earnestly to improve his performance.

When Reichart was a senior his school instituted a program in gymnastics and a competitive team was established. Bill's track coach encouraged him to try out for the gymnastic team and informed the gymnastics coach of the boy's prowess in motor skills and extreme dedication. Bill worked diligently on the still rings and parallel bars. As a high school senior he was the most improved gymnast on the team and later, as a freshman in college entered the sport. Bill continued with his gymnastic work in college and as an upper classman placed nationally in competition on the still rings.

QUESTIONS

1. What principles were followed by the coaching personnel in satisfying the interests and desires of Bill Reichart? Do you feel that he might have enjoyed more success at some track event other than high jumping? Why?
2. If you had been acquainted with Bill Reichart, what sports would you have advised him to enter in view of the activities offered?

JUAN MORRO

Juan Morro played football for two years in high school and was selected as an all-conference tackle during the season of his junior year. He was extremely well-skilled, large, and possessed an uncanny instinct for diagnosing offensive team maneuvers. Morro was well liked by his peers and seemed to be doing well in his school work until midway through the football season of his senior year.

As a senior Morro developed a poor attitude toward practice sessions and deliberately missed two days in order to go on a hunting trip. His coach visited him and informed him that if he missed one more practice session his suit would be picked up. It was thoroughly explained to Morro that he should understand the training rules since they had been in effect for the two previous years and there was no excuse for missed practice. It was also emphasized that the athletic policy of the school allowed one warning for an offense prior to a boy's dismissal from the team.

The week following Morro's warning he was selected as the outstanding lineman in the district and was placed among the newspaper's candidates for the mythical all-state team. The day after the article in the newspaper appeared Morro again skipped practice. The next afternoon Morro reappeared and found that his equipment had been removed from his locker and that he could no longer consider himself a member of the team. He protested vehemently that such treatment was not fair to the team, and that as an "all-state" player he deserved greater consideration. The coach handed Morro a copy of the training rules and without another word walked to the practice field.

QUESTIONS

1. Do you believe that the coach was correct in his handling of Juan Morro? Should he have extended more consideration to Morro because of his prior contributions as a football player?
2. If Morro had been allowed to continue as a player, what problems might have arisen in regard to team morale? In regard to the attitude of Morro himself?
3. Do you think that the coach owed Morro a more lengthy explanation when he was dismissed than merely handing him a copy of the training regulations?

JEFF LARUE

Jeff Larue was an extremely capable football player and an outstanding student. When he was two years old Jeff's father had died and left only the boy and his mother. They had managed financially throughout the years and Jeff was well liked by all his friends. He worked to help support his mother and was therefore kept busy during the summer months; he did not have much opportunity for a social life of any kind.

Larue played football only. He did not have time for other sports due to his academic and work commitments. He played throughout his junior high years and was a varsity guard as a sophomore in high school. Jeff was even more outstanding as a junior and was considered by his coach to be the finest lineman that he had ever had the privilege of coaching.

When Jeff was a senior he was elected captain of his team and felt a great moral responsibility toward the team members. One afternoon early in the season he reported to the coach with a very difficult problem. After practice he was employed at an ice cream bar and had to work until one or two o'clock in the morning three nights a week. He said that he didn't want to give up football but that he needed at least two afternoons a week in which to catch up on his homework. Jeff's coach, Mr. Ingalls, sympathized with the boy but informed him that in the interest of the other players the matter would have to be placed before them for their decision.

A team meeting took place and Coach Ingalls presented Jeff Larue's case. The boys listened attentively and then unanimously agreed that Jeff should be allowed special dispensation to miss practice two days per week. They believed that in view of his family circumstances and prior dedication he should not be deprived of either football, which was his only luxury, or a chance to succeed academically.

When the news "leaked" that Larue had been granted two days

practice leave per week an irate mother of one of the other ball players called Coach Ingalls and demanded an explanation of why this had been allowed. Coach Ingalls patiently explained the situation, but to no avail. The mother called the parents of other players and apparently received no sympathy because the incident prompted no additional phone calls or discussion. Larue later continued his education in college and graduated with distinction from a reputable school of engineering.

QUESTIONS

1. Do you believe that the coach placed undue responsibility on his team by asking them to decide upon the fate of Jeff Larue as a football player? If so, why? If not, why?
2. Why should Jeff LaRue's case have been handled any differently than any other athlete? In whose best interest did the coach act?
3. As a parent of one of the other ball players, how would you have reacted to the decision made in the Larue case? How would you have reacted if your son had been the understudy for Jeff Larue?
4. What lessons can be learned about human relationships from the Larue case?

CYNTHIA WEST AND MISS RADFORD

Cynthia West was the daughter of a local business executive and was an outstanding student. She was an exceptionally tall girl who demonstrated a great deal of skill in basketball. She was not particularly interested in sports generally ascribed to the "country club set," and was ridiculed by some of the girls who believed competitive basketball to be an "unladylike" activity.

Cynthia went to Miss Radford, the girls' basketball coach, to ask if she would talk with her mother. It seemed that Mrs. West had been listening to some of the other mothers and believed that Cynthia should drop basketball because it was giving her an image of being masculine. Cynthia, on the verge of tears, maintained that she not only liked basketball but also it was the only sport in which she enjoyed a measure of success and therefore hated to give it up; at the same time she did not wish to displease her parents.

Miss Radford asked Cynthia if she would bring her mother to school to discuss the matter. An appointment was made and Mrs. West reluctantly agreed to attend the meeting. Mrs. West and Cynthia both stated their opinions regarding their feelings toward basketball and Miss Radford listened patiently. Miss Radford then raised the question as to whether Mrs. West had ever really tried to appreciate the grace of movement and the necessary strategies inherent in basketball. Mrs. West admitted that she was not too familiar with the game.

Miss Radford arranged for Mrs. West to accompany the girls' team on a trip to a nearby community so that she could judge for herself the feminine quality and social graces of the youngsters on the team. During the trip Miss Radford became better acquainted with Mrs. West and asked her directly if she was perhaps more aware of the social pressures which had been brought to bear upon her daughter than of Cynthia's interests and mental health. Mrs. West pondered the question for a time and admitted that perhaps she had been somewhat blind to what was happening; she further stated that she might also have been more interested in remarks which she felt could damage her own social status. After the trip Mrs. West told Cynthia how much she had enjoyed the outing and that Cynthia should continue playing basketball with the blessing of her parents.

QUESTIONS

1. Do you believe from reading the West-Radford case that there is a certain stigma attached to women's sports that might deter some girls from participation? What can be done to eliminate such stigma, if it indeed exists?
2. If Cynthia' mother had not allowed the girl to continue her basketball, might there have been additional strained relationships within the family?

SUGGESTED RELATED READING

Lewin, Kurt, *Principles of Topological Psychology.* Translated by Fritz Heider and Grace Heider. New York: McGraw-Hill, 1936, and Films (Xerox Co.), 1969.

Maslow, Abraham Harold, *Motivation and Personality.* New York: Harper, 1954.

Maslow, Abraham Harold, *Toward a Psychology of Being,* 2nd ed. Princeton, N.J.: Van Nostrand, 1968.

Sheldon, William Herbert, *The Varieties of Human Physique.* Darien, Conn.: Hafner Publishing Co. 1940. An introduction to constitutional psychology.

Sheldon, William Herbert, and S. S. Stevens, *The Varieties of Temperament.* New York: Harper and Brothers, 1942. A psychology of constitutional differences.

Williams, Jesse F., *The Principles of Physical Education,* 8th ed. Philadelphia: Saunders, 1964.

LIVING IN A FISHBOWL

Teaching is a unique profession in many respects. Whether the teacher prefers it or not, he lives under the constant surveillance of many people. His life style is scrutinized and criticized by students, colleagues, administrators, parents, and the local school board members. He is also the subject of discussion among those who belong to political organizations, tax research committees, legislative committees, and other governmental agencies. The teacher and his profession are characterized by various groups as being too liberal, too conservative, selfish, dedicated, overpaid, underpaid, overworked, underworked, interfering, not being involved, civic minded, lacking civic pride, practical, fuzzy thinkers, thrifty, financially overextended, and occasionally other adjectives that are unprintable.

Historically the teacher has been regarded as a public servant and his work has been difficult to evaluate in terms of absolute production. The students with whom a teacher comes into contact represent the end product of the labors of the educator, and, as such, are difficult to assess in terms of material worth. Unfortunately, the vast number of well-adjusted youngsters who are products of American education do not get the publicity that is accorded the minority radical element.

Teachers and parents alike prefer not to be associated with the wrongdoers of our culture, however both may have had a significant impact on the lives of these recalcitrants. As a profession that is continually in the public eye, however, we present an eternal target for those who would damn as well as praise. The behavior of one teacher in an entire school district is often taken as characteristic of all those who are employed. Thus the position of a coach or physical educator, who is supposed to exemplify certain qualities, is even more subject to scrutiny than the academician who is subject to less public exposure.

The physical educator is often stereotyped as being one who possesses a fine physique, neither smokes nor drinks, and should always be available to work with the Y.M.C.A., church youth groups, Boy Scouts, Girl Scouts, or other similar agencies. It is surmised by the general public that this man or woman is available should the need arise to provide leadership for the betterment of youth. Also physical educators are frequently regarded as individuals who are somewhat incapable of abstract thinking because they are not endowed with very profound powers of intellect. Sadly enough, many coaches and physical educators have not read widely or endeavored to polish their speech and vocabulary whereby they might convey a better image. A college president once remarked, after hiring an extremely eloquent young man to head his department of physical education, that "finding this man was like plucking a flower from an intellectual dung heap." This was certainly a sad commentary on the verbal skills of a large number of candidates, but was unfortunately a sincere observation after interviewing a great number of people who had applied for the position.

A recent case was recorded in California where a female physical educator was dismissed from her position because she was so obese. Another instance, in a southwestern state, cited as reason for dismissal the fact that a coach was found guilty of drunken driving. In other instances, teachers were fired for social discrepancies which would have been overlooked if committed by members of another profession. This serves only to illustrate that regardless of how a prospective teacher may view his private life, he is still vulnerable to the public and can be held legally accountable for his action. Furthermore, unless he is on tenure, he is not even entitled to a hearing.

The private life of any human being must necessarily be confined to those things which are within the realm of legality. However, the teacher is confronted with certain obligations not usually incumbent on members in other walks of life. The educator's life is mixed rather deeply with lives of others, and is difficult to separate. He may desire a private life, but his students and their parents may not view the situation in the same way. In teaching it is very difficult to ascribe to the philosophy of "do as I say, not as I do." To live by such a dual standard could well alienate a teacher from many students who would be highly desirous of emulating him.

Teachers are often misquoted by students and some parents are prone to attack the veracity of what has been said without checking the facts. Teachers are also often misquoted by fellow educators. It is difficult for a teacher to convey exact information to some students, but every educator should be cautious about conversations which involve fellow teachers. The problem of communication with members of the public is difficult enough, and falsely drawing one's colleagues into such discussions is highly unethical to say the least.

Many business and professional men stop by a tavern or similar establishment for refreshment on their way home from work. Teachers are often criticized for frequenting such places and occasionally take issue with the administration or school board when admonished for their actions. The most innocent intentions are sometimes misinterpreted by the public and especially by students who see their teachers entering drinking establishments. Some school districts have initiated policies which forbid teachers from patronizing establishments which serve alcoholic beverages and have made these policies a condition of employment. The rationale behind one such policy is that although the school board and the administration did not particularly frown upon moderate social drinking, the public would not stand for it from "their" teachers. It was further emphasized that the "public" was especially concerned about physical education teachers and coaches who drank. The constitutionality of such policies is open to question; however, any new teacher would be wise to investigate the existence of such guidelines prior to accepting any position. Some administrators are aware that the adult population of the community believes that their children should not be exposed to seeing teachers enter taverns. This is usually an excuse used by parents who don't wish to be known as prudes, but who do wish to convey the fact that they disapprove of teachers who drink, even moderately.

Proper dress for teachers has become a controversial matter recently because of some styles and color combinations that are currently being worn. A teacher occupies a position in which he must be the focal point of attention for his students. They should be more interested in what he has to say or do than in the clothing he wears. He should dress in a moderate style that is not distracting and maintain a neat and clean appearance at all times. The physical education teacher usually wears some type of uniform during class that allows for freedom of movement necessary in demonstrating skills, but should wear a suit or sports jacket and slacks during extra class periods. The women should likewise wear a suitable uniform while in class, and not wear micromini skirts or similar unique fashions while out of class. Such attire is really not too functional when a person must stoop, bend over a filing cabinet, or sit in an awkward position. Those who feel that their personal rights are being assailed by dress codes must remember that the position they occupy demands some considerations not often found in other forms of work. Extreme styles of dress may endear the teacher to some students but may in turn alienate others. A middle of the road policy is usually best and leads to fewer problems. After all, the primary function of a teacher is to educate by communicating his or her skills and knowledge, not to conduct a concerted drive to advance a personal philosophy or life style.

The demeanor of the teacher, both in school and out, may be a deciding factor in determining his success or failure. Suffice it to say that in *all* dealings, both directly related to the school and the community at large, a teacher should conduct himself in a mannerly fashion. He should be honest in his business dealings, and not be known as a poor credit risk, a chronic complainer, or one who is desirous of completely remaking the community. A new teacher should meet people in the community and would be well advised to become a good listener before he begins to make any arbitrary assessments or suggestions for change. Good manners and a positive approach to community affairs should carry a person a long way on the road to success.

FIRST- OR SECOND-CLASS CITIZEN

Educators have long been the butt of many jokes about their financial status as well as their occupation. The Washington Irving character, Ichabod Crane, and the cartoon caricatures of the "old maid school marm" have provided stereotypes of teachers that have been difficult to eradicate. Education itself has progressed much further than its public image. It is the duty of the profession to change this image because such changes most certainly cannot be effected from any other source. This being the case, the individual teacher must undertake to consolidate his position in the community in order to effect group acceptance of teaching as a true profession.

It is unfortunate that people often judge the success of others by the material objects possessed such as a new automobile, boat, large home, expensive clothes, and other factors such as membership in the country club or similar exclusive organizations. Young people throughout this nation are reassessing their values and beginning to consider the genuineness of the person more than his wealth. Hopefully this trend will grow until humans are judged by their fellows on the basis of personal integrity and the contributions made to society.

Until recently teachers have not taken a very active position in the nation's politics. Few had the money or opportunity to run for public office, and some have not been allowed to do so because they could not get time off from their jobs to attend legislative sessions or similar functions attendant to the office they might seek. School boards are now beginning to understand that teachers who are politically active can be a definite asset to a school district, as well as to the community at large, and are extending leaves of absence to those who have been elected to public office.

Political activity should be positive and *constructive*, not negative and *destructive*. The educator who is desirous of influencing a political party should work within the establishment in a democratic manner and not resort to revolutionary tactics or anarchism as a means to attain his goals. The democratic process is slow and tedious but can be productive and involve a great many people in the decision-making process. A teacher who becomes actively involved will quickly discover that he makes some interesting associations in the process, and may even emerge as a political leader. He should however always be careful to avoid mixing his personal politics with his classroom activities. A subjective private life does not mix well with one of professional objectivity.

Civic clubs provide the teacher with an inexpensive but worthwhile avenue of approach to community affairs. Most civic organizations are constantly searching for men and women who desire to render service, and will generally welcome teachers with a genuine interest in community betterment. The membership of most civic clubs is varied and this in itself affords the educator an opportunity to meet people from divergent backgrounds and at the same time have them become acquainted with him. The aims and objectives of various organizations differ, therefore a prospective member should become thoroughly informed about a club prior to membership. Also, the meetings of some organizations are held at times which conflict with the school schedule and would tend to rule out membership for teachers.

On joining an organization, the teacher should be willing to share in the duties and responsibilities placed upon the membership. He should become well acquainted and perhaps will discover that he has the opportunity to discuss his school program with individual members. At no time should a teacher criticize his administration or school board. He must present the positive side of education regardless of his personal opinions or bias. "Dirty linen" should always be aired within the profession and not in public. Such criticism serves no worthwhile purpose and indeed can be detrimental, not only to the profession but to the students whom it serves.

PERSONAL FINANCE AND THE TEACHER

The existence at college for a student is often a period of relatively low income with little to spend on items other than necessities. After graduation beginning teachers frequently sign contracts for salaries representative of a much larger amount of money than they have been accustomed to spending. Often the neophyte educator purchases a new automobile, and perhaps a number of other items, on credit and later discovers that after the necessary deductions his actual take-home pay is somewhat less than he anticipated. As a result, he may become disgruntled, worry a great deal about his credit payments, and perhaps accept an evening job of some kind to augment his income.

Many young people have the mistaken idea that they should

immediately be able to purchase the same kind of merchandise and afford the same type of house that their parents have worked thirty years to obtain. No teacher should have to live in a hovel or drive an old battered automobile, but they should use discretion in their purchasing. As their salary increases they can then begin to afford some of the luxuries they desire. It is probable that teachers' salaries will never rise to a level earned by physicians or lawyers, but the trend for better salaries for teachers has placed them in a more satisfactory financial position than once occupied.

The "moonlighter" is really compromising his position as a teacher. Education is a full-time job and demands a great deal of planning if proper instruction is to result. The easy life of a teacher, with short hours and many vacations, is a myth. A conscientious instructor will work well over forty hours a week and will spend many summers attending graduate school and conferences, mainly at his own expense. The teacher who assumes that his day begins with the arrival of the students and ends with their departure, is cheating not only his pupils but also himself. The satisfaction of doing a job well, and the contacts one makes with his students while supervising extracurricular activities, are the factors that make teaching worthwhile. All of these extra-class duties do not allow the teacher to perform wage-earning functions other than those pertaining to his chosen profession.

Many school boards have seriously considered various schemes of merit pay for teachers. This type of pay in the form of bonuses and extended salary has been found to serve as an inducement in other areas of endeavor. The end product of education is not easily measured, but the time and effort involved in planning and organizing can readily be determined by observing the effectiveness and efficiency of the teacher during instructional periods. It is not too difficult for a perceptive administrator to determine which of his teachers are teaching and which are merely baby-sitting. It would not be surprising to see more merit-pay schedules emerging throughout the country.

It would be foolish to imply that teachers are a breed of individuals whose only interest is their profession and that they should therefore compromise the financial returns received for their labors. Even though the educator himself gains great satisfaction from his position, his family cannot. His family is not operating within the same frame of reference and exposure; therefore their feelings may differ entirely in matters of compensation and life style. Often families make financial demands upon the head of the household that just cannot be met by a teacher's salary. If money is the prime target of an individual, he would do well to choose a profession other than teaching before he determines his college major. The teacher will be miserable and so will his pupils, if he concerns himself first with finances and second with students.

THE TEACHER IS AN ADULT

The public is rather possessive of teachers because they comprise a large segment of those who are paid from tax revenues. In some communities such a furor has been raised because teachers have "been seen downtown" during the school day that boards have initiated policies which prohibit teachers from leaving the school at any time during school hours except for dire emergencies. Most teachers have enough to do at school without going to town, but occasionally a situation arises when a faculty member must go to the bank, consult an attorney, visit a realtor, or engage in other business transactions. If the teacher has a preparation period, and has prepared his lesson at home so that his "prep" period could be utilized for a particular business appointment, he should be allowed to take care of his private affairs. The school districts of this nation *must* begin to realize that teachers devote a great deal of their own time to counseling, extracurricular activities, lesson planning and grading of papers; therefore they should be able to leave school occasionally when they are not teaching in order to transact their business. Nothing is as demeaning as to be called before the superintendent and treated as a truant child because "you have been seen in town during school hours." Obviously, teachers should not abuse the privilege of leaving school and they should inform the secretary of their whereabouts in case they are needed, but to deny the privilege in the first place is an administrative error which automatically relegates the professional teacher to a position of inferiority in the community.

Teachers as a group, generally have been considered good credit risks. This is partly due to the educational level of the people in the teaching profession and also because educators realize that they can be dismissed from their job for failure to pay their bills. It seems only fair that they should be accorded the consideration of an adult role in conducting their affairs and not have to beg for special favors.

Individuals engaged in certain businesses and professions are exempt from jury duty in various states if they sign a statement declaring their duties are such that they cannot be replaced. In some schools the administration insists that teachers excuse themselves from jury duty on the grounds that their classes will suffer if a substitute is employed. This type of demand is a direct violation of an individual's rights to assume his place as a responsible citizen and should not be countenanced by any school board. Any attorney can testify to the difficulty of impaneling a competent jury, and the automatic elimination of school teachers only compounds the problem. It would seem only logical that a person on trial, perhaps for his life, should receive the consideration of the most intelligent jury possible, yet the elimination of teachers from jury duty excludes a large segment of the educated population of any community.

GET TO KNOW THE OTHER HALF

Schools serve many publics, and their students come from all walks of life. Pupils vary in ability, socioeconomic background, attitude, size, interest, and a myriad of other factors. The teacher is faced with the problem of communicating not only with students from different backgrounds, but with their parents as well. Some parents respect the teacher because of his educational background and some distrust him because he represents an educational level above theirs or their associates. Because schools represent authority and control over children, the teacher is sometimes looked upon as one who interferes with the rights and privileges of parents.

By becoming members of a civic organization, teachers can meet people of various backgrounds. However, schools must expand their public relations programs in an effort to contact all of the parents, and teachers should exert themselves in areas where the school cannot. Many teachers have found that summer jobs offer an opportunity to contact segments of the population that do not often visit schools. Working with labor crews, migrant workers, and other unskilled members of the society have proven a valuable experience for many teachers. First it must be understood by any teacher who is involved in common labor as a summer job that the people with whom he is working depend upon that type of endeavor year-round for their livelihood. The astute educator should not demean those working with him and would be well advised to become acquainted gradually with his fellow workers. He can ask questions, show a definite interest in the job and try to understand the problems that arise. By working with people from other backgrounds, the teacher may discover that they have suggestions and comments which may well be of value in assisting him in dealing with their children. Furthermore, the "other half" should begin to realize that teachers are human beings and have many problems and aspirations similar to their own.

Often as a teacher works in an occupation other than education he finds that his co-workers are interested in the schools and what they are teaching. They have many searching questions and comments that would never arise in a P.T.A. meeting, and they are more willing to communicate these feelings because they are functioning within their own "territory." Many of these questions and comments reflect very sound native intelligence, despite the fact that the person from whom the question or comment originated may have had little formal education. In our society we often falsely assume that formal training should supersede native intelligence and that those who have had little educational background are not qualified to make sound judgments; this is just not true. Many citizens who are poorly educated in the formal sense have very astute powers of observation and should be listened to, especially when considering matters in which their children are concerned. Even if the observations made are erroneous, the teacher has the opportunity of clarifying misunderstandings and thus forwarding the cause of education.

Physical education is a widely misinterpreted discipline and the opportunity to discuss the values of physical education and athletics should be seized upon whenever possible. People are prone to believe that all school programs are similar to those to which they have been exposed. If they personally suffered from a poor program of physical education, they will probably assume that the present offerings are the same. Unless this misunderstanding is corrected, the expected support from the concerned individual will not be forthcoming.

College professors and public teachers find that it is often easier to remain in their ivory towers and theorize rather than to personally investigate problems and situations at the level they occur. It would be difficult to interest ghetto children and their parents in any kind of curriculum without personally attempting to determine their desires, interests, and aspirations. Likewise, the value of a program as it relates to rural children often depends upon their manner of thinking and what has been communicated to them before. Teachers cannot afford to isolate themselves from the citizenry. Education is a cooperative enterprise and therefore all of the interested factions—students, parents, teachers, administrators, and school boards—are going to have to open lines of communication if they are to resolve common problems. This is not meant to imply that every idea or opinion of those concerned can be implemented within the program or that the formal training of professional educators should be ignored. It means simply that the interpretation of school programs, their aims, objectives, and necessary changes of direction, can best be understood by all people through the medium of open lines of communication and interest.

THE TEACHER AS A LIVING EXAMPLE

Youngsters emulate those whom they respect. They idolize athletes, musicians, motion picture and television performers, and yes, even some idolize their parents and teachers. The teacher who conducts himself in a professional manner by living the type of existence he prescribes for his students is a person whom they can respect. The physical educator who advocates one type of life style for his students and leads an existence which is contrary to his teachings is viewed as a hypocrite by his students. They may not openly criticize an instructor, but nevertheless their actions might well indicate their true feelings.

It seems inconceivable that a physical education teacher who is grossly overweight and indulges in virtually no physical activity could effectively impart to his students the benefits of proper nutrition and vigorous exercise. The logical question for the students to ask of such a person would be, "if nutrition and activity have values for us, why not for you?" It would indeed be difficult to answer such a query in a manner which would indicate that the teacher genuinely believed in those things he was teaching his classes.

All teachers are human and usually exhibit the emotional characteristics peculiar to any other group of people. Some individuals in other professions enjoy the luxury of being able to display their feelings in a more forceful manner than the teacher is permitted. There are times when emotions run high and the educator would like to "blow off steam," but to do so would only place him on the same plane with the volatile youngster whom he is counseling. It is difficult to maintain one's composure at times, but with practice it can be done. Moreover, when the students perceive that their teacher approaches problems with logic rather than emotion they begin to realize that perhaps his approach is much better than one which is predicated on rage and misunderstanding. If an individual is of such temperament that he cannot control himself emotionally, he should perhaps seek a profession other than teaching. Physical education classes and coaching present many opportunities for displays of temper. Any situation which involves an active and competitive endeavor will be charged with emotional pressure, and may result in chaos unless the instructor maintains his composure. It is the responsibility of the teacher or coach to control and direct his classes or sport; therefore, he must be in command of his faculties at all times and cannot afford to resort to emotional outbursts, whatever the circumstances. Perhaps teaching and coaching would produce fewer ulcers if less emotional control was demanded, but that is not possible if order is to be maintained.

It is very difficult for a coach or teacher to remain emotionally detached under certain circumstances. However, the true professional must learn that whatever the situation he must be objective in order to critically evaluate and immediately make corrections which hopefully will alter the behavior of his students or players in a positive manner. To do otherwise only compounds the problem, and if the teacher or coach becomes actively involved in an argument or dispute it is analagous to throwing gasoline on a fire. It has been learned that volatile coaches and teachers tend to produce volatile students and players; this is certainly not to be desired and may have a crippling effect on the entire school program.

School boards and administrators frown upon teachers who create unrest and dissension in the school and community. The professional educator who continually fights the establishment and conducts himself in an unprofessional manner is inviting trouble. Beginning teachers must learn that they can only effect positive change through positive means. Change takes time and patience and negative behavior only generates animosity and distrust. Change in an organized and democratic society is usually a product of evolution rather than revolution. If a teacher desires the admiration of his students and sincerely wishes to affect them in a positive manner he will set the example. For those who advocate a policy of hypocrisy in their own lives it would be well to paraphrase Confucius who was reputed to state, "What you are speaks so loudly that I cannot hear what you say."

DON'T CATER TO INFLUENCE—TO THINE OWNSELF BE TRUE

Every community has a power structure. That power structure may include bankers, lawyers, doctors, dentists, influential housewives, and usually anyone of wealth. Often, those who comprise the power structure of a community belong to various civic organizations, lodges, and the country club, and sometimes are school board members. Many of those who occupy positions of influence are responsible public-spirited citizens who are sincere in their attempts to improve upon the social environment in which they live. Unfortunately, some individuals seek positions of power selfishly and are only interested in their own self-aggrandizement.

The youngsters who attend our public schools represent every socioeconomic element in the community and are not responsible for the conditions into which they were born. Teachers owe each and every youngster in their classes the moral obligation of equal opportunity regardless of background or parental influence. Most individuals of every profession desire success and should do everything ethically possible to attain their goals. Young teachers occasionally discover that the quickest way up the ladder to success is to "know the right people." In their attempt to make themselves known, some individuals believe they should join the right organizations and socialize with the elite of the community. In their attempt to "climb" some find that they progress much faster if they ingratiate themselves to others by performing special favors or paying special attention to the children of those who exert influence within the community. To prostitute oneself professionally by becoming obligated to any individual or pressure group in the interest of personal advancement is inexcusable as well as completely unethical.

When class assignments are made or team positions assigned, the procedure should be based exclusively upon the personal merits of the individual student and should never in any way reflect the social or political status of their parents. Public schools are not intended to be private institutions for those of position, but are designed to afford equal educational opportunity for all children in order to assist them toward a better life not only for themselves, but the nation as a whole. In a truly democratic society, there is no room for favoritism and discrimination.

One may observe that often the valedictorian of a particular class or the captain of a debate team comes from a higher than average socioeconomic background. In most instances, the relationship between school success and economic background is the result of the family's access to selected magazines, books, and information gained through communication with friends, not because of special treatment at school. In physical education classes and athletics the poor youngster may well succeed because of his motor ability rather than because of his home environment. Likewise, he may be handicapped due to malnutrition or other environmental factors. However, successful students in physical education and athletics reflect a broader spectrum of the society than is generally true of those who succeed in the arts. This does not imply that physical educators are more interested than other teachers in the equality of human beings, but does illustrate that socioeconomic background has a more profound effect upon the arts than upon motor skills.

People should enter the teaching profession with a missionary zeal and a conscience that would not permit them to be swayed by community or social politics. As a teacher goes through his or her daily duties, he should continually ask himself, "what am I doing, and whom do I serve." If at any time the answer reflects favoritism or inequality of student treatment, that teacher should immediately reassess his goals and objectives to determine whether personal aims have superseded those of the profession. If the self-evaluative process reveals interests contrary to those of a dedicated professional, steps should be taken to ameliorate the condition. Some individuals, regardless of their chosen profession, will elect the quick road to what they equate with success, namely position and/or money. A few teachers have even used the teaching profession as a vehicle to make themselves known so that they could later enter a more lucrative business. However, it is doubtful that *any* parent would welcome the use of his child as a stepping-stone.

QUESTIONS FOR DISCUSSION

1. What are some of the factors that have previously placed teachers in the position of second-class citizens?
2. Why do many parents expect more exemplary personal behavior from physical educators and coaches than they would expect from teachers of academic courses?
3. What are some of the means by which a teacher can become better acquainted with the citizens of the community?
4. What possible values could a teacher or coach accrue from spending a summer working with a laboring crew, packing house, or maintenance department? Is this realistic or not?
5. Of what significance is a community's power structure? Who usually comprises such a structure?
6. Are there certain forms of entertainment which are generally accepted by the public in which teachers cannot indulge? If so, why? If not, why?
7. Are there reasons why students from middle-income groups succeed in arts better than those from the lower-income groups? Can you think of any competitive sports in which socioeconomic background might well have an influence?
8. Why are some teachers living examples of hypocrisy? How would you assess these individuals as true professionals?
9. Why is the teacher not truly free to "do his own thing"? Who, other than himself, would be affected?
10. What has the management of personal finances to do with one's acceptance or rejection within the community in which he lives?
11. If you were a school board member or administrator and you were called by a parent and chastized because one of your teachers was downtown during school hours, what would your reply be to that parent?

CASE STUDIES

SALARIES AND CORPORATE PROPAGANDA

A number of years ago a state in the Southwest was plagued by rapidly rising educational costs due to the population influx. Taxpayers voiced their usual complaints about wasteful educational expenditures and corporate interests became aroused as never before in the history of the area. Many firms sent representatives to school board meetings throughout the state to "investigate" fiscal policies and frequently these individuals represented themselves only as "interested and concerned citizens."

One rather large corporate enterprise purchased two pages in a metropolitan newspaper and published the name of every school employee in the state along with his hourly wage. The figures for the published wages were easily obtained inasmuch as such salaries are a matter of public information. However, the manner in which they were presented was somewhat biased to say the least. Each person's hourly wage was predicated on the actual number of days in which the school operated and the classroom hours that the individual taught. All vacations were eliminated in the computation as were hours on non-teaching duty, preparation periods, all extracurricular activities, and days utilized for in-service training or similar projects. Absolutely nothing was mentioned about the hours spent in grading of papers or any related professional obligations. To the average person who read the paper and was unfamiliar with the manner in which the figures had been computed, the hourly wages of teachers seemed indeed astronomical when compared to the wages of others.

Teachers and administrators alike were incensed at the manner in which they had been treated by the advertisement and therefore prevailed upon their state education association to counter the article with accurate facts and information. The state association was forced to expend a substantial amount of money and time in compiling and printing information which would offset the damage done. Fortunately, the common sense and perception of school boards was not adversely affected by spurious figures and no permanent damage was done. However, the particular state in question was not one in which the school budget was placed before the general public for passage. Each independent school board at the time was responsible for setting and adopting the budget, and the taxes were adjusted accordingly. In a state where school budgets were voted on annually, the results of such articles could have been calamitous.

QUESTIONS

1. What are your observations regarding the conduct of agencies who use tactics similar to those cited in the case regarding the publishing of teachers' salaries? Is this legal?
2. What should be done to "head off" similar situations before they ever arise?

Outline a plan of public relations that would not allow professional personnel to be placed in such a compromising position.

MR. EDSON

Mr. Edson was an excellent high school civics teachers. He had the respect of his students and many believed that he was the finest teacher they had. He always planned his lessons in detail, stimulated interesting classroom discussions, conducted field trips to the various city and county offices, and brought in many guest speakers to enhance the subject area.

Edson was a pool player of some skill who frequented one of the two local billiard parlors as a recreational outlet. He played only for fun and did not gamble. He became friendly with many people of the "lower socioeconomic" citizenry and believed he not only had an opportunity to enjoy himself but also he was able to converse with youngsters who were seriously considering leaving school. The pool hall that Mr. Edson attended did not serve liquor and there was never any trouble on the premises.

Mr. Edson was called into the office of Mr. Milford, the superintendent, and asked about his social life. Edson was rather surprised to discover that "a certain board member" had requested that he stay out of pool rooms and other such unsavory places of doubtful repute. Milford patiently explained to Edson that teachers should reflect the finer things in society and that he was casting a rather poor image of both himself and his profession. Edson countered that he had never misbehaved or gambled in the pool room and believed that his associations with the youngsters and parents who frequented the establishment were of benefit to the educational process. Mr. Milford accused Edson of being stubborn and uncooperative. He further informed Edson that unless he stayed out of the pool rooms he was left with no choice but to terminate his contract at the conclusion of the school year.

Mr. Edson consulted the officers of his local education association to find out whether or not he could enlist their support in combating what he felt to be an arbitrary decision by the superintendent. He was informed that since he was not a teacher on tenure he had no recourse. Moreover, during the discussion of the matter it was insinuated that what he was asked to sacrifice was so inconsequential that it wouldn't be worth "rocking the boat about." Edson went to the superintendent's office and handed in his resignation, effective at the conclusion of the school year.

QUESTIONS

1. Do you believe that Mr. Edson was acting in a professional manner by frequenting a pool hall? If so, why? If not, why?
2. Why shouldn't teachers be allowed to frequent billiard parlors or similar establishments in the pursuit of recreation? Is there any way in which you would care to qualify your answer?
3. If you had been an administrator who was confronted by the Edson case what would you have done? Is it the prerogative of any single board member to exert pressure in such a case?
4. How do you feel about the reaction of the officials of the local education association in regard to Mr. Edson's case?

MISS TILLSON

Miss Tillson had just been graduated from a state college with a degree in health and physical education. She had earned her way through college by performing various campus jobs and acting as an assistant hall resident. She was an outstanding student who belonged to many honor organizations and had no difficulty in being placed in a fine teaching position.

Miss Tillson had never possessed much money in college to spend on personal things and her first annual salary appeared to her as an extremely large amount of money. She purchased a new automobile, furnished an apartment, bought a stereo set, and completely outfitted herself with a new wardrobe. All of her purchases were made on credit with a minimal down payment. She had carefully totaled her payments and found them to be well within her budget and therefore anticipated no financial difficulties.

In her budgetary considerations Miss Tillson had not considered deductions from her salary for state retirement, income taxes, health insurance, and professional dues for various organizations. Neither had she considered that on entering the teaching profession she would be prevailed upon to contribute to charitable projects or certain school funds. As a result of these deductions she found that her check did not leave her with enough take-home pay to meet her monthly installments on personal purchases.

Miss Tillson was left with only one alternative, she would either have to sell some of the items that she had purchased on credit or allow them to be repossessed. She was advised by friends to borrow from her credit union, pay off her debts, and then sell her car for whatever she could get, hopefully enough to pay the balance due as she did not, at the time, have any substantial equity. She was granted the loan and liquidated her debts as advised. However, she sold the car for just enough to pay it off, and was left with no money and no automobile. After a few months, however, she was able to purchase an older secondhand auto which served as transportation for short trips. It took Miss Tillson approximately five years to regain a sound financial status and during that time she had very little money to spend for personal pleasures.

QUESTIONS

1. What advice should be given to college graduates in regard to the expenditures they might expect on their first job? Is it, indeed, the business of anyone to interfere in such matters by giving such advice? Would you as a student appreciate such advice?
2. Do you believe that restrictions should be placed on credit-buying to prevent people such as Miss Tillson from getting involved financially to such an extent? What measures would you suggest?
3. Do you think that such financial involvement as mentioned in the Tillson case could cause disruption of her professional life? If so, why?

MR. MCAULIFF

Mr. McAuliff was the principal of East High School. He had previously been a teacher and coach and had also served for a period of three years as vice principal. He was extremely interested in athletics and maintained that the disciplinary values inherent in the interscholastic program could be found nowhere else in the school curriculum.

McAuliff frequently informed his coaches that he believed the manner in which they handled their athletes on trips was most important. He stated that he did not believe in catering to lazy youngsters and that all student athletes should learn to be punctual. He further told his coaches that they should establish deadlines for students to meet at the school bus in order to return from games played at other schools, and if any youngster was more than five minutes late the bus should leave without him.

East High was playing basketball against a school some 50 miles distant. After the game was over the boys ate their postgame meal and were dismissed after being told to report to the bus at an appointed time. At the predetermined time all the boys were back except one, George McAuliff, the principal's son. After waiting approximately ten minutes the coach told the bus driver to leave and George was left behind. Fortunately George was given a ride by one of the parents of some student spectators but arrived home three hours after the bus.

Mr. McAuliff was waiting in the school parking lot for his son when the bus returned. The coach explained what had happened and McAuliff concurred with the decision but was visably shaken by his son's unexpected absence. The next morning McAuliff asked the basketball coach to his home and then proceeded to verbally chastise his son George in the presence of his coach. George apologized to both his father and his coach and the matter was forgotten. The coach thanked Mr. McAuliff for his support and stated that perhaps he had been a bit hasty in his decision to leave the boy behind. McAuliff replied that he believed rules were rules and they should apply equally to all concerned without any consideration to the position of the persons involved.

QUESTIONS

1. What do you think of the decision made by the basketball coach in the McAuliff case? Would you have acted differently? If so, why? If not, why?
2. How would you evaluate Mr. McAuliff as an administrator after reading the case? Do you believe that his rules were too severe or too arbitrary?
3. What might have been the repercussion if George had been the son of the chairman of the school board? Should you ever cater to *any* special interest group?

SUGGESTED RELATED READING

Davis, Jerome, *Character Assassination.* Introduction by Robert M. Hutchins. New York: Philosophical Library, 1950.

Hook, Sidney, *Academic Freedom and Academic Anarchy.* New York: Cowles Book Co., 1970.

Hook, Sidney, *The Paradoxes of Freedom.* Berkeley: University of California Press, 1970.

Langdon, Grace, and Irving W. Stout, *Helping Parents Understand their School.* Englewood Cliffs, N.J.: Prentice-Hall, 1957. A handbook for teachers.

Marshall, Max Skidmore, *Two Sides to a Teacher's Desk.* New York: Macmillan, 1951. Dedicated to students, teachers and bystanders.

Newman, Edwin S., *Civil Liberty and Civil Rights.* Dobbs Ferry, N.Y.: Oceana Publications, 1964.

Rope, Frederick Thornton, *Opinion Conflict and School Support.* New York: Teacher's College, Columbia University, 1941.

9
THE TEACHER
AND
PROFESSIONAL CONSIDERATIONS

WHAT IS A PROFESSIONAL PERSON

The definition of a professional implies that the individual engaged in a profession is one who conforms to the standards of his chosen occupation. The term profession has also been associated with certain types of endeavor that are basically performed as services to other individuals, for example, the ministry, law, medicine, pharmacy, and social work. It is assumed that the sincere professional practitioner is one who is more dedicated to his work than to the financial rewards that he might receive for his services. To assume however that a physician, lawyer, or teacher would not be at least *concerned* about his salary or fee would be ridiculous in our present society. The matter of professional performance and remuneration for services rendered is really a matter of priority; hopefully, the educator would consider his professional obligations as the priority of first order. It is doubtful that anyone would wish to place himself under the care of a neurosurgeon who was more interested in his fee than he was in conducting brain surgery. It is just as doubtful that a parent would wish to entrust the future of his children to teachers who could care less about youngsters and were just marking time from payday to payday.

As one examines the various professions, it becomes apparent that there *are* individuals who are professionally incompetent and should seek some other form of employment. Physicians, lawyers, and dentists are self-employed and must be competent practitioners or lose their clientele. Teachers are employed by private or public schools and, as such, public school teachers practice their skills upon a student body which is compelled by law to attend classes. Therefore, the selection of a public school teacher by his students is not a matter of electing him because of his competence, but because he is the person assigned to the position.

A large number of public school teachers operate under *tenure* laws whereby a teacher cannot be dismissed from his position unless the district can prove that he has been grossly negligent in his duties, insubordinate, or morally unfit to teach. Furthermore, the teacher on tenure is entitled to a hearing prior to dismissal and may answer, in the presence of legal council, any charges leveled against him. Tenure laws were enacted to protect teachers against the whims of arbitrary administrators, *not* to provide them with a shelter under which they could engage in professional hibernation and mark time until retirement. Tenure laws place the administrator in a rather compromising position in that many times he has difficulty ridding the profession of "deadwood." Very few administrators gain the assistance of members of the teaching staff in eliminating poor teachers; this is unfortunate. If teaching is to be considered a true profession, the classroom practitioners should be just as interested in policing their ranks as should the administration or school board. It has been hypothesized that the teaching profession will never present a united front against incompetency until there is parity between teachers and administrators in both recognition of importance and salary. It has even been suggested that perhaps one way to insure even greater unity would be for school administrators to be selected by school faculties rather than appointed by the board.

Physical educators and coaches are often one and the same person. Some coaches perform exceptionally well as professional physical educators and are extremely conscientious about their teaching duties. However, in some instances, the individual is hired primarily because he can coach a particular sport and not because he can teach physical education. School administrators and board members who are more concerned about the image the athletic teams project than they are about the instructional process should review their philosophies very critically. If they are concerned only about the coaching aspect of a position, then they should employ persons who will perform that function alone. If, on the other hand, they are equally concerned about both instruction in physical education and coaching, they should be very specific in their job descriptions and their subsequent evaluation of an individual's performance in both areas. If the teacher-coach is found to be deficient in either his teaching or his coaching and does not improve his performance, he should be dismissed from his position. Physical educators who coach have a dual function and should remember that they are employed to serve *both* the students in the service course program and the athletes, not one or the other.

The professional should respect all his fellow teachers and should learn to work in harmony with them. In many colleges and universities the men's and women's physical education departments are separated from one another. Such separation during the period of teacher training is often carried over into the public schools and results in many conflicts relative to the use of equipment, facilities, and budget. Physical education and athletics should be concerned with *students*, not males or females. It is therefore mandatory that men and women physical educators and coaches learn to work together for the welfare of *all* youngsters. Mature professional physical educators of both sexes should work *together* to improve offerings in both men's and women's programs. Furthermore, for teachers to engage in a perpetual dispute over emphasis and direction is indeed stupid. Naturally there should be differing philosophies relative to men's and women's programs, but professional people must learn to understand and appreciate differing points of view, not involve themselves in an eternal debate over who is right and who is wrong. If men and women of the profession learn to cooperate more fully, they will ultimately discover that mutual support will yield far greater educational returns than will mutual discord.

PROFESSIONAL ETHICS

The ethics or moral principles as related to education encompass a multitude of factors. Professional ethics involve every aspect of teaching, from the respect for one's colleagues to the discussion of individual student's problems in the faculty lounge. A listing of professional ethics for teachers is tantamount to a code of conduct and should seriously be considered. The physical educator must learn that among other things he should conduct himself in a manner that he himself would prefer to be treated. Many of the ethical procedures attendant to the teaching profession are those found in the everyday proceeding of civilized social intercourse. Others more specific are as follows:

1. Never adversely criticize another teacher, administrator, or board member.

2. Never violate the confidence of *anyone* who entrusts information to you in good faith.

3. Do not apply for a position known to be held by another, even though you know that the person holding the position might be dismissed from his employment.

4. Do not threaten your employer by telling him that you will leave your position unless certain conditions are met, or that you have been "offered" another position and will seriously consider it if your present situation doesn't improve.

5. Treat equally all personnel—administrators, teachers, students, custodians, and clerical help. These people are human and deserve the same consideration you desire extended to you.

6. Conduct all your business dealings, both private and professional, in a forthright and honest manner. Do not accept any kickbacks from salesmen, or other inducements which are designed to influence your purchases.

7. Admit your mistakes, do not try to excuse your shortcomings, and make every effort to improve yourself.

8. Don't try to "feather your own nest" by flattery or politics.

9. Observe proper protocol relative to students and professional associates. Follow the prescribed chain of authority in all of your duties.

10. Never play favorites or fall into the trap of showing special consideration for athletes or other select student groups. Be objective and fair in all of your deliberations.

11. Do not shirk your professional duties as a member of campus committees, class sponsor, or assistant at any extracurricular function.

12. Consider all budgetary funds allocated to you as moneys belonging to others. Do not spend money for unnecessary items or "pad" your budget in any way.

13. Maintain all equipment in a manner whereby you waste nothing. You are accountable for everything in your department.

14. Do not allow personal bias to interfere with professional relationships and obligations; maintain an open mind and be receptive to new ideas.

15. Stay abreast of developments in your discipline. Join your professional associations and *read* their journals.

Professionalism is not synonymous with blind allegiance. If you sincerely believe one of your superiors or colleagues to be wrong, you should call his attention to factual evidence which supports your contention. It would be a gross injustice to adhere to a fallacious policy when you have evidence to demonstrate its shortcomings. However, to engage in criticism without providing your associates with the opportunity to alter their position is highly unethical. Professional disagreements should take place from time to time, but they must remain on a high plane of behavior and be supported by facts rather than emotion. In a truly democratic administration, the machinery exists whereby differences can be resolved without resorting to namecalling and backstabbing. The objective teacher who sincerely desires to effect positive change should be willing to confront his superiors and colleagues as a professional. He may discover that fellow teachers, principals, and superintendents are willing to listen to logic and will alter their positions if presented with adequate and convincing evidence. He may also occasionally discover that he does not have all the facts in the matter being studied and thereby must alter his own position.

There is no reason why educators cannot disagree on professional matters and still remain the best of friends in private life. Conversely, people do not necessarily have to be friends in order to be professional allies. It is often difficult for teachers to separate their private and professional lives, but through practice and objective thinking it can be done. The teacher must learn to respect the opinions of his associates and not take every criticism of professional philosophy as a personal affront. Many legislators, at both the state and national levels, have found that they may differ markedly in political philosophy and yet remain close personal friends. For teachers and administrators to do less would be a sad commentary upon education.

PROFESSIONAL ORGANIZATIONS—SERVICE OR MUTUAL ADMIRATION?

Professional organizations at the local, state, and national levels are basically structured to provide the following:

1. Cohesiveness of the profession.
2. Communication between individual members.
3. Dissemination of research and ideas pertinent to the field.
4. A forum for discussion and debate of various philosophic positions.
5. A means of distributing costs of publications among the members.
6. Fellowship and a kindred spirit among those of a like profession.
7. An opportunity to serve one's profession.

The majority of the members of any professional association are dedicated to the service of the organization and also to the profession in general. Those who write for journals and research publications render a valuable service by providing others with information which might otherwise be unavailable. Most of these people serve without consideration of either time or money. The truly professional physical educator must put forth the effort and expense to better himself even though it might infringe upon his recreation or social life. It is frequently inconvenient to serve on a committee or engage in similar activities after school hours or on weekends, but the hours of a professional person cannot as easily be regulated as those of industry or the building trades. The nature of education dictates that the school hours are consumed by the teaching or administrative functions and professional obligations often encroach upon an educator's free time. Some physical educators maintain that they perform to capacity during the school hours and therefore fail to perceive the values inherent in a professional association. What they really fail to perceive is that they often remain unaware of professional advancements and frequently do not incorporate the most up-to-date methods or materials in their instruction; this is grossly unfair to the students.

If one is to succeed in any endeavor, personal contacts with others in the field are imperative. Sound educational ideas should be shared, not hoarded, by one individual. The educational recluse is not only cheating his students by failing to utilize the best thinking of others, but he is also slighting his colleagues by not imparting his own ideas to them. How far would our industrial technology, medicine, law, or educational system have progressed if it had not been for the sharing of knowledge?

One of the practical functions of a professional association is that of serving as a clearing house for employment. The American Association for Health, Physical Education, and Recreation offers a placement service to all of its members. State associations usually do not establish a formal placement bureau, but nevertheless the membership is generally cognizant of vacant positions, and personal contacts made through organizational functions are beneficial to those seeking employment. It has always been apparent that personal recommendations are usually given more credence than those from persons unknown.

Any organization of size will be plagued by drones, or people who are more interested in self-advancement than professional goals. There are those who join both state and national associations who are primarily interested in professional recognition purely for personal reasons; fortunately, these individuals are in the minority and do not constitute a threat to the integrity of the entire group of dedicated members. If one takes the time to investigate the leadership of his state or national association, he rarely finds the noncontributor in a position of leadership. It is only human nature to desire recognition, but very few of the leaders in physical education have sought to place themselves in the spotlight at the expense of their profession. Leadership in any professional education association demands great personal sacrifice. Those who would criticize the works of others should first thoroughly investigate their own contributions and shortcomings. It has been observed that those who rise above the common herd are often criticized by others who aspire to great recognition but are too indolent to achieve it.

The virtues of membership in professional organizations have long been espoused in college classes dealing with the preparation of teachers. Many teachers join their state and national education associations, but relatively few join the associations which are directed toward a specific discipline.

Teachers have frequently been heard to say that most of the dues for professional organizations are collected on an annual basis at the outset of the school year and that they simply cannot afford such a large deduction from their initial check. The American Association for Health, Physical Education, and Recreation offers memberships at various times during the year in order to afford the teacher an opportunity of choice. It would perhaps be advantageous for all professional education associations to stagger their dues so that payments would be spread over a greater period of time. It is one thing for a teacher to feel quite strongly in favor of professional obligations, but it is often difficult for a husband or wife to feel the same way when he or she is confronted with a multitude of monthly bills to pay. In the event that payment of dues exerts a financial burden, money should be saved on a monthly basis to defer payments when they arise. It should also be noted that professional dues are deductible from income taxes. It would seem that if the government believes in the values inherent in keeping abreast of professional advancement, the teachers themselves should be even more concerned.

There are many organizations which the physical educator may join. It would be wise however for the prudent teacher to be selective in his choice of professional affiliations and choose only those which he believes to be of the most value to him in his work. Joining an organization only as a matter of record is to be frowned upon. Every member should be willing to contribute to his professional organization to the best of his ability. If active contributions are not possible, a member should at least budget his time so that he can read his journals and discuss the articles with his fellow teachers. If each and every teacher would apply to his classes the knowledge available through the professional literature, our public schools would progress at a much more rapid pace. Unfortunately, some teachers receive their periodicals, file them away on the shelf, and remain completely oblivious to the contents. Perhaps the only answer to this dilemma would be compulsory in-service training sessions where teachers would be held responsible for reading assignments as are their students.

Any worthwhile organization must have competent leadership, and that leadership can be no better than the membership which elected it. Those who excuse themselves from joining professional organizations because they deplore the quality of the leaders are to be deplored themselves. Any teacher who is conscientious in his desire to see his profession grow should exert every effort to seek positions of responsibility in his professional organizations. To do so involves hard work, but to sit on the sidelines and criticize the efforts of others is despicable.

THE SCHOOL COMMUNITY AND THE PHYSICAL EDUCATOR

The physical education teachers and coaches are often isolated from the rest of the school community by virtue of the gymnasium's location in relation to the rest of the school campus. In addition, they teach a unique subject which may be described by a few academicians as a "frill." To compound matters even further, those who coach inter-scholastic teams usually receive more publicity than all the rest of the teachers combined. Physical isolation from fellow faculty members, and extreme public attention to certain aspects of the school's program, do tend to breed misunderstanding and often contempt.

Physical educators are often involved in extracurricular activities such as coaching, intramural sports, supervision of sport clubs, individual corrective programs, and other activities which frequently prevent them from participating in faculty and school committee meetings which are after school hours. Every physical educator and coach should undertake to ensure attendance at any faculty gathering he can. If the administration insists upon holding meetings during conflicting periods, someone from the physical education and athletic department should attend, even if only on a rotating basis. Further-more, department members should volunteer their services in assisting with functions other than physical education and athletic events whenever possible. They should take an active part in faculty discussions, panels, and committees, and should at all times conduct themselves in a manner which is acceptable to any segment of the school community.

The matter of attire may seem of small concern to some, but it has been a thorn in the side of professional educators for many years. The physical education teacher should dress in the same fashion as other teachers; the uniform worn during class should be donned after arrival at school, not before. To go about the campus and into the office clad in shorts and blouse or tee shirt is poor taste except where unavoidable. Such actions tend to further separate the physical educator from his associates. Some may argue that the only major concern a teacher should have is how well he functions as an instructor in the classroom. Unfortunately, society and many colleagues do not have the same perspective, and it is with these people the physical education department must coexist. To combat the codes of the society in which a person finds himself, trivial though they may seem, is just poor politics and may actually endanger the chances of gaining faculty cooperation in forwarding the all-important physical education pro-gram. It is sometimes far better to lose a battle or two than to lose the war.

Teachers, like other human beings, tend to be possessive of those things which they believe to be within the realm of their personal responsibility. The gymnasium does not belong to the department of physical education and athletics any more than does the auditorium belong to the drama department. Naturally, any conscientious teacher does not desire to see the facility in which he is teaching abused. Playing floors should be protected against undue scuffing and other abrasions, but to deny access to the gymnasium to those other than athletes is ridiculous. Cooperation between teachers is the essence of success and job enjoyment. A schedule of gymnasium use should be established, and physical education activities and athletics should take precedence; after all, they are the primary purposes for which the facility was constructed. However, if proper footgear is worn during noon hour when no activities are scheduled, or at other times when the gymnasium is not in use, there is no reason why student groups who want to dance or engage in recreational play should not be allowed on the floor. All educational facilities should be used to their full potential whenever possible.

Equipment as well as buildings is often jealously guarded and withheld from the use of individuals other than those directly connected with a particular department. Cooperative use of equipment, and mutual respect for the care of such equipment, should be established by administrative policy. To safeguard the lending of equipment, an accounting system should be established and time limitations set so that a department's equipment is available for use when needed by those for whom it is intended.

Cooperation between individual faculty members and departments does not just happen. Like many other behavior patterns, it must be learned. Mutual sharing of facilities and equipment on a *systematized basis* lends greater cohesiveness to the school community by bringing people together, and also results in considerable savings in school budgets. With the increased attentiveness to school finances by taxpayers, it is imperative that schools exert every opportunity to effect economy of operation in areas that do not impede instruction or impair learning, and more intelligent use of facilities and equipment would certainly further the cause.

Physical education and athletics should be a part of, not the focal point of, the school curriculum. Physical educators or coaches who believe that their programs should take precedence over other activities such as band, orchestra, debate, drama, exhibits, journalistic endeavors, and academic instruction, should realize that their offerings constitute only one component of the general education offered by an institution.

It is not enough to merely recognize that other educational offerings exist on campus, they should be actively supported, even by those whose views may differ somewhat. All teachers must learn to paddle the same "educational canoe," and they should be willing to pull together to advance the progress of all youngsters through cooperative effort.

The public and the press tend to glamorize athletics almost to the exclusion of other aspects of school life. Such press coverage is not the fault of individual schools, but has become a part of the culture in which we live. No sponsor of other curricular or extracurricular functions resents athletic publicity per se, but they do resent the fact that coaches frequently evidence disdain for other school programs and sometimes convey this feeling to students, even if only by innuendo. The coach who engages in such practices is certainly to be pitied for his narrow-minded attitude and ultimately discovers that general faculty support for his program may wane. If all coaches would actively encourage youngsters to take part in those programs in which they might enjoy success, they might find that their personal and professional relationships with other faculty members would improve immensely.

Schools sponsor many clubs and activities that are not directly affiliated with the physical education and athletic department. These clubs must have advisers and those who coach and teach physical education should assume some responsibility for advisement. Historically, student professional organizations have been dominated by girls simply because women have volunteered their services as advisers. If more men would assume leadership in organizations such as Future Teachers of America and student preprofessional physical education associations, a more satisfactory balance between male and female membership would evolve and mutual understanding of the role of the male and female teacher would develop. The excuse for nonparticipation in club advisement by many teachers of physical education and coaches is that since they are so busy with their interscholastic athletic program, it is the duty of others to carry the load of advisement. The teachers of the academic courses could easily counter that excuse by stating they not only have the additional responsibility of grading many papers, but also they are not paid extra for their efforts as are the coaches.

Some school districts have adopted a policy of paying hourly wages for duties such as ticket-taking, ushering, and other responsibilities related to athletic contests. Very few schools, however, will compensate teachers for class advisement, club sponsorship, or similar duties. The districts that do compensate teachers for extra duty frequently schedule such duties on a voluntary basis. If extra pay was awarded for club sponsorships, it could well be that the teacher assigned might be more interested in the financial returns than in the responsibility of the assignment itself. Such an attitude would indeed be a travesty of education.

Teachers are human beings, and as such some are prone to take advantage of others. It has been common practice in some schools to dismiss certain students from classes to attend special programs and retain others, who are not interested or involved, to study. Occasionally, a teacher has found he has only two or three students left in his classroom, and rationalizes that they will not study anyhow so they might just as well be doing something in which they are interested. Such teachers sometimes believe that the gymnasium is the place to send all "leftover" students and thereby have them taken care of. It is the professional responsibility of the physical educator to supervise only his own students unless he personally agreed to look after students from other classes. He has no obligation to serve as a baby sitter for youngsters throughout the school and should hastily make his position known. If a new teacher is confronted by this situation, he should contact the teachers involved and apprise them of the fact that the gymnasium or field is an instructional area, and two or three students from twenty or more classes constitute a number which he does not feel obliged to supervise. He might also add that, if the facilities are available, students from other areas are welcome during extra-class hours, but during instructional time his responsibility lies with his own students. No administration should allow some teachers to take unfair advantage of others; however, this occasionally occurs and, when it does, should be remedied immediately.

The term "jock" has come into common usage of late and refers to those engaged in physical education and athletics who evidence something less than an inclination toward the arts. Among physical educators the term denotes the teacher-coach whose primary and consuming interest is his interscholastic team. This individual usually rolls a ball to his "fiz ed" classes and takes no active part in the school community other than what directly relates to his "team." He is a poor teacher, often boorish, and frequently inarticulate and uninformed in fields other than athletics. The "jock" is often tolerated by his fellow faculty members, but thought of as a bumpkin or dolt who has been caught in the backwash of the educative process and has affixed himself to the school system as a parasite upon the profession.

Physical education and coaching is a combination that can be executed successfully if the teacher is conscientious and extremely capable. It demands extensive preparation and dedication to both teaching and working with athletes. However, when a person is seeking employment it is only fair to provide him with a job description clearly defining his duties and compensation. Some administrators have refused to allow their physical educators to assume the duties of a head coach because past experience has shown that in some instances the two positions are incompatible. The prevalent belief among such administrators was that preparation for athletic practices took precedence over physical education classes. It would be fallacious indeed to condemn all physical educators for the shortcomings of a few, and the only logical solution to the problem is perhaps careful selection of personnel in all positions, whether a combination of teaching physical education and coaching or coaching and teaching another discipline. Any coach who neglects his teaching duties, regardless of the discipline, should be released from his position. Incompetence at any level in education cannot and should not be tolerated. If education in general, and physical education in particular, is to claim true professional status, those who use our profession as a stepping-stone to coaching careers without competently teaching their classes should be summarily dismissed. The only way in which we can ever attain the recognition to which we as physical educators aspire is to (1) clean up our own ranks, and (2) offer a comprehensive and viable program to those we teach.

YOU AND THE ADMINISTRATION

School administrations are usually established on a line and staff basis with the superintendent directly responsible to the board of education. The principals are responsible to the superintendent, vice principals and department chairmen to the principals, and teachers are responsible to their particular department chairmen and all other administrative officials. When making requests and conducting other school business, a chain of command should be prescribed in which items are routed through channels to the administrators concerned. Some items may not be processed by any person other than the department chairman and some may have to be routed to the superintendent. Any item, however, should pass through the principal to the superintendent as a matter of both courtesy and good business practice. Teachers who have complaints, and make "end runs" around their principal enroute to the superintendent, are not conducting themselves in an ethical manner. Even though a teacher knows that his principal will disagree with a particular item of consideration, he owes it to his immediate superior to consult him about the matter. Many minor matters may never even reach the principal if they can be resolved by the actions of the teacher and the department head.

From the preceding discussion, it can readily be determined that the larger the school district the greater the hierarchy of administrators. In exceptionally large school districts, such as in metropolitan areas, individual teachers often never have the opportunity to meet the superintendent on an informal basis. Small school districts on the other hand, afford a much greater intimacy between staff and administration, and usually function in a more democratic fashion.

Education cannot afford to be conducted in an impersonal manner because it deals with people. Administrators, teachers, custodial and clerical staff, and students must learn to work harmoniously in order to effect a proper climate for the learning experience. Cooperation between administrators and teachers is most difficult when lines of communication are strained and neither faction fully appreciates the position of the other. All discussions between teaching faculty and administrators should be frank, honest, and forthright without being disrupted by emotion.

In any form of endeavor which involves a hierarchy of positions, people tend to think that they must resort to a certain amount of apple-polishing in order to gain recognition. Some are even afraid to live by their convictions for fear that every thing they say will be taken personally and precipitate further trouble. Teachers *should* live by their convictions if they are founded upon logic and fact and are therefore defensible. Cooperation and courtesy are the antitheses of dissent and rudeness, and should always be included in any dealings a teacher may have with his administrator. However, cooperation and courtesy do not imply the sacrifice of principles; to do so would be tantamount to intellectual dishonesty. No professional progress of any real import has been made by yes-men who grovel at the feet of the administration and whose only goal is self-interest. Furthermore, *competent* administrators in either business or education have little respect for those who will not battle for their own convictions and most assuredly will never place them in positions of responsibility should the occasion arise.

Administration is a lonely job and one that is extremely demanding. A good democratic administrator needs all the allies he can get, and his teaching staff should assist him wherever possible. Perceptive administrators soon learn that if they want the backing of their staff, they in turn must be willing to support, when necessary, those whom they supervise. Cooperation by teachers and administrators is a two-way street, and it must be equally trod by both parties.

Every staff has a few individuals who insist upon making trouble for the administration over the slightest provocation, unfounded or otherwise. These teachers are possessed by a psychological negativism that seems to border on paranoia when confronted by any figure of authority. Frequently the attack upon the administration is not a frontal assault, but a rearguard action premised upon allegation and rumors that are carried downtown for all to hear. This type of individual has no place in any social organization; he is usually his own worst enemy, and can virtually wreck a sound school system and the careers of all its teachers with his slander. Constructive criticism of any school system is beneficial and should be carried on openly by the members of the school community without fear of administrative reprisal. However, to cast aspersions and spread rumors about people who are attempting to carry on the business of education, even though in complete disagreement with their philosophies, is childish.

Progressive administrators should provide a forum of some kind so that their teachers can air their professional views *within* professional ranks. They should encourage innovation in teaching and not be content with status quo. To do otherwise would halt the progress of the schools and the education of the students therein. Prior to engaging in debate relative to the merits of certain teaching procedures, a teacher should document his remarks with as much evidence as he possibly can obtain. Some physical educators who advocate movement education, as well as some who are in violent opposition to the concept, have presented their arguments with absolutely no evidence to support their contentions whatever, and then wondered why they were not listened to. Extravagant claims have often been made in support of virtually every discipline taught in our schools, however, many times documentary evidence to substantiate these claims is never mentioned. To engage in an argument with any learned individual, without adequate background information, is an open invitation to lose the debate.

Physical education teachers who are sincere in their attempts to impress the administration need only show a professional interest in that which they were employed to do. They should be ready and willing to establish curriculum guides showing rationale, scope, sequence, and proper progression of activities. All equipment and supplies should be properly maintained, accounted for and stored; facilities should be clean and show no abuse, and the students should be totally involved in the instructional process. The teacher should demonstrate to the administrator that he respects his position by showing him that his directives and policies have been carried out and that the students are receiving the best possible physical education instruction in the district.

Performance is always rated far above discussion. The administrator who actually *sees* that his teachers are competent performers on the job will be far more impressed than the administrator who just *hears* about it. If the opposite is true, then the administration should busy itself by getting out of the office and onto the field to see what is happening rather than making judgments and promotions by hearsay.

QUESTIONS FOR DISCUSSION

1. What are the obligations of a professional person and how do they compare with the obligations of a trade?
2. What is the definition of the term *ethics?* What are some of the ethical practices teachers should observe in their relationships with fellow faculty members?
3. What is meant by blind allegiance? How could such allegiance lead to inferior physical education programs?
4. Are professional and personal obligations intertwined to such an extent that they cannot be separated? If so, why? If not, why?
5. What are the functions of a professional organization and why is it important for teachers to belong to such organizations? Do you think that the school district should pay teacher's professional dues? Substantiate your argument.
6. Who is primarily responsible for ridding the teaching profession of those who refuse to carry their work load? Why do you believe as you do?
7. Why should physical educators and coaches have to bother with attending faculty meetings? Don't they have enough work handling extracurricular activities to warrant their absence from such meetings?
8. How can cooperative effort alleviate intrafaculty problems?
9. How do you feel about extra pay for extra duties? Is this really a component of professionalism?
10. What should a teacher's relationship be with his administration? Can he ever disagree with his immediate superiors? If so, why? If not, why?

CASE STUDIES

MR. DODGE

Mr. Dodge was employed by Fernley Junior High School as a physical educator and coach. He was well liked by his students because he was friendly and entertaining. However his administration and colleagues became very irritated by his actions after only a few weeks of associating with him.

Dodge engaged in a "moonlighting" occupation of house plastering in order to augment his teaching income and was regarded by many in the construction industry as an excellent plasterer. He worked at this occupation on Saturday and Sunday and after school when he was not busy with his coaching duties. It became apparent that Dodge was a competent coach but that his physical education classes consisted of nothing more than a recreational period of whatever activity the students seemed interested in at the time. He would enter class and ask the students what they would like to do, then provide the equipment for them, and stand on the sidelines to watch while they played. No skills were taught, discipline was completely lacking, and Dodge apparently assigned grades by some random method known only to himself.

After the football season was over, Dodge contracted some plastering jobs in a distant community to occupy himself on the weekends. Frequently Dodge would come to school an hour or so late on Monday morning, take his class roll, and then spend the remainder of the time sleeping on a tumbling mat. When his actions became known to Mr. Weatherton, principal of Fernley, he was called into the office for a conference. Mr. Weatherton, being a person who believed in reaching the point immediately, proceeded to apprise Dodge of his responsibilities as a teacher and informed him that if he heard of any more malingering it would be necessary to fire him immediately. Dodge replied that he did not like Weatherton's attitude and he could not see what he had done wrong in the first place. He did admit being late for class on one or two occasions, but had frequently noticed Mr. Weatherton was not in his office either. Weatherton informed Dodge that often he had business at the central district office which took him away from his own school, and then dropped the matter.

Dodge continued with his poor habits of instruction but did manage to arrive at school on time. However from the time of his first formal altercation with Mr. Weatherton, Dodge proceeded to cast public aspersions about the district in general, and Mr. Weatherton in particular, whenever he believed that he had an audience. He castigated the entire school district in the presence of his students and told various untruths in public whenever the opportunity arose. Dodge's fellow faculty members would not speak to him, except to inform him that they felt his antics were highly unprofessional and uncalled for in view of his own conduct as a teacher. At the conclusion of the year, Dodge was released from his position and unfortunately was employed in another school district.

QUESTIONS

1. How would you evaluate the professional attitude of Mr. Dodge? Do you think he was justified in his actions? If so, why? If not, why?

2. If you were Mr. Dodge's principal, what kind of recommendation would you write for him? Do you believe that Dodge was a stable personality judging by his actions?
3. How would you, as a fellow faculty member, react to the conduct of Mr. Dodge?

MR. ANDERSON

Mr. Anderson was regarded as an excellent physical education teacher by both his students and his colleagues. He was always ready to assume duties beyond those required of him and supported many programs besides his own. Anderson was never known to have said a bad word about anyone and he conducted himself as a model citizen within the community.

During the first week of school, general faculty meetings were called for purposes of orientation and preparation for the coming year. At these meetings the matter of professional obligations would arise and the subsequent discussion would invariably lead to the consideration of membership in local, state, and national professional education associations. Anderson, ordinarily considered as the personification of a professional person, would become completely incensed at the idea of paying dues to an organization he did not believe in and stated that he felt such organizations were superfluous to the educational enterprise anyway. Usually his protestations were met with silence from the group or the subject was changed. As a result of his refusal to join professional organizations, Anderson was never seen at state conventions but did manage to read every monthly journal that was shelved in the library.

QUESTIONS

1. Why do you suppose Mr. Anderson was so vehement in his protests regarding membership in professional associations? What in his background could have led to his negative attitude?
2. Why would Anderson refuse to join his professional associations and yet read their journals?
3. As his administrator would you talk with Anderson? If so, what would you say? As a colleague of Anderson's what would be your response to his protests?

NELSON AND BRICE

Mr. Nelson was the head football coach at East High School and Mr. Brice was the band director. Both had taught at the school for

approximately the same length of time and both were equally dedicated
to their respective extracurricular tasks. Mr. Nelson was known to be a
coach who got along well with his players, colleagues, and members of
the community. Mr. Brice, on the other hand, was the type of
individual who spent most of his time by himself, infrequently went to
the faculty room, and constantly made demands upon the time and
talents of others in the interest of furthering his own program.

Prior to homecoming game Coach Nelson's quarterback, who also
played first trumpet in the band, asked to be excused from marching in
the homecoming parade because it ended just before the kickoff at the
football game. Coach Nelson believed this to be a legitimate request,
and, inasmuch as it was two weeks before the homecoming festivities,
felt that Brice could get a substitute trumpet player without undue
difficulty. Nelson asked Brice if he would excuse the boy and Brice
replied that he would not do so under any circumstances because it
would interfere with his plans. Brice also added that if Nelson
"badgered" him anymore he would take the matter to the administration. The coach retorted amicably that he had always cooperated with
Brice's band by marking the practice field for them and had arranged
for other considerations relative to effective band productions at the
games. Brice immediately began to berate Nelson and placed the entire
matter before the school principal.

The principal arranged to meet with Brice and Nelson to gather all
of the facts in the case and was somewhat surprised to discover that
Brice was most uncooperative and adamant about the boy marching in
the band or being dropped from the music program. At this juncture,
the principal called the boy in and asked him what his alternatives
would be under the circumstances. The student replied he would like to
continue his music but if given only one choice he would prefer not to
march. The wishes of the boy were complied with and he was dropped
from the band but continued to play football.

QUESTIONS

1. How would you characterize Mr. Brice and Mr. Nelson? Which of the two
   would you rather work with and why?
2. What are your feelings regarding the manner in which the principal handled
   the Brice-Nelson conflict?
3. Do you believe that Nelson was wrong in requesting that his quarterback be
   excused from marching in the band? If so, why? If not, why?
4. What should have been the primary concern of both Brice and Nelson in their
   deliberations?

MISS KELLEY AND MISS GIFFORD

Miss Kelley was a geography teacher who had taught in the public schools for many years. She had served diligently on local, state, and national education committees and had been instrumental in developing student interest in preprofessional organizations such as the Future Teachers of America. She was an attractive individual who carefully prepared her lessons, treated pupils fairly, and believed that all people were basically good. Her idealism was tempered somewhat by her tailoring of lessons to suit the mental capabilities of the various groups with which she worked. Her only complaint in life seemed to be the inability to understand why some pupils thirsted for knowledge and others seemed to care very little. Her discipline was outstanding and no student ever wondered for a moment just what was expected of him. Course outlines were provided for students and Miss Kelley was always available for individual counseling and guidance.

Miss Gifford was relatively the same age as Miss Kelley and taught English in the same high school. She was rather permissive in her discipline at certain times and very strict at others. She directed many school plays and was always ready to receive the acclaim of the student-parent audiences at the conclusion of each performance.

Miss Gifford was not too active in professional associations but played quite a part in the social life of the community. She belonged to the "correct social set" and often fawned over the school principal at social gatherings, never failing to refer to him as "the boss." The principal seemed to enjoy Miss Gifford's antics; however, he informed othe faculty members that he really thought Miss Gifford was somewhat "artificial" at times.

Miss Kelley and Miss Gifford were apprised by the administration that they were both eligible to apply for sabbatical leaves which were being granted to acceptable candidates by virtue of a newly adopted school board policy. Both of the ladies had taught within the district for the required minimum of seven years. In fact, Miss Gifford had taught for ten years and Miss Kelley for nine.

Under the sabbatical leave policy each applicant was required to submit a proposal for study and/or travel to the principal who would then submit it to the superintendent and school board. Accordingly, Miss Kelley and Miss Gifford completed the necessary forms in detail and submitted them. Miss Kelley was interested in pursuing the doctorate in her discipline and had made the necessary arrangements for admission to the graduate program at the state university. Miss Gifford's request listed an itinerary of travel which culminated in a tour of various New York Broadway productions that "would furnish valuable information relative to the production of school plays and possible future musicals."

Two weeks or so after the forms had been submitted Miss Kelley and Miss Gifford were informed as to the board's decision regarding the awarding of their sabbatical leaves. Miss Gifford's leave was approved without question. Miss Kelley was informed that her leave was disapproved because "she had been in the district one year less than Miss Gifford and also in all probability would not continue in public school teaching after receiving the doctorate. Miss Kelley appealed the decision based on the fact that she had fulfilled the minimal time requirement and would be bound by the sabbatical agreement to return to the district for at least two years following her leave. The appeal was quickly denied.

QUESTIONS

1. How would you professionally evaluate Miss Kelley and Miss Gifford? Which would you rather have for a teacher and why?
2. Do you suppose that Miss Kelley handicapped herself by not engaging in more social activities? Do you think the board judged the sabbatical applications objectively or subjectively? What effect could administration endorsement have upon such applications?

SUGGESTED RELATED READING

Bucher, Charles A., *Foundations of Physical Education*, 4th ed. St. Louis: C. V. Mosby, 1964.

Kroll, Walter P., *Perspectives in Physical Education*. New York: Academic Press, 1971.

Nixon, John E., and Anne E. Jewett, *An Introduction to Physical Education*, 7th ed. Philadelphia: W. B. Saunders, 1969.

Voltmer, Edward F., and Arthur A. Esslinger, *The Organization and Administration of Physical Education*, 4th ed. New York: Appleton-Century-Crofts, 1967.

THE PROBLEM OF GRADING

Grading of students has long been a matter of controversy by both teachers and administrators. There are many ways to evaluate students and no single method has yet been found that is not without fault. A method perfectly acceptable to one instructor may well be cast aside by another whose philosophy differs in relation to grading or evaluation.

Grades are awarded for the purpose of indicating the progress which a student is making in a particular discipline. They constitute a report which is given to the student and to his parents and which is also a component of his permanent record. In general, the grade indicates whether a student is above, within, or below the class average. In practice, however, most teachers tend to grade high by giving the student the benefit of any doubt when considering borderline cases.

The overall evaluation of students is used to compute grade point indices for awarding honors, admittance to certain school organizations, grouping of students, and college admission requirements. We live in a society that places great faith in numbers and performance scales. Unfortunately, many times the numerical grade is derived in a haphazard manner and is really not indicative of the ability of the student. In order to establish a marking system to be as fair an evaluative tool as possible, many factors must be considered.

The primary consideration of any grading system must be the discipline for which it was designed. There are those who extol the virtues of physical education as a most "unique" offering. They say that physical education contributes to the development of students in many ways not accomplished by any other discipline; yet some of these same individuals continue to grade their students upon the basis of their skills and knowledge and tend to ignore such factors as behavior, leadership, attitude, cooperation, and other psychosociological factors which are among the foundation blocks of physical education. If physical educators do perform a unique function, and physical education is indeed a unique discipline, then it would seem logical to have a grading system which would encompass those qualities we profess to teach. Physical educators should be vitally concerned about devising a marking system that truly evaluates the discipline of physical education rather than worrying about whether or not the marks they award will be equated with those given by the teachers of the academic subjects.

Physical education as a discipline should stand on its own merits and be graded accordingly. There is no reason why physical educators should be defensive about their grading procedures if the procedures are carefully designed to conform to the prescribed objectives of the subject area. Physical education is founded upon different objectives than those of the various academic disciplines, just as the objectives of mathematics differ from those of music, art, industrial arts, journalism, or English. All disciplines should concern themselves with evaluative techniques to measure performance in their particular subject matter. They should never subordinate the needs and desires of the students in the interest of expediency or concern for "what others might think."

Secondary schools throughout the United States categorize subject matter areas into "solid" and "nonsolid" classifications. Physical education for many years has been placed in the "nonsolid" category and as a result physical educators, in some instances, have felt professionally impuissant when compared to those teaching in the "solid" or academic areas. Disciplines should not be categorized in any rank order. To do so is to assign a lesser value to some subjects than to others and is similar to the categorization of sports into major and minor offerings, a practice which is abhorrent to anyone who has ever participated in the so-called "minor" activities.

High schools frequently publish an "honor roll" at the conclusion of each grading period. Occasionally a student will attain high marks in his "solid" subjects and not perform quite as well in a "nonsolid"; thus his overall grade point average is below the cutoff point required for admission to the honor roll. Because of parental pressure some school administrations have not considered the "nonsolid" subjects in the computation of grade point averages for honor roll students. It would seem fair that a true honor student should be one successful in all disciplines and a well-rounded person. However, it has been easier for some school administrators to placate parents by taking the line of least resistance and deleting "nonsolid" courses from the honor roll rather than by justifying the logic behind overall performance. If a discipline has any educational value it should be included in grade point computation for all purposes; if it has no educational value, it should not be included in the curriculum of the schools in the first place.

When determining grades for physical education many factors must be considered. These factors include the physiological, psychological, and sociological contributions as well as the skills and knowledge pertinent to a particular unit of study. The philosophy of the individual instructor would determine in part the weighing of each factor in the computation of the final grade that the student should receive. All of the objectives of physical education should receive a share of consideration in evaluating students.

The policy of the particular school district should determine whether or not the grading scale was a numerical one or whether it was premised upon the pass or fail concept. In any event, a rating scale would have to be established whereby justification could be made for the numerical or letter grade, or the passing or failing mark. The mechanics for either method might well be the same with percentages computed to determine the grade or pass/fail mark. An example of such a grading scheme is presented as follows:

Percentages	*Point Values*
20% Skills	11 — A
20% Knowledge	10 — A minus
10% Attitude (general)	9 — B plus
10% Attendance	8 — B
10% Cooperation (with instructor)	7 — B minus
10% Relations with other students	6 — C plus
10% Leadership (ability to direct)	5 — C
10% Followership (ability to follow direction)	4 — C minus
	3 — D plus
	2 — D
	1 — D minus
	0 — F

To compute the grade for the student, point values for the performance would be multiplied by the percentage allotted to the particular factor and then totaled. The total, as indicated in the sample below, would indicate the letter grade the student receives for the grading period. If the grading system was predicated on a pass or fail basis, a percentage of the total possible number of points (11 points in this instance) would be the cutoff point to determine a passing grade.

Subject: John P. Jones

Skills	$7 \times .20 - 1.40$
Knowledge	$5 \times .20 - 1.00$
Attitude	$11 \times .10 - 1.10$
Attendance	$5 \times .10 - .50$
Cooperation (instructor)	$8 \times .10 - .80$
Relations (students)	$2 \times .10 - .20$
Leadership	$2 \times .10 - .20$
Followership	$1 \times .10 - .10$
	5.30*

*From the point values indicated it can be seen that a total of 5.30 would constitute a grade of "C."

In using the preceding technique of determining grades, the teacher could devise a point scale or weighting arrangement to suit himself. He might also wish to combine some of the elements in order to expedite grading if his classes were too large to render the above system practical. Philosophy and emphasis would be the determinants of any scale and the example was presented *only to serve as a guideline.* Obviously, a grading chart would have to be maintained for each student in order to determine the final point assignments given to each of the weighted factors. Such charts can be marked periodically during the grading period and would lend themselves to a certain amount of subjectivity in items such as attitudes, cooperation, student relations, leadership, and followership. The information relative to the marks obtained in skills tests, knowledge tests, and attendance would be automatically recorded from test results and daily roll sheets. All student evaluation sheets or cards should be maintained as a matter of record in the event that a student, parent, or administrator should desire to see just how a particular grade was derived and what justification was used. Any physical educator who arbitrarily assigned grades to students without an analytical and systematized approach is grossly deliquent in his duties. No grade should ever be assigned without full justification and evidence for that justification.

Grades are important to all youngsters and should be *earned.* There have been instances where grades have been arbitrarily raised for students engaged in athletics and need such grades to ensure their eligibility. This is a practice which is potently dishonest and should never be countenanced under any circumstances. Every youngster enrolled in a physical education class should be extended the courtesy of equal and fair treatment regardless of whether he is a star quarterback or has never competed in an athletic contest in his life. The same rationale would also apply to those enrolled in drama classes and who also participate in class plays or similarly related activities. No student should be extended special grading privileges in any class based on his performance in an extracurricular activity. This should be a matter of administrative policy as well as a matter of professional integrity.

TEACHING UNITS ARE NOT JUST "HAPPENINGS"

Teaching units must be structured and well planned in order to be effective. They must include proper scope and sequence and be detailed enough so that the progression and organization of the material is presented in a logical manner. Teaching units should be an integral part of the curriculum guide; they should be reviewed, evaluated on an annual basis, and kept up to date by incorporating the latest techniques and methodology set forth by the profession.

A comprehensive teaching unit should be blocked out in a week-by-week progression of instruction and should be compatible with the time allocated for the particular unit. The teaching unit should be drafted *before* the time allocation is placed on the yearly calendar. It seems ridiculous that a calendar would be drafted and then the teaching units arranged to conform accordingly; yet this has been done in numerous instances. The primary function of a teaching unit is an instructional plan, not subject matter tailored to a calendar. The time allocated for different units may vary considerably depending upon the material being taught. Some units of instruction may be completed in three weeks and others may take six. However, the unit cannot be taught in a haphazard manner in order to complete some ethereal schedule which dictates that one shall take only four weeks for badminton, two weeks for tumbling, three weeks for volleyball, and so on. To place administrative expediency before acceptable instructional practice is unsound and should not be allowed. A variety of programming is desirable, but not when it means that instructional time is cut to the point whereby learning is minimal or nonexistent.

Teaching units are outlines which serve as guidelines for the formulation of daily lesson plans. They should be comprehensive enough to leave no question as to what material will be presented during a specific week and therefore should be structured on a weekly basis. It should be remembered that the units will generally relate to beginning and advanced instruction and should encompass all of the necessary items pertinent to each level. In some instances three levels of competence are considered: beginning, intermediate, and advanced. These tri-level programs are usually assigned to very complex activities such as tumbling, gymnastics, and games that demand a great deal of strategy in addition to basic skills. Some prime examples would be football, basketball, power volleyball, and soccer.

In all instances a unit of instruction should include information related to the following considerations:

   I.   Facilities and equipment to be used

  II.   Objectives of the unit

III.   Organization and presentation of the unit

      A.   Class organization

      B.   Method of instruction

          1.   Lecture

          2.   Demonstration

      3. Audiovisual Aids

      4. Written assignments, workbooks, etc.

      5. Evaluation (tests of skills and knowledge)

IV. Content of the unit

    A. This would include those skills that are actually going to be taught and a progression of difficulty ranging from the simple to the complex. It should be considered that some students, more than others, will be more familiar with a given activity, and yet it cannot be *assumed* that any of them are thoroughly knowledgeable. No detail should be left to chance or given only cursory treatment. It is sometimes assumed that students are far more sophisticated than they actually are.

Immediately after a unit of instruction has been completed, it should be evaluated in terms of its successes and failures in communicating the skills and knowledge to the students. It should further be determined whether or not facilities, equipment, and instructional time were adequate and if audiovisual or other instructional aids were needed. All evaluations should reflect the objectives of the unit and determine whether these objectives were met, and if not, why. Any deficiencies found as a result of the evaluation should be noted and measures immediately implemented to rectify the situation prior to the next offering of the unit. Procrastination in evaluation leads to a situation whereby pertinent information is neglected and a true perspective of the course is often lost. The evaluation of the unit necessarily should be a component of the unit and should receive as much attention as the teaching process itself. The unit cannot be considered as complete until final evaluation and subsequent corrections in procedure have been made.

WHEN TO EVALUATE AND WHAT TO LOOK FOR

Evaluation must be a continual process. One does not evaluate instruction only at the completion of a unit, it should take place during and immediately after each instructional period. The teacher therefore should ask himself the following questions:

    1. Was student interest high?

    2. Were the objectives of the lesson accomplished?

    3. Was there a lag in time during which restlessness took place and class control might have been lacking?

    4. Was ample time allowed to answer questions asked by students?

5. Were questions solicited by the instructor?

6. Was there any discernable difference in performance at the conclusion of the class as compared to the beginning of the class?

7. Were all of the students involved in the instructional process during the majority of the class period? Were all students working on skills or inactive while waiting for others to perform?

8. How much individual attention was given to students who were having trouble performing skills in an acceptable fashion? Were the names of the skilled and unskilled performers noted for future reference?

9. What was the physical setting of the lesson? Was the temperature too high, too low, or correct for the activity? How was the lighting?

10. Was there enough equipment available and was it checked out and returned in a systematic manner?

11. What, if any, discipline problems arose?

12. Do you believe that you attempted to cover too much or too little material in the time allowed?

13. Do you believe that the lesson was taught to the best of your ability or that you should have prepared yourself better before teaching it?

14. What procedures would you advocate for the improvement of this lesson the next time it is taught?

If the teacher can answer the previous questions in a positive manner, obviously nothing needs to be done to improve the instructional process. However, if any question is answered negatively, procedures should be undertaken to change the situation so that in the future students will profit from adjustments made in the lesson plan.

A beginning teacher will soon discover that a check sheet may assist him in answering the questions about his instruction. If he completed the check list at the conclusion of each class and then made a thorough evaluation at the conclusion of the day, with proper notations on his lesson plan, it would be of great help to him. Even the experienced teacher must involve himself in the evaluative process. Experience should be accompanied by a greater degree of wisdom in planning and should not be used as an excuse for less preparation.

The questions used for evaluating an individual lesson can be the same for evaluating an instructional unit. Moreover, daily checklists derived from each lesson, and notes made thereon, should serve as valuable points of departure in examining the entire unit. If more than one teacher is involved in teaching the same unit, group process in evaluation procedures should be used. The pooling of knowledge to assist in problem-solving can be of great help, especially to the beginning teacher. In all deliberations the evaluator must be as objective as possible and not rationalize his or her actions in any way. Excuses for poor teaching have no place in evaluation. If you have planned ineffectively, admit it and rectify your mistakes; don't just shrug your shoulders and proceed to repeat errors. No instructional unit or individual lesson will be perfectly executed; there is always room for improvement. However, improvement can only result from polishing instruction by evaluation and subsequent correction of the mistakes which have been made. As the units and lessons are repeatedly taught, evaluated, and corrected, a more satisfactory teaching situation should result. There will always be room for improvement or alteration but the teacher will have the satisfaction of knowing that the best attempt possible was made toward the perfection of instruction.

One facet of evaluation frequently overlooked by teachers is their personal habits during the teaching process. The only way in which objectional habits can be overcome is to have them called to the teacher's attention by an observer. Some teachers have called upon their colleagues to observe their classes and assess any personal "quirks" that might impair instruction; others have chosen to implement student-rating forms. Student-rating forms are beneficial because the teacher can detect a pattern of behavior and adjust accordingly. Student-rating forms must be carefully constructed and should be handed in unsigned. This way the student feels he is not going to be chastised for telling the truth. The format for such forms should be simple and explicit. The checklist with room for comments is most satisfactory because it is easiest to tabulate. Some students will purposely answer every query in a negative manner and insert a few caustic comments in an attempt to be funny. The spurious forms are not too difficult to detect and should make little difference compiling results from a large sampling of students. A larger sample is better than a small one because a more composite pattern of response can be ascertained.

Prior to the distribution of student evaluation forms, the teacher should explain very patiently why the forms are being distributed and what their ultimate use will be. It should also be pointed out that the students must be objective in their evaluation and eliminate person-alities from their deliberations. Some teachers have been afraid of student opinion, mainly because they fear the truth. Teachers who have utilized student evaluation forms and have eliminated their poor habits found the experience most rewarding. The psychological effect of student evaluation also makes the student feel that his best interests are being considered and gives him a more positive feeling toward the entire educational process. It then seems only logical that the students served by the physical educator should be able to participate in the process of evaluation. It is, of course, true that students do not necessarily possess the mature judgment of adults, but even elementary school pupils are perceptive enough to determine whether they are really learning something or just marking time in the classroom. As adults, many people can readily reflect on their days as students and on their teachers. The outstanding teachers are recalled without much difficulty, and those of lesser ability are sometimes easily forgotten unless remembered only for their incompetence. If it is possible for adults to evaluate teachers over a span of many years, it should be much easier for students to do so while currently enrolled in their classes. No teacher should be ashamed to receive a poor report relative to certain facets of his teaching and he should then rectify his habits. It is much better to improve one's efforts as a result of a poor evaluation than it is to ignore the evaluative procedure completely and continue to stumble along in a manner distasteful to students and fellow faculty members alike. A truly professional person should seek any means of improving himself to be outstanding in his field rather than being content with mediocrity and willing to survive only by virtue of his rationalization or the security of tenure. Those who are afraid of being evaluated by others are generally insecure in their profession, but if one is to improve his performance he can do so only by first ascertaining his mistakes and then taking proper measures to ameliorate his performance.

EVALUATION—ENTHUSIASM OR COMPLACENCY

The demand for teacher evaluation has been voiced by many parents, board members, lay people, and students in the past few years. They are greatly concerned about allowing inferior teachers to continue in public education and are becoming more and more vociferous in their remarks as time goes by. The demand for program evaluation has not been as distinct as that for teacher evaluation, but college and high school students alike are now raising some rather pointed questions about programs in which they had unsatisfactory experiences.

The teaching profession owes much to the public which supports it, and one of its most important obligations is to program evaluation and necessary revision. All teachers and administrators should enter into the evaluative procedure with enthusiasm and not regard the matter as just another mechanical chore to please the general public. The teacher who simply goes through the motions of showing up for class and giving cursory instructions to his students prior to "rolling out a ball" to play with soon becomes bored and even more lackadaisical. He soon discovers that his major concern is how to get through the school day without much effort and at the same time avoid going to sleep while the class participates. In any endeavor one obtains only as much satisfaction as he is willing to exert effort. The teacher who constantly assesses his performance and strives to improve will discover that the satisfaction of teaching can be tremendous. The days pass much more rapidly and the response of the students to improved instruction lessens problems and tensions to a significant degree.

Students tend to question only things from which they receive little or no apparent enjoyment or benefit. If they can perceive values in a class they become enthusiastic and willing to participate to the best of their ability. Placed in a boring situation in which a minimal amount of learning takes place, they become disenchanted with the entire discipline. The athlete generally responds to coaching with enthusiasm because practices are usually well planned and the instruction is organized and carried out with dispatch. They know that their coaches spend long hours preparing for practices and therefore are receiving the best instruction possible. This preparation is perhaps initiated since the coach knows that his product is going to be placed in display before the general public and a well-coached team means job tenure. It then follows that the same amount of evaluation that goes into postgame reviews could also benefit education if a like amount of effort was put forth in postclass and postunit reviews. Unfortunately the reason this does not frequently occur is that the physical education teacher is not placed in a position of having to display the talents of his students to the general public on a scheduled basis. It should be remembered, however, that although the general public does not actually see a demonstration of class activities, the students fully realize they are being "shortchanged" in instruction and strongly resent it. Students may not become as vocal as the hometown crowd who witnesses a poorly coached football team each week, but their feelings may well be evidenced in later years when voting on the fate of the local school budget. In many instances the student is afraid to voice his opinion of the instruction because he fears his grade will suffer. However, he may still harbor a distinct resentment toward the subject and the teacher of the class where he feels slighted.

Teachers frequently blame students for being apathetic, and indeed many of them are; however, an apathetic teacher generally has the effect of infecting his classes with the same demeanor. Teaching is a difficult job in that the teacher cannot relax for a moment during the time he is involved in the instructional process. He must be in control at all times and must be cognizant of times when activity lags and his students become restless. He must continually ask himself "What is wrong?, Why are the students reluctant?, Why has the lesson or unit gone sour? Moreover, he must be prepared to rectify the situation regardless of his pride. If he has been at fault in his instruction he owes it to both his students and to himself to do a better job of planning and teaching and the only way he can discover his errors is through the evaluative process.

PROGRAM EVALUATION INVOLVES EVERYONE CONCERNED

The school administration should seize the initiative in implementing program evaluation for all disciplines. This should be a matter of policy formulated by the school board and carried out by superintendent and principals of the various schools. In conjunction with the building principals, the department chairman of physical education and his staff members should be delegated the responsibility for evaluating those facets of the program for which they have primary responsibility. After the individual evaluations have been completed, a composite of these studies should be drafted and results submitted, through proper channels, to the superintendent and school board.

Everyone who has an equity in the physical education program should be involved directly or indirectly in the evaluation procedure. Establishing the mechanics for evaluation is a process that demands collective thinking and should not be done by any single individual. The school administration, physical education staff, parents, and students should be represented on any committee charged with responsibility of establishing evaluative techniques. There are many aspects of physical education that would lend themselves to a different evaluative technique than might be found in other subject areas. The direction or goals of evaluation would be the same for all disciplines, but the mechanics and information gained would vary.

Each of the representative groups—students, parents, teachers, and administrators—would probably be inclined to emphasize slightly different aspects of program evaluation and all these aspects must be considered. The initial deliberations of an evaluative committee would be to assess those factors of the program which they feel need to be evaluated and to what degree. The following items are offered as a suggestion for topics to be considered for evaluation. These topics could be considered as major headings; they should be broken down into specific areas depending on the organization of a particular school.

1. Teaching effectiveness
2. Time allotment for instruction
3. Ability grouping of students
4. Utilization of team teaching (specialists for specialties)
5. Equipment
    a. Purchase
    b. Accessibility
    c. Quality
    d. Quantity
    e. Maintenance
    f. Storage
6. Facilities
    a. Adequacy
    b. Usage (maximal or minimal)
    c. Cleanliness and attractiveness
    d. Projected needs
7. Teaching Units
    a. Strengths
    b. Weaknesses
8. Individual Lessons
    a. Strengths
    b. Weaknesses
9. Preparation
    a. Time
    b. Depth
10. Summary, conclusions, recommendations and projections for future program content and conduct.

Teachers universally are busy people who follow extremely crowded schedules and therefore must utilize their time in a most efficient manner. Evaluation takes time but pays great dividends in terms of satisfaction. The most satisfying experience a teacher can enjoy is to see his program grow in a positive manner and be readily accepted by both his students and his colleagues. Evaluation must proceed beyond the theoretical stage and be incorporated into the daily practice of the teacher and the school. Inasmuch as time is of the essence, evaluation must be thorough but efficient. A committee charged with the responsibility of establishing evaluative criteria and procedures must always consider methods which are as objective as possible and easily implemented, yet thorough in coverage of those things being investigated.

Program analysis is the result of daily analysis. In order to analyze daily instruction and its strengths or weaknesses, it is necessary to use some form which is simple to complete and not time-consuming and so detailed that it would detract from the teaching function. Checklists which can easily be completed and yet are comprehensive enough to be of value can be utilized, later reviewed, and the information synthesized into a comprehensive evaluative report. Frequently, instructional weaknesses occur which are mentally noted and then forgotten. The time for recording is the moment of occurrence, not after the issue has become clouded and vague due to a lapse in time. If such "on the spot" notations are made, they will serve to jog the memory later on when it is time to evaluate the entire unit of instruction.

In addition to devising evaluative forms, a system has to be established whereby the forms are systematically filed, reviewed, synthesized, and later used in program revision. It is obviously of no value whatever to evaluate and then ignore the information that has been gained by the process. At the conclusion of every school year the comprehensive evaluation should be used to alter the curriculum for the coming year. Individual teachers should alter lesson plans to overcome mistakes made in the previous units taught, and administrators should ensure that curriculum guides are revised and that the revisions are kept on file for future reference by those concerned. In this way, curriculum revision is continually fostered and the physical education program therefore enjoys growth and progress rather than stagnation.

A modern progressive school district would be prudent to draft job descriptions for all of its teachers and spell out the duties which are incumbent upon them. These job descriptions would be specific for each area but a general teaching job description should be included in the faculty handbook and the duties pertinent to the evaluative process should be stipulated. It should be further emphasized that *all* teachers will take an active part in evaluation. If evaluation is undertaken only by the department head or the school administration, it will certainly not meet with the enthusiasm of the general faculty. It is human nature to desire to become involved in deliberations which directly affect one's daily life. When evaluation is imposed from without it is not as effective as when it comes from within. The program, as previously stated, belongs to those who are actively engaged in its conduct. To make arbitrary evaluations and program alterations at the administrative level is tantamount to telling faculty members that they don't really have any grasp of what they are doing in the first place and therefore need to be told what is proper by the administrative head. No one knows better than the individual teacher what his shortcomings are and what he should do to rectify errors. Also, students are most directly affected by any program and due to their different point of perception are invaluable in assisting in evaluation. If people are actively involved in any enterprise, and receive credit for their knowledge and intelligence in their respective field, they will usually respond in a much more positive manner than when they are eliminated from those deliberations which most vitally determine their lives as either professionals or students.

QUESTIONS FOR DISCUSSION

1. What are some of the problems of grading? Should physical education be graded in some manner other than that used to grade students in academic disciplines? If so, why? If not, why?
2. What items should be included in a grading scale and why?
3. Is there any reason why physical education should be graded at all?
4. What justification can you provide for grading physical education on a pass or fail basis rather than on a numerical or letter basis?
5. How would you improve or alter the example of grading procedure given by the text and why? Justify your answer by referring to the basic objectives of your program.
6. Of what value is a written teaching unit? Would it be just as satisfactory to take each day as it comes and not worry about any instructional guidelines?
7. What should be incorporated into a teaching unit? Why would units of instruction differ from one school to another?
8. Who should be involved in the evaluation of instruction? Why?
9. Do you believe in student evaluation? Do you believe that the students have the capability to evaluate teachers objectively and fairly?
10. Why must evaluation be a continual process? Would it be just as effective and less time-consuming to evaluate every five years instead of annually?
11. Why does evaluation have to be in written form? Why would an experienced teacher have to evaluate by taking notes rather than merely mentally noting successes and failures?
12. Why should evaluation be performed by both teachers and administrators? Should teachers or administrators be more concerned about evaluation?
13. If teachers, students, and administrators do not properly evaluate instruction, whose responsibility should it become?
14. As an individual project, draft an evaluative checklist for a particular unit of instruction and let your classmates critique it for you.
15. Of what value is record-keeping in the evaluative process?

CASE STUDIES

MR. CUTLER

Mr. Cutler taught physical education and coached all sports at a high school which enrolled approximately three hundred students. Cutler's physical education curriculum was progressive and comprehensive, and he was a well-liked and competent teacher and coach. The athletic program was fundamentally sound with a great deal of emphasis being placed upon basic skills. Cutler's teams were not "fancy"; they worked hard and executed their movements with precision and determination. Many boys participated in the interscholastic competition and physical education was required of all students.

Cutler's grading seemed to follow a fairly normal curve for the most part, but all of the boys who participated on interscholastic teams were awarded A's during the season in which they were competing and could never earn above a B when they were not out for a seasonal sport. Thus, football players received A's during the football season but if they did not report for basketball they would receive no higher than a B regardless of what they did in their regular physical education class. When the boys asked about this inequity Mr. Cutler replied that a true athlete should compete in *all* sports, not just *one*, and therefore believed they were not performing at their level of capability when they did not even bother to turn out for a team. Boys who were non-athletes could earn A's in Mr. Cutler's classes even though they were obviously less skilled than some of the athletes who were not competing at the time. The logic behind Cutler's thinking seemed vague to his students, but they liked and respected him so much for his other virtues that they made no real issue of his grading practices.

QUESTIONS

1. As a student, how would you react to Mr. Cutler's grading philosophy? Do you think that Cutler favored athletes?
2. What was his purpose in assigning grades no higher than B's to athletes who were not competing?

MR. WILDING

Mr. Wilding had entered South High School as a new teacher and had initiated an excellent physical education program. He had worked diligently in developing a sound curriculum guide and evaluation system which was based upon skills, knowledge, attitude, participation, leadership, and the ability of students to get along with one another. His grading system was complex but organized to the extent that he could account for every mark given and logically explain the final six-week grade without difficulty.

Parents who were displeased with the marks their youngsters received in physical education were generally satisfied with the explanations furnished by Wilding and indeed most were favorably impressed with the thoroughness of his approach to grading. After one particular marking period Mr. Wilding was summoned to the principal's office and asked to explain his procedure to the administration. The principal had just received a telephone call from the junior high school principal whose son was in Wilding's class and had just received a failing grade for the six-week period. Wilding patiently explained that his entire grading procedure was presented in the curriculum guide approved by the principal. He also carefully explained the methods he used by which grade points were computed and the standards he employed to obtain these points. At this juncture the principal became very angry and verbally chastised Wilding for having the audacity to "set standards" in the first place. The principal staunchly maintained that every student should be evaluated as an individual and that no *standards* should ever be used in determining grades for any student. The principal further stated that Wilding's entire curriculum was as far removed from sound educational philosophy as were his grading procedures, and that it should immediately be revised. Wilding retorted that the curriculum guide had previously been endorsed by the administration and therefore he could see no reason to revise something that had only been in effect for less than a year. The principal stated that the guide had obviously been approved hurriedly and regardless of Wilding's protests to the contrary the curriculum would have to be altered. Wilding refused to revise the curriculum; the principal was supported by the superintendent and Wilding subsequently was fired for insubordination.

QUESTIONS

1. How would you regard Mr. Wilding as a professional person? Do you agree or disagree with his grading procedures? Why?
2. How would you characterize Wilding's principal? Do you believe he was correct in his assessment that teachers should not set standards? If so, why? If not, why?
3. What would you have done in Mr. Wilding's position as a teacher who was confronted by such a problem? What recourse should Mr. Wilding have had in such an instance?

MRS. MANLY

In the same school with Mr. Wilding was Mrs. Manly who taught American History. Mrs. Manly was an excellent lecturer and read extensively to keep herself informed in her field. She related well to the youngsters and was liked by her colleagues. Mrs. Manly had a few discussions about discipline with her principal but everything had been resolved to the mutual satisfaction of all parties concerned.

At the conclusion of a particular semester the homeroom teacher of one of Mrs. Manly's students walked into the faculty room to ask Mrs. Manly about a report card the student had received that seemed to be in error. The student had been awarded a failing grade for each of the six weeks of the eighteen-week semester, a marginal grade for his term project, a failing grade for his semester exam, and a *passing* final grade for the semester. Mrs. Manly explained that the student was a nice young fellow and caused no trouble, therefore she had not wished to retard his progress by failing him in a required course. She had consulted the principal on this matter and he had concurred with her decision.

QUESTIONS

1. Do you suppose that Mrs. Manly was playing politics by her attitude toward grading in the case cited? Why would a professional person resort to placating the boss instead of abiding by her convictions? What do you think her true convictions were?
2. How do you suppose students would react when Mrs. Manly's grade card was shown to them, as it most assuredly was? What would you as a student think of her grading practices?

MR. STEBBINS

Mr. Stebbins was a firm advocate of program evaluation. He was an active member in his professional associations and was always on the lookout for new and better methods of teaching physical education. At the conclusion of each teaching unit Stebbins would thoroughly evaluate the unit by referring to notes made on lesson plans and would also hand out evaluative sheets to his students to gain their reaction regarding various aspects of the unit. The students would complete the evaluation forms and turn them in unsigned. Most of the items on the sheets were arranged in a manner that could easily be tabulated and graphed. Stebbins was careful not to discard any of the student information, regardless of how biased it might be. He believed that the rational and objective students would outnumber those who were just trying to be obstinate and that the final tabulations would favor objectivity.

Stebbins was kidded by some of his colleagues for his diligent efforts to evaluate, but most of them secretly praised his efforts and admired his professional attitude. His principal and superintendent commended him many times in the presence of others as a man teachers would do well to emulate. Stebbins was not the type of person who could be accused of "buttering up the boss." In fact, he had the tenacity of a bulldog when discussing a controversial matter with his principal. However, he was always calm and objective in his thinking and never became belligerent even though losing an argument while knowing within himself that his point of view was correct.

Stebbins continued his teaching career at the high school level despite having been offered positions in higher education. He believed he had found his niche and wanted to remain with the younger boys and teach activities. He was liked by his students and respected by his superiors as a master teacher who continually strived for improvement in his person and in his profession. Perhaps, as one colleague stated, "Mr. Stebbins' finest attribute is his ability to mind his own business and to set an example of excellence for others to see rather than to hear about."

QUESTIONS

1. How would you evaluate Mr. Stebbins as a professional person? Why do you suppose Stebbins was so conscientious and gave so much time to evaluation when it was obvious that others did not, although probably receiving as much or more money for their services?

MR. FARROL

Mr. Farrol taught three sections of general science and two of biology. He was a great conversationalist in the faculty room and a good organizer of extracurricular activities such as dances, parties, and similar events. He stated on many occasions that he believed education to be primarily a socializing process and the subject matter presented in class was of a secondary nature because very little of what was learned was relevant anyway.

Farrol maintained his grade book but never recorded anything other than absences. At the conclusion of a six-week period he would assign an arbitrary grade to his students, usually an A or B. The only students who ever made a mark below the two top grades were those who had missed a number of classes for which they had received unexcused absences. Farrol's only justification for his actions was that the grades assigned by him were a valid professional judgment of the student's performance and his only criterion for such evaluations was personal observation.

When questioned about Farrol's grading practices, the administration informed inquisitive teachers that all of Farrol's students were of low ability and his grading methods served "a real need" for that type of student. The administration also maintained that Farrol was a teacher with tenure and would shortly retire, therefore creating a disturbance over the situation would only "tend to compound the problem."

QUESTIONS

1. What do you think of Mr. Farrol's "professional" opinion?
2. What do you think of the attitude of the administration toward Farrol? If Farrol was in your employ, how would you have handled his case? What about the administrative attitude toward Farrol's students?

SUGGESTED RELATED READING

Clarke, H. Harrison, *Application of Measurement to Physical Education*, 3rd ed. Englewood Cliffs, N.J.: Prentice-Hall, 1959.

Davis, Elwood Craig, and Earl L. Wallis, *Toward Better Teaching in Physical Education*. Englewood Cliffs, N.J.: Prentice-Hall, 1961.

Davis, Elwood Craig, and John D. Lawther, *Successful Teaching in Physical Education*, 2nd ed. Englewood Cliffs, N.J.: Prentice-Hall, 1948.

Kozman, Hilda C., ed., *Group Process in Physical Education*. New York: Harper, 1951. Written by the staff of the Physical Education Department at University of California.

Kozman, Hilda C., Rosiland Cassidy, and C. O. Jackson, *Methods in Physical Education*. 4th ed. Dubuque, Iowa: Wm. C. Brown, 1967.

Resick, Matthew G., Beverly L. Seidel, and James G. Mason, *Modern Administrative Practices in Physical Education and Athletics*. Reading, Mass.: Addison-Wesley, 1970.

Scott, Harry A., and Richard B. Westkaemper, *From Program to Facilities in Physical Education*. New York: Harper, 1958.

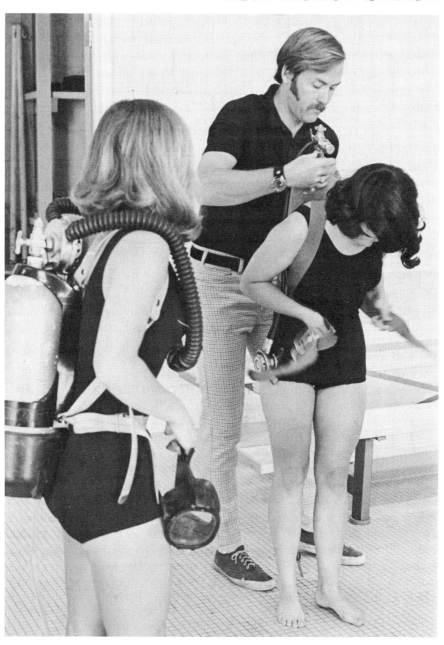

IMAGINATION IN PROGRAM DEVELOPMENT—
DARE TO BE DIFFERENT

Creativity is the essence of progress in any society. Early man devised ways of propelling projectiles and thus enabled himself to be more effective as a hunter and also protect himself and his family from adversaries. As society developed, laws were created to control the use of weaponry and thereby protect citizens without having them resort to violence. Housing, by virtue of creativity and inventive genius, has progressed from the cave of our ancestors to the modern apartment of our present generation. New construction materials which have added to our comfort have been developed and many recent advances have brought the relative cost of comfort within the means of many more human beings. Now, we are faced with the need for additional creativity, such as inventions to recycle or effectively dispose of some of the things we enjoy as creature comforts and now wish to discard. Hopefully man's creative brain will devise solutions to our dilemma and we shall produce an environment more conducive to living than the one we now occupy. If man can create to destroy, he should certainly be able to create those things which are beneficial.

Physical education has enjoyed the fruits of creativity and has incorporated into its programs activities such as basketball, invented by Dr. James Naismith and which, by virtue of its playing court, provided us with the laboratory space in which we conduct most of our other indoor activities. Games such as volleyball, flickerball, speedball, and cage ball are relatively new and were devised by individuals as original concepts of play, or were adapted from other similar activities. Nonetheless, the individuals responsible for creating the activities we use in our service course program made a significant contribution to the discipline.

It has occurred to people such as Mosston (1965), Metheny (1965), Smith, *et al.* (1968), and others in the field of physical education that there is more to the discipline than a mere teaching of skills. It has now been postulated that students must have a thorough knowledge of movement and the whys of movement before they will have a complete understanding of physical education. These authors have worked diligently to present their message to the profession and have been extremely creative in their approach to what they believe to be vital to the program. The movement program has been incorporated into many elementary schools throughout the country and certainly added a long-needed new dimension to the offerings of physical education.

Education generally has been apathetic toward innovation and change when compared to industry. Many people are appalled when they consider the short period of time in which aviation has progressed from the early flights of the Wright brothers to the development of supersonic transports, or from the experimentation by Goddard with rocketry to the moon landing of the Apollo space vehicle. Industry thrives on competition and must be innovative in order to survive. It can readily be determined that the Ford Motor Company would have been out of business long ago had they continued to produce the Model "T" in the face of competition from other automobile manufacturers. In many respects, education is still in the Model "T" stage and innovation and experimentation are the only ways by which it can become extricated. There is a dire need for professional people whose minds and energies lend themselves to attempt new techniques and methods.

Coaches have been forced by competition into devising new formations and game strategy, and they have met the challenge admirably. In conjunction with coaching and athletics, rules committees have convened annually and initiated procedures whereby games are more interesting and exciting even though complex and difficult to teach. It would be safe to assume that if the classroom teacher was forced to alter his technique in order to meet the competition from students enrolled in other classes, he would either arise to the occasion or leave the profession.

Medicine has continually improved over the years and dramatically so in the past quarter century. Educators may argue that both medicine and industry have been blessed by supported research which has demanded huge sums of money. However, this is not true of athletics which has made advances mainly by virtue of dedicated and innovative coaches. Should less be said of education? Why is it that physical education is still doing the same things essentially that it has done for the past fifty years? Is it because of lazy teachers, apathetic students, lack of funds, administrative reluctance toward new programs, lack of research, or a composite of all of these factors. Mathematics has made tremendous advances in conceptual education in the past few years. Are mathematicians more creative than physical educators? Have they received more funds for their research? Are they more dedicated to the education of youngsters or just what is their key to success? The basic key to the success of any program is personnel. People make programs and people carry them out.

We have many astute people in positions of leadership in the field of physical education, and their writings are indeed worthy of reading.

However, due to the shortage of teachers in the United States many people have felt secure in their positions and have not kept abreast of new concepts and ideas because it was not necessary to do this to hold a job. Teacher training institutions were unable to be selective and school administrators were confronted by the same problem. Job security and salary raises were equally automatic whether performances were outstanding or just mediocre. The average teacher has not been faced with the competition necessary to compel him toward better performance. Now, for the first time in the history of our nation, the supply of teachers has overtaken the demand and hopefully competition for jobs will result in a more dynamic educational process.

Teacher-training institutions are going to recommend only those physical educators whom they feel will accomplish the objectives of physical education, and they will be more concerned with excellence than just filling vacant positions. There will most certainly be mistakes in the evaluation of some teaching candidates; however, the general picture should be brighter than ever before. In order to create additional competition, school boards must institute some form of merit pay in an attempt to reward competence and eliminate those content with status quo. Through such rewards, creativity and innovation should provide a much more viable program in physical education than we now have. Those people who desire to remain in the teaching profession will, of necessity, have to be aware of the innovations of others and consequently will have to take a more active part in their professional organizations and avail themselves of the recent literature in the field. In general it has been conceded that most humans function better while working under the lash of compulsion, and the present supply and demand of teachers will indeed serve to compel excellence in those who wish to enter the profession. Celeste Ulrich spoke eloquently at the 1970 AAHPER convention on the topic of "New Wine in Old Bottles." She pointed out the fact that the basic objectives of physical education have not changed appreciably, but the course content and the approach is being revised daily. If physical education is to infuse its clientele with the available "new wine," then hopefully the teachers who are charged with the development of the new product will produce a vintage far more palatable than the old. The "grapes" for the new wine of physical education will be the ideas and creations employed in the teaching process and will come either from the minds of new teachers or from the thoughts of those already in the profession who are dedicated to the proposition that creativity leads to progress and that progress leads to excellence and the recognition of one of the most important disciplines in the public schools.

Equipment and apparatus are expensive, and frequently the beginning teacher discovers that certain aspects of his program are contingent upon items of equipment which he does not have or the budget will not provide. Weight-training programs obviously cannot be conducted without weights. Some inventive teachers have manufactured weights from lengths of pipe inserted into concrete-filled one-gallon cans. These weights are somewhat cumbersome but will suffice until more satisfactory weights can be purchased in sufficient numbers to meet the needs of the program. Inclined boards for abdominal exercises can be contructed of plywood, balance beams can be made by school woodworking shops, and other pieces of apparatus such as horizontal bars, peg boards, Swedish boxes, hurdles, ram racks, stall bars, or even bicycle ergometers used for adaptives or measurement can likewise be constructed by maintenance personnel or industrial arts people. The physical education instructor who has some mechanical aptitude can do much to improve his situation in the area of equipment acquisition and can also aid the women's program by assisting them in the construction of items they might need. Satisfactory whirlpool baths, tape rollers, and storage racks for training rooms have been constructed by creative people who were ambitious enough to remedy an equipment shortage by substituting a little work for a ready excuse. Some homemade items of equipment have even been patented by their inventors and later marketed by major suppliers at a handsome profit to their creators. The physical educator who has no knowledge of how to make things for himself can often prevail upon his colleagues to assist him. If physical education teachers have good rapport with their maintenance staff and industrial arts personnel, they soon discover that these people often are looking for projects they can build in their shops or utilize for basic instructional purposes. It should be remembered, however, that when an item of equipment is constructed by the maintenance department or an industrial arts class, a letter of commendation and gratitude should immediately be forwarded by the physical education department to those who have given assistance. In this way better relations can be fostered between school personnel, and future projects will be looked upon with greater favor. A word of thanks is little enough compensation for a job well done, but it may pave the way for a much better program in the future. In addition, the physical educator should always be ready to reciprocate if one of his colleagues requests assistance on a project of his own. Positive intraschool relationships are a two-way street.

A unit may be interesting or boring, depending upon the manner in which it is presented. For instance, an archery unit would be much more interesting if a field course was established after the fundamentals have been learned. This would provide the students with an opportunity to test their skills on a range which offers different targets at varying distances and which are approached from odd angles and positions. Such a course can easily be established with a bit of ingenuity and adds an entirely new dimension to the unit. Some teachers have utilized an occasional Saturday morning to take archery students to a field range or to help them establish one that can be used under field conditions. Putting greens can be readily constructed on existing turf fields merely by keeping the grass mowed very low and sinking a cup into the turf. Such greens are not as satisfactory as those found on a golf course, but they do provide an opportunity to chip and putt that might not otherwise be available. Some teachers have worked diligently to develop unique circuit-breaking courses which have been successfully utilized in units relating to physical fitness. All of these creations require additional effort on the part of the teacher and usually cannot be constructed during school hours. Evenings and an occasional weekend are frequently used by enterprising teachers who are more concerned with the education of their students than they are with their own personal welfare. No one would advocate that a teacher give all of his free time to the profession, but one has to reflect only momentarily to discover that the truly outstanding people in *any* profession are those who are willing to devote some of their free time to their work. Also it has been discovered by talking with these diligent workers that the dividends reaped from working a few extra hours far outweigh the inconvenience involved.

DON'T BE AFRAID TO TRY YOUR WINGS

Inexperienced teachers, especially those new to a large school district, are often reluctant to attempt innovative methodology for fear of criticism by others. The teacher who embarks upon his career in a small school enjoys the advantage of not feeling restrained by conformity and frequently finds that he can incorporate new approaches and methods more easily than if functioning within a very prescribed curriculum. Little progress can be made in education if everyone is afraid to attempt new approaches and techniques. However, the experimentalist must be prepared to accept the fact that his unorthodox methods might meet with failure. The experimenter should not give up in the case of failure, but should evaluate his success and failures and attempt to restructure his teaching in light of what he has learned. No teacher has any assurance that a method will work until it has been tried, but he can be assured there will never be progress until he has made an honest attempt. If Dr. Salk, or other similar researchers, had given up after their first attempt we would never have the polio vaccine. Therefore, the key to success is perseverance. Hindsight is always more valid than foresight, but the educator must always be thinking in terms of future performance and must use his hindsight only as a matter of evaluation.

Teachers have discovered that students themselves can aid in the learning process by being assigned certain segments of instruction to present to others. Students who are encouraged to develop plays and strategy for game situations gain a sense of belonging that can be attained in no other way. Their ideas may be a bit radical, but nevertheless they should be presented, analyzed, and discussed by the students and instructor to determine which features are valuable and why, and which features should be eliminated and why. No teacher should ever pursue the philosophy that he has all of the answers, but should encourage students to develop solutions of their own. It is in this way that students become actively involved and begin to realize that the class is *theirs* and not the exclusive property of the instructor.

In movement education provisions have been made to involve the student in experimenting with various movement patterns and to incorporate these patterns into games of low organization which the students themselves devise. This type of instruction has been favorably received by elementary school pupils and similar efforts should be made to incorporate the process into the teaching of games and skills of high organization. Some physical educators have argued that time does not permit much student involvement. The obvious counter argument would be that at any time students are *not* involved in an activity the activity has ceased to be of value. The function of the teacher is to impart knowledge, not to establish himself as a pillar of wisdom who knows and tells all and therefore should remain unquestioned. The objective of teaching is to ensure that skills and knowledges are acquired, and it follows that the method is not as important as the result. Time should certainly take a backseat to learning. Learning is *always* of primary importance; time is only a vehicle within which learning takes place. All too often teachers find that in their conformity to orthodoxy they religiously follow a time schedule that acts only as a detriment to the learning process. In many instances classes have been observed in which youngsters are on the very brink of mastering a skill when a whistle blows and they are moved to something else, thereby losing all which has been gained. Certainly time must be considered but never at the expense of knowledge.

Problem-solving is a process of inductive reasoning that must be learned and to be learned must be practiced. Physical educators have an exciting opportunity to assist youngsters in problem-solving, but few have seized upon it. Perhaps this is because they themselves are not completely familiar with the problem-solving process. Any skill or strategy poses a problem and that problem must first be identified before a solution can be formulated. After the problem is identified and reduced to its component parts, possible alternatives toward a solution should be posed and analyzed. When the student is involved in such analysis and determines why certain methods are better than others, he becomes a part of the process and his interest is whetted. If a student given a simple solution without any rationale whatever begins to become dependent upon others for all his solutions, he thereby assumes the characteristics of a robot who merely reacts and does not think for himself. Such is not the intent of learning. Internalizing material by rote memory must be done in some instances, but is no substitute for conceptualization and analytical thought.

Teacher-training institutions must begin to emphasize the conceptual approach in order to expect their graduates to utilize the same techniques in their own professional lives. The instructional approach that emphasizes conceptualization requires extensive planning and patience on the part of the teacher. However, when students begin to learn to reason inductively and apply this logic to their everyday deliberations much will have been accomplished. It should be reiterated that the problem-solving technique does not imply permissiveness to the extent where the student is free to do anything he wishes. He must apply logic based upon his past experiences and that which is compatible with the society in which he lives. In other words, he must structure his ideas and concepts in accord with the rules and regulations of the game or skill being learned, not in a helter-skelter design which satisfies only his desires and ego. During a period of conceptualized instruction, discipline is a must not only on the part of those involved as teachers but on the part of students as well.

Teachers must be allowed to experiment in their instruction but the experimental design they use must be based on sound psychological principles. Experimentation just for the sake of doing something different is not justifiable. Any approach to instruction which differs from accepted practice must entail the following factors:

1. The objectives to be attained.
2. Class control and direction.
3. Use of facilities and equipment.
4. Sound teaching principles based on the psychology of learning.

5. Conformity to existing rules and regulations in the conduct of any game governed by such rules and regulations.

6. Conformity to basic principles of physics and kinesiological function.

If an experimental unit is taught, a very careful analysis and evaluation must be undertaken at the conclusion of the unit to determine its value. Such evaluation should be systematic and the new method should then be compared with a standard approach to objectively assess relative merits. At no time during the experimental instruction should a teacher ever criticize an existing method of teaching used by others, even though it is obvious that his own method is yielding superior results. Sound experimentation should definitely be encouraged but should never violate the rights of others either directly or indirectly. Any experimental unit should be supported by its own merits. If the advantages of a new method are conclusive, the method should then be offered for general adoption. In all evaluations, the experimenter must be objective, in fact even critical. No physical educator should allow his own personal interests or bias to affect his evaluation of instruction. The experimenter must always keep the welfare of his students in mind and therefore subordinate his own personal desires and ambitions.

THE USE OF HANDOUTS AND THE ANNUAL REPORT

Physical education encompasses a body of knowledge that should not be kept from the students. In most secondary schools a text book for physical education is not required due to the variety of subject matter presented. In lieu of a textbook, the conscientious teacher should provide students with handout material which is pertinent to the subject being taught. Handouts may include rules, strategies, diagrams of play, physiological, psychological, and sociological information relative to physical education, and such things as training procedures. If handouts are used they should be maintained by the students in a physical education notebook. Such materials can then be used as a point of departure for knowledge tests and other related assignments.

Much of the material concerning the physiological, psychological, and sociological implications of physical education is not generally available to students but can be abstracted from textbooks and journals by the physical education instructor and duplicated for distribution to the students. Past experience revealed that these materials, if properly used in classes, can be of inestimable value in a number of ways. The students gain the concept that physical education classes actually have a body of knowledge which is of value and many youngsters will share this information with their parents who in turn become more appreciative of the discipline. By using handout material, the instructor is provided with a much better point of departure for purposes of testing and can therefore devise more meaningful and comprehensive evaluative procedures.

Handouts should not be used indiscriminately; they should conform to the material of the unit being presented and should be checked out to students systematically. It takes a great deal of time to adequately prepare a good handout, and the paper and duplication of these materials cost money. If the students get the mistaken idea that handout materials are automatically replaced when lost, they will not be cautious about properly filing them in their notebooks. A prudent method of ensuring that handouts are kept by the students is to charge them for any necessary replacements and then turning the acquired funds into the main office for purchasing paper and duplicating materials. The replacement of a few articles of dittoed material doesn't in itself imply much of a financial loss to a school, but when the "few" articles are multiplied it can become quite costly and public schools have absolutely no funds to spare.

An annual report may sound like a formidable and distasteful undertaking that is time-consuming and perhaps not worthwhile; however, the report does not have to be extremely detailed and once the format is developed it can be compiled in a matter of a few hours. An annual report should be written in an anecdotal form with only the tables or numerical information necessary to illustrate such things as participation or other data that must be placed in tabular form. Some annual reports contain pictures of activities which have been taught during the year or perhaps one page of composite photographs used as an introduction. The primary purpose of the annual report is to convey to the administration and/or lay public what happened during the year in the physical education and athletic program. If the use of pictures renders the cost of the report prohibitive, a simple mimeographed format will suffice. It is advisable to send the report to parents, but again if cost is a factor, it should only be forwarded to the administration and school board. Annual reports have not been as widely accepted by education as by industry, but they do serve a worthwhile purpose in conveying information about the program to those who are vitally interested in the conduct of the public schools. School board members generally do not have the time to devote to the investigation of departmental offerings due to the fact that most are in business or professions that are time-consuming. Therefore, board members do not have the opportunity to undertake a thorough investigation of all facets of the school curriculum. Ideally an annual report for physical education and athletics should be incorporated in an *all school* annual report.

When drafting the annual report, the physical educator should dwell on both the strengths and weaknesses of his department. He should never convey the concept that everything has been 100 percent successful or it would be difficult to justify additions or deletions in future programming as well as additional budget requests for needed equipment. The report should be objective and should demonstrate facts which illustrate the program as it is presently being carried out as well as the goals it hopes to attain. The report should emphasize participation, subject areas taught, and materials used in the instructional process. It should further elaborate upon any program innovations and their successes or failures, and above all it should present an *honest* appraisal of the situation, not a colored version that does not accurately depict the program in its truest sense.

Some large school districts have condensed their annual report and have then included it as a supplement in the local newspaper. In a large community the newspaper may be willing to assist with the layout and take photographs of various school activities to add interest to the report. The wide distribution of the newspaper should ensure that an annual report receives the attention of a large audience and is an item certainly newsworthy and informative to the general public. By keeping the public informed as to the character of the schools, individual readers become more cognizant of school programs and problems and are often more sympathetic toward public education than they might otherwise be.

Prior to submitting an annual report for publication, the administration should circulate a sample copy to all staff members to determine whether or not the material is accurate. Comments or changes should be made on sample copies before the completion of the final draft and subsequent publication. All printed copy should be kept on file from year to year so that improvements in format and presentation can be made. By regularly submitting material during the year and following a routine procedure, the writing of an annual report should become an easy and pleasurable task that is self-satisfying to complete. If the task is approached in a positive manner with the thought in mind that the school program will ultimately benefit, the job of compiling an annual report can be an interesting and profitable experience.

CARE IN PICKING THE BRAINS OF OTHERS

Physical educators should be aware of innovations which are being implemented within their discipline, and if they perceive a concept with merit they should attempt to incorporate it within their *own* program. No teacher should be adverse to using the ideas of his associates, but he should take care in determining which ideas to use and which not to. A change in teaching method, just for the sake of change, is undesirable. However, if an idea is analyzed carefully and discovered to be sound in terms of educational values, it should be attempted. In analyzing new ideas the problem-solving approach should be used to determine values, and in all instances the selection of possible alternatives should be based upon logic. Occasionally one discovers a drill that someone else is using to teach a skill, and outwardly it appears enjoyable and profitable to the students. However, upon close examination the drill may be found extremely lacking in its relevancy to the game or activity for which it was designed. Any drill that is used should approximate actual game conditions insofar as possible. Frequently conditioning drills and skill practices are conducted under conditions which are artificial in relation to the entire activity and are therefore of little value, regardless of the enjoyment the students might experience.

Publications such as the *Journal of Health, Physical Education and Recreation; Research Quarterly; Scholastic Coach; Athletic Journal;* and other professional periodicals provide material that is valuable and should be read by all teachers and coaches. No method or drill should ever be placed in the program without first considering the facilities, equipment, and staff necessary to its proper conduct. Teachers of physical education and athletic coaches who work with high school students occasionally utilize methods and drills that have been found successful in professional athletics. Without considering the fact that professionals are much more sophisticated athletes than high school students and that they function under a different psychological drive, the teacher or coach may be rendering an injustice to his students simply because they aren't equipped either physically or mentally for the tasks the drill demands. In order for any teaching method to be successful, it must be tailored to the age group for which it is going to be used.

When searching for a new method of instruction, the physical educator should first consult the literature to determine what methods have been successful in similar instances. If a good idea is discovered which, when thoroughly analyzed in terms of the age group, staff, facilities and equipment, is found to be acceptable, *use it*. Give credit where credit is due if students ask the source of a new drill or method. Don't let pride goad you into the position of gleaning ideas from others and taking credit for them yourself. In the determination of drills and teaching methodology, no teacher should be discouraged from experimentation, but such experimentation should *always* be premised upon research and logic rather than upon whim and personal preference.

PUBLIC RELATIONS AND HORSE SENSE

Public relations is a field that schools should pursue continuously, not merely at the time of a budget or bond election. The public schools should make every effort to communicate with the public through news releases and personal contact at every level. Athletics receives much public attention because of the nature of the activity. Sports-minded people become emotionally involved with local athletic teams and consider high school athletic events to be newsworthy. Every department within the schools should submit articles to the administration for release to the news media. All material should be properly channeled through one individual charged with the responsibility for news releases. In many instances this job is handled by the journalism instructor who works closely with the administration. Whether or not the news media chooses to use releases is something over which the schools have no control. However, to assume that news will not be released and thus withhold information is erroneous. Any newsworthy item should be released in hope that it will be assimilated by the general public.

In conducting a systematic program of public relations, it should be remembered that there are many publics to contact. These publics consist of parents, students, interested organizations, such as property owners, whose children are not currently in school, the financial community and corporations whose taxes are used for educational purposes, the school board, and other concerned elements of the community. The publics should be identified not only as to who they are, but also as to what their particular interest in the school might be. Information which would tend to answer the questions that these special interest groups would have can then be compiled.

A program of positive public relations should be as carefully planned as a curriculum and should contain essentially the same factors such as objectives, method, and evaluation. Each department should be involved in the planning of a public relations program and contribute its own pertinent information accordingly. Physical education and athletics should furnish press releases on service courses and intramural activities in the same manner in which they are furnished for athletics. Obviously the amount of material available for public consumption from the physical education classes and intramural program is not usually as voluminous as that from athletics. However, regular releases which inform the public of what is happening in the realm of men's and women's class and intramural activities are appreciated by those students who are involved in these programs as well as by their parents.

Interested groups should be brought into the schools to observe procedures and practices such as equipment storage and maintenance, cleanliness and sanitation, and demonstrations of classroom activities. It is not enough to merely invite people to the school, a concerted effort must be made to ensure that the public actually makes the visitation. Open houses are one way in which the publics are attracted to the schools, but they must be widely advertised and should consist of something other than a cursory tour of the school facilities. Some schools have discovered that an open house held three or four times a year is far more satisfactory than just one all-encompassing program. If each open house program emphasizes a certain segment of the school program, such as social studies, physical education and athletics, science, vocational education, and the language arts, four or five such programs can be held each year without imposing upon any one group of faculty and also without duplication of programming. Parents and other interested people who attend open houses offered only once a year often find it difficult to talk with all of the instructors. There are usually so many different activities going on at one time that many people never have an opportunity to investigate any one area in depth and as a result leave the function with unanswered questions.

The annual report, as previously mentioned, is a positive approach to public relations, however, it is not enough. The annual report should be supplemented with handout materials, information disseminated at P.T.A. meetings, parent conferences, and news releases. In the publication of such materials every effort should be made to be objective and factual. It is not enough to be informative about only those aspects of the school program which are positive. The public has the right to know about things which need to be improved. Such information could relate to every aspect of the school program from curriculum to student conduct. The public is investing millions of dollars in its school systems and has a right to know just what it is getting for its money, good or bad. Hopefully the positive aspects of education would outweigh the negative and should of course be stressed, but not at the expense of the truth.

The basic objective of any public relations program should be to dispel rumors and false information related to the enterprise in question. Therefore, some schools have distributed surveys or questionnaires in an attempt to determine which facets of the school program need clarification. After the results of questionnaires are tabulated, a public relations program can be initiated which attempts to depict the entire field of education in its proper perspective but emphasizes those features about which there is the most controversy.

Physical educators frequently refer to physical fitness programs in public relations campaigns, but neglect to provide the physiological rationale or values which underlie such programs. Few people understand the psychological or sociological aspects of physical education, or for that matter even realize that they exist. In communicating with the public, it is imperative that *all* aspects of any discipline be considered if the public relations program is to be complete. Common sense would dictate that factors considered by physical educators to be implicit might not be considered as such by the lay public.

Public relations must concern itself with four major subdivisions: research, communication, action, and evaluation. The public relations program in physical education and athletics must therefore research the areas of the program to be considered, communicate with the public in an effective manner, demonstrate its product to the various publics, and evaluate the results in terms of acceptance or rejection. No program of value can be undertaken without adequate planning in the four subdivisions. Research for a public relations program may reveal that the schools have an opinion of themselves which does not coincide with that of the publics they serve. The image that physical education projects to its professional workers may be completely different from the image envisaged by the students, parents, or, for that matter, the school board. Such a situation would make it the duty of the physical education department to alter public opinion by following their research study with adequate communication and action. If the evaluative process, which may include questionnaires or interviews, reveals that the image of physical education has been altered favorably, the same type of public relations program should be carried out in the future. The failure of the various publics to perceive a new image of physical education makes necessary a different approach which hopefully will alter their views.

Public relations programs should be designed so that new subject areas are "sold" to the public prior to the time they are actually incorporated into the curriculum. The public must be acquainted with new school programs by advance publicity rather than by advertising after they have been in operation. The adverse opinion of public education voiced by many people is merely a reflection of ignorance; however, it is imperative that we *know* what the public really thinks in order to remedy the situation. Ignorance stems from either misinformation or no information, and the public schools are guilty of both. Asking school patrons and others to attend board meetings or an occasional open house is only a fragment of a good public relations program. In any school district where positive educational advances have been made, an informed public can be found. For physical education or any other discipline to progress, it must be sold to the public and this can only be accomplished through a well-planned public relations program which functions as a continual process within the school district. Crash programs serve poorly because they reach so few people and do not thoroughly educate the publics that must be contacted.

QUESTIONS FOR DISCUSSION

1. Of what importance is creativity in education and upon what concepts should it be based?
2. What economic value would creativity be in the field of physical education? Can you think of ways in which a creative teacher might save money for his department?
3. How does creativity by the teacher affect the learning process of the student?
4. In what ways does a small school offer opportunities for teacher creativity that are not possible in large school districts?
5. What factors should control experimentalism in education?
6. In what way is an annual report valuable and how should it be formulated?
7. How would you adequately define public relations?
8. Of what value is a public relations program and which publics should the schools attempt to reach?
9. Is timing important in public relations and why?
10. What purposes are served by providing students with handout materials?
11. What are the four main subdivisions of a public relations program and how can they be best used by physical education in "selling" its product to its publics?
12. Should a public relations program be continuous or executed on a periodic basis? Why?

BIBLIOGRAPHY

Metheny, Eleanor. *Connotations of Movement In Sport and Dance.* Dubuque, Iowa: Wm. C. Brown, 1965.

Mosston, Muske. *Developmental Movement.* Columbus, Ohio: Chas. E. Merrill, 1965.

Smith, Hope, *et al. Introduction To Human Movement.* Reading, Mass.: Addison-Wesley, 1968.

CASE STUDIES

MR. STIENER

Mr. Stiener was an innovative fellow and a fine teacher. He spent many years teaching high school students and then accepted a position on a junior college faculty. One of his activity assignments was a class in basketball which he had taught previously to younger students, but he believed that more depth should be presented to college freshmen and sophomores.

After introducing the unit Stiener proceeded to give assignments to each student. The students were responsible for developing offensive and defensive patterns and specific drills pertinent to the various aspects of the game. The students were not only to devise the drills and patterns, but were also to instruct the class in the conduct of the activities they designed. After each instructional period the class was critiqued by Stiener and the strengths and weaknesses of the drill or pattern were analyzed by the class. The student's method of teaching was not questioned because the class was not designed for professional students. However, many of the students employed various charts and diagrams and some even used film loops which were checked out to them by the media center. One-half of each period was utilized by the students for instructional time over a period of five weeks. The class met three times weekly so that there was ample time for all students to present their contributions. After the five-week instructional period, a tournament was established and the skills and patterns learned were utilized in a practical game situation. The response of the class was overwhelmingly favorable to Stiener's methodology and many of the students indicated they had enjoyed the teaching and preparation of their units so much that they themselves were considering teaching as a profession.

Stiener succeeded so well with his basketball class that he adopted similar techniques in teaching his other activity courses and with great success. After the basketball class completed the final examination they were asked to hand in an unsigned evaluation of the experience. The majority of the students was definitely in favor of the manner in which the class had been conducted, some had minor reservations, but all believed they had profited from the exposure and encouraged similar methodology to be used in other activity sections.

QUESTIONS

1. Do you believe that Stiener's method of presenting his basketball unit would be successful with younger students? If so, why? If not, why?
2. Do you feel that Stiener was taking a lazy man's approach to his teaching duties? Why or why not?

MR. GROVER

Mr. Grover, a junior high school physical educator, annually taught a unit in physical fitness. In his teaching unit he included a variety of calisthenics, rope climbing, and running. His students complained about the unit by stating they did not really see any value in using time that could be devoted to play and the activities themselves were no fun.

Grover began to evaluate his fitness unit in terms of the effects it was having on students and came to the conclusion that it was not very innovative and perhaps even less informative. He therefore spent much of his spare time devising something he believed would provide more of a challenge to his students and perhaps be equally stimulating to him as a teacher. He analyzed the unit and scrapped virtually everything in the form of calisthenics in favor of activities that were unique.

The new unit Grover devised was established as a circuit course involving an agility drill, balance apparatus, strength development on a multi-purpose weight-training machine, a hop-scotch course using suspended elastic ropes arranged in a grid pattern, an endurance run, and a vertical jumping sequence. Grover also drafted a handout which included basic physiological principles that were directly related to each activity; these were thoroughly discussed in class prior to the activity portion of the unit.

Written tests were given periodically during the course of the fitness unit and performance records were maintained by all boys. At the conclusion of the unit a final performance test and written examination were administered followed by a student evaluation. Comments about the unit were solicited and for the most part appeared to be sincere. Some were obviously facetious and reflected nothing more than a shallow attempt on the part of a small number of students to be humorous.

Suggestions were made about the sequence of the stunts in the circuit and comments were voiced about the handout material. These suggestions and comments were duly noted and the information of value was incorporated in the unit the following year. Grover altered various aspects of his fitness unit from time to time and was well pleased with the reception of the material as compared to his previous experience.

QUESTIONS

1. Why do you believe that Mr. Grover's physical fitness unit, as originally presented, was a failure? Should physical fitness be taught as a separate unit or should it be integrated into all units of instruction?
2. Of what value was Grover's follow-up of the unit?

MR. GIRARD

Mr. Girard had coached track and field for a number of years in a high school which was located in a rather cold climate. He usually received complaints from the boys about the weather during the early weeks of the season and their inability to train properly without wearing bulky clothing which restricted their movement. Girard had thought seriously about using rubber or plastic warmup jackets of the type that wrestlers wore, but his budget was limited and the expense for a large number of boys seemed prohibitive.

From his knowledge of physiology, Girard realized that his major problem was retaining body heat and a plastic membrane of some type might just accomplish his purpose. He first tried using plastic bags from a cleaning establishment. He had the boys cut holes in the bags for their head and arms, then don the bag over a tee shirt and pull on a sweat shirt over the plastic. The plastic did not allow the boy's perspiration to evaporate and therefore soaked into the cotton undershirt but the boys remained warm. However, the shirts became thoroughly soaked and caused some skin problems. The sweat shirts remained dry and provided enough insulation for adequate warmth even in extremely cold weather. No clothing was worn over the lower extremities except heavy cotton sweat pants.

Mr. Girard discovered that a heavy grade of cotton undershirt absorbed more perspiration and remained relatively dry when compared to the lighter ones customarily worn. However, he found that the plastic bags soon became torn and had to be replaced almost daily. He insisted upon dry undershirts each day and the skin problems diminished as did a rather malodorous condition in the locker room.

One day Girard passed by the school cafeteria when the custodian was cleaning. He noticed that large heavy plastic bags were being used to line the garbage cans. He inquired as to the source of the bags whereupon the custodian gave him a half dozen or so to experiment with. Girard discovered that the bags were available through grocery stores, were inexpensive, and could be purchased in a variety of sizes. They were much heavier than the bags he had procured from the cleaning establishment and could be rinsed off in the shower for reuse.

Mr. Girard experimented with the plastic refuse can liners and found them to be most satisfactory. He discovered they were long enough to cover the hips of most of his runners, and the boys found they were so warm that many of them requested short-sleeved sweat shirts. Girard cautioned the boys about overheating and the possible consequences thereof. He passed all of his information on to his coaching colleagues and was pleased to hear that the football coach readily consented to try the new method during late season practices and games. After just one year of experimentation by various athletic teams it was discovered that a judicial use of plastic can liners was not only satisfactory, but it also helped the performance of the athletes and substantially reduced the prospects of having to expend funds which simply were not available.

QUESTIONS

1. What uses could Mr. Girard's discovery have other than warmth?
2. What type of research projects could stem from Mr. Girard's experiments?
3. When one experiments, as did Mr. Girard, what precautions must he take? What precautions did Girard take?

MR. WESLEY

Coach Wesley accepted a position as wrestling coach at a high school which had entered the sport initially with a part-time coach. Many youngsters reported for the wrestling team but the townspeople did not turn out to support the program. Wesley was a fine coach and a good disciplinarian who commanded the respect of his team. He was an excellent fundamentalist and his teams made an enviable record in conference matches but did not receive as much public acclaim as boys generally like to have.

Mr. Wesley contacted his local sports writer on numerous occasions and received publicity in the paper prior to all of his matches. He still did not believe that people were attending the matches in the numbers they should. He therefore actively pursued a project that he had previously considered but had done nothing about. He contacted the editor of the local newspaper and asked his permission to insert a special folder in the Wednesday edition of each local paper; permission was granted.

Coach Wesley composed a cleverly written supplement in which he explained the history of wrestling in its various forms and thoroughly explained all of the rules. The explanation of the rules was accompanied by diagrams and "stick figures" which served to illustrate various basic movements used in wrestling. The supplemental insert was then placed on a duplicating machine and enough copies were made so that each newspaper subscriber could have one. Members of the wrestling team reported to the newspaper office and "stuffed" each paper as it came off the press. The papers were then delivered via the regular routing system.

The response that Coach Wesley received in regard to his newspaper supplement was gratifying. People who had never seen an amateur wrestling bout in their lives became curious upon reading the material and attended the Friday evening matches to satisfy their curiosity. Apparently many spectators informed their friends that wrestling was something which should not be overlooked and the crowds became very regular in their attendance. Wesley was informed by many people that they would have been coming to the matches long before had they only known something about the rules and objectives of the program. From a rather inauspicious beginning emerged a program that subsequently became a major feature of the high school interscholastic athletic program.

QUESTIONS

1. What do you think of Mr. Wesley's idea in relation to public relations? Do you suppose that the principle he used could be applied to other areas of education? Give examples.
2. What does the public reaction to Coach Wesley's project tell you about things we too frequently assume?

MR. RIFKIND

Mr. Rifkind was the sponsor of a lettermen's club interested in buying a motion picture camera and film to be used for photographing high school athletic contests. The organization was blessed with many boys who had boundless initiative and imagination. They did not believe that car washes, cake sales, dances, and similar projects would net them the amount of money required for their needs. They further believed they should initiate a project that could be conducted annually with some assurance of success and with yearly income.

Rifkind met with the executive body of the organization and acquainted them with the technique of "brainstorming" an idea. He conducted a practice session with the boys who in turn would expose the other club members to the technique. Many of the ideas for money raising were unrealistic but some had definite merit.

When the regular brainstorming session was held with all members present, every conceivable idea was noted and the executive board then proceeded to weed out those which showed no promise. Two major projects were considered. The first was to enter the annual Chamber of Commerce fair as a civic organization and purchase the right to operate a concession booth of some sort. This idea was presented to the Chamber of Commerce with the rationale that any funds earned were to be used by the lettermen in their camera project. The boys explained that moneys so earned would possibly eliminate having to ask for school funds and thereby effect a savings in the athletic budget. Their plea was heard and approved.

The second project was proposed by a young fellow whose father owned a dairy. It seemed that the cattle pens needed to be cleaned monthly and if they would undertake the cleaning chore, the fertilizer from these pens would belong to the lettermen. The boys agreed to clean the pens and then sell the fertilizer during the spring and fall months. The dairyman agreed to let them store the residue from the pens on his property and rented them a large dump truck which was to be paid for on a percentage basis. The project was an immediate success and each customer who bought the product in the spring was asked whether or not he would like a repeat order in the fall. After seeing the bargain they received for their money, virtually all of the customers reordered.

Both projects undertaken by this lettermen's organization paid off very well and the photographing of athletic contests became a reality. The townspeople believed the boys not only received the benefit of the funds they earned, but also were favorably introduced into a business enterprise that provided valuable on-the-job training and experience.

QUESTIONS

1. Do you think that Mr. Rifkind followed the usual procedures in stimulating his boys to develop moneymaking projects? Why?
2. What similar projects do you know about that have been of benefit to school and civic organizations?
3. What principles of business management were learned by Rifkind's boys?

MR. BUFORD

Mr. Buford accepted a superintendency in a small school district notorious for its inability to have the annual budget approved. At the initial fall faculty meeting Buford requested all administrators and department heads to begin keeping a record of significant aspects of school life. Many people were rather critical of the plan but agreed that if it would serve a worthwhile purpose they would do as directed. Buford entered into an agreement with the editor of the local newspaper to print highlights of the school activities each month and then compile the more significant factors into an annual report.

After the annual report had been edited to an appropriate size, Buford asked the board for special funds to have it printed in the local paper in a special edition. The funds were granted reluctantly, and the material was published just two days prior to the budget election. Unfortunately the budget was defeated. Buford then took the material from the annual report and submitted it to the local radio station and asked them to use it as a feature prior to the next budget election. The manager of the station discussed the matter at length with Buford and convinced him that segments of the report should be broadcast daily, rather than in only one installment. At the next budget election a budget was presented which had been altered very little; however there was a greater total vote and the budget passed.

QUESTIONS

1. What advice could you give to Mr. Buford in his approach to acquainting the public with his annual report?
2. How could the faculty have been more satisfactorily involved in the compilation of the annual report?
3. What are the implications of the timing of Mr. Buford's report?

MISS MERRICK

Miss Merrick was confronted by a problem which arose very suddenly with regard to her summer teaching schedule in a small college. The staff member who was scheduled to teach a course in Community Health Problems was suddenly incapacitated by severe illness and could not teach. None of the other instructors believed themselves competent enough in the health field to teach the Community Health class and inasmuch as Miss Merrick was the department chairman she believed it an obligation incumbent upon herself to resolve the problem.

The students had planned their schedules so that they could complete Community Health Problems at the designated time; for some, graduation was contingent upon the course. Miss Merrick decided to instruct the course herself and diligently endeavored to restructure the offering in order to compensate for her own lack of background. She planned a series of introductory materials for each unit, then scheduled a progression of films, guest lecturers, and field trips which utilized the outstanding resource materials and personnel in the surrounding area. Miss Merrick spent many hours personally contacting people and making the necessary arrangements for field trips. She patiently explained to each person or agency the nature of her problem and all were more than willing to cooperate. Time schedules were completed, the course syllabus was drafted, and all final arrangements made just prior to summer registration.

Miss Merrick informed the students at the initial class meeting of the nature of the Community Health class and why it had to be restructured. She also told them that she had been unable to arrange for college transportation on field trips due to budgetary considerations and they would have to pool their own automobiles. The students understood that a great deal of effort had been undertaken to ensure the offering of the course and were very willing to cooperate.

At the conclusion of the summer session Miss Merrick called for a student evaluation of the Community Health class. The response was enthusiastic to say the least. Many of the students believed the experience was one of the most valuable they had ever encountered since they not only studied about the problems, but also were better able to conceptualize the difficulties because of their field trip experiences. Some stated that they had always been aware of such things as sewage treatment plants, water filtration, garbage disposal, and other related enterprises, but had *never* fully appreciated the complexities of these things which most citizens are willing to take for granted.

Miss Merrick was satisfied with the manner in which the course had been accepted but was somewhat reluctant to convey the enthusiasm of the students to the regular instructor who had previously used a traditional approach. However, after discussing the matter thoroughly with the professor, she was relieved to discover that he too was as enthusiastic as the students and promised to pursue the matter even further in refining the approach used by Miss Merrick. Subsequent classes were even better organized than Miss Merrick's. Also the regular instructor was much more adept at presenting introductory material and concluding remarks due to his thorough knowledge of the community health field.

QUESTIONS

1. How could a course plan such as Miss Merrick's be implemented in a public school situation? What would be some of the problems in scheduling?
2. If you had been in the position of the instructor whom Miss Merrick replaced, how would you feel toward her conduct of the class? Do you believe that "character" sometimes plays an important part in the acceptance of ideas from other people? Why?

SUGGESTED RELATED READINGS

Adams, Alexander B., *Handbook of Practical Public Relations.* New York: Crowell, 1965.

Bernays, Edward L., *Public Relations.* Norman: University of Oklahoma Press, 1952.

Marston, John E., *The Nature of Public Relations.* New York: McGraw-Hill, 1963.

Robinson, Edward J., *Communication and Public Relations.* Columbus, Ohio: C. E. Merrill, 1966.

Stahl, LeRoy, *The Art of Publicity.* Minneapolis: T. S. Denison, 1962.

12

THE TEACHER'S ROLE
IN THE
GUIDANCE SERVICES

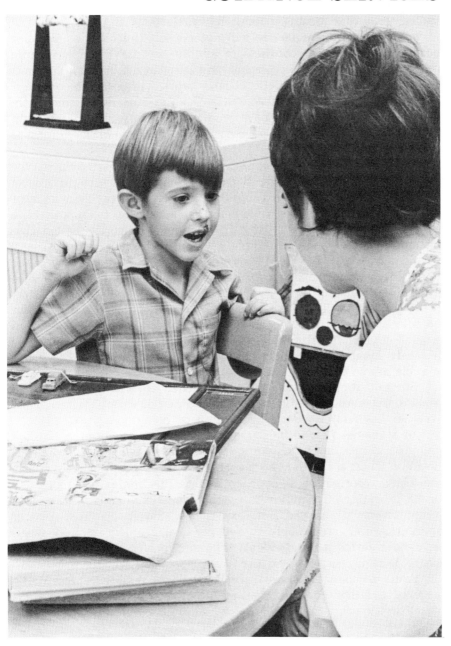

YOU ARE NOW A COUNSELOR—LIKE IT OR NOT

Counseling and guidance are not restricted to those who are hired specifically as counselors. Every teacher in the public school system must at some time assume a counseling role due to the very nature of his work. Students frequently will not consult the regular counselor because of personality conflicts or simply because they place more confidence in a particular teacher and respect his or her judgment. Physical educators and athletic coaches work with students on a less formal basis than do some academicians and as a result are frequently sought out by students who have problems. Such problems range from those of a personal nature to general and specific considerations of vocational interest.

The problems which confront youngsters often seem to be insignificant by adult standards but the student regards such difficulties as extremely consequential because they happen to be the basic areas of interest he has at the time. Experience has taught most adults that life is filled with complexities, many of which are not worthy of extreme concern, and that time heals many wounds. The student is usually impatient with himself as well as with those around him and perceives many things rather superficially because he has had little experience with which to relate. Because of his lack of experience, the youngster with a problem will seek out someone who is willing to listen to him and who has had experiences which may aid in determining a solution to his dilemma. Unfortunately, many adults are not willing to listen to seemingly insignificant problems, and the student then turns to a less desirable source for his counsel.

Students soon discover that some teachers are willing listeners who have a sincere desire to aid youngsters in directing their activities. Once a teacher has established the reputation of being concerned with the lives of students, he will be sought as the person in whom to confide when difficulties arise. There are certain problems that a physical education teacher would be capable of handling, such as sports counseling, information relative to college life, minor personal difficulties, providing information to parents, vocational counseling related to the teacher's personal past experience, and many other *general* topics. However, any deeply rooted personal problems should necessarily be referred to individuals who are professionally trained as psychologists or psychiatrists.

Some teachers, because of their personal qualities, present the image of a father confessor; others do not. The teacher who finds himself in the role of an involuntary counselor should be gratified that students will confide in him but should not establish himself as a savior of mankind and undertake to solicit additional clients for himself. Humility is a quality all teachers should possess and especially those who are blessed with the intangible "something" that draws students to them. Certain teachers are warm and personable and perform a valuable role in the counseling function. Others are less personable, but nevertheless excellent teachers, and should not be criticized for their lack of personal attraction. Such people often are vitally concerned about the welfare of their students but do not have the personal qualities and characteristics conducive to counseling.

CONFIDENCE, QUALITY, AND QUACKERY

The physical educator who counsels students should have confidence in his ability and should increase his proficiency by taking additional course work in counseling and guidance, and by reading extensively in the literature of that field. However, the teacher-counselor should also be the first to realize his own limitations and shortcomings and be ready to refer students to more competent personnel should the occasion arise.

Students who discuss their private lives, or personal aspirations, with teachers expect that such discussions will be held in confidence. A teacher should never violate the confidence of his students by reviewing their discussions in the faculty room or in the presence of other students. Such deplorable, nonprofessional behavior, occurs occasionally and should be discouraged by both the administration and colleagues of the guilty party. Many problems that youngsters bring to their teachers are indeed humorous, but not to the student. If students become aware that their counseling sessions or confidential conversations are being repeated to others, they will quickly lose respect for their teachers and will cease to seek their assistance. Young people cannot be blamed for becoming distrustful of their elders when they discover that their problems have become the subject of idle chatter by those in whom they confide.

Teachers who counsel students must have a variety of information available to them if they are to counsel effectively. Cumulative records which indicate general background, test scores, family status, and other pertinent information are extremely valuable. Such records are usually kept in the school counselor's office but should be used by all teachers. Some filing system should be established whereby one set of records is available to the school counselors and a duplicate set centrally located for the teachers to use. Records must not be removed from the filing center because they are used by many people and also might fall into the hands of students thereby disclosing confidential information. Cumulative records are only a part of the total profile of the student. Many of these records are incomplete because the student has transferred from school to school and occasionally pertinent information is lost or has not been accurately recorded.

No student should ever be stereotyped because of information appearing on a cumulative record. Frequently teachers will discover that a student is not performing well and will consult his cumulative folder to determine his I.Q. If the student's I.Q. is found to be below normal or borderline, the teacher may assume that the youngster is not capable of better performance. This assumption may or may not be valid, depending upon the number of I.Q. scores available, cultural background, conditions under which tests were administered, or previous mobility of the student from school to school. In an attempt to gather information relative to a student's behavior, the teacher should consult many sources other than the cumulative record. Other teachers may be able to provide information about a particular student and such empirical data gathered by observation may be of help. Cumulative records should be used only as an *initial* source of information and in all instances the student should be given the benefit of the doubt. Written remarks relative to a student's behavior in the elementary or junior high school may not be relevant upon examination of that same student in later years. Maturation exerts a considerable influence upon student behavior, as does a change in physical environment and the conditions one encounters by making new friends.

A competent counselor must base his evaluations of a student upon a broad spectrum of information and must interject his own findings into those of others. Students frequently have clashes with some teachers due to personality conflicts or diversity of interest. Youngsters should learn that they must get along with many people whom they do not necessarily like, but the same could be said of some teachers. Hopefully, an experienced teacher would be more objective in his evaluation of a youngster than the youngster would be of the teacher. However this is not always the case and therefore a diversity of opinion is desirable in evaluating students.

Youngsters who become disciplinary problems, and must be counseled accordingly, frequently resort to poor behavior as a result of problems that are beyond their control. Occasionally a health problem may precipitate poor behavior and yet not be considered as a causative factor by teachers. Health records are usually located in the health suite or nurse's office and should be as readily available to teachers as the cumulative folders. Physical educators should have a duplicate of each student's health record on file and be aware of any problem that a youngster might have. Sports counseling, as well as placement in many physical education activities, may be affected by consulting health records. Records of any type are of no real value unless used regularly by both teachers and administrators. Health records should be kept up to date and contain a complete history of all innoculations, injuries, illnesses, and other pertinent health data.

Teachers should consult professional school counselors at any time the need arises. They should seek the advice of the counselor in the same manner that they would seek advice from the administration regarding problems about which they need additional information. The student is not the property of any one individual within the school system; he is the concern of each and every person with whom he comes into contact. Custodians and grounds keepers may occasionally provide valuable information about a student's behavior because they see him in a very informal setting. School bus drivers are also a good source of information and can frequently furnish facts about a student's behavior away from school which are of great value to the counseling function.

LISTEN, LISTEN, LISTEN

Good counselors are good listeners. A youngster occasionally desires nothing from his counselor other than an opportunity to "let off steam" and purge himself of his frustrations. He may have a problem that really is of no consequence once he has talked about it and has come to perceive it in its true sense. It is human nature to desire to share one's troubles. However, it is sometimes difficult to find a sympathetic person who is willing to listen to problems that are of no mutual concern. The counselor who is willing to listen attentively to either logic or mere rambling soon earns the reputation of one who has the interest of the students at heart.

Listening objectively without making snap judgments takes practice. The listener should maintain eye contact with the speaker and should learn to jot down notes pertinent to what is being said. He should assure the speaker that these notes are merely for reference and should make sure he, as listener, understands clearly what has been said. Such attentiveness reassures the speaker that he is being heard and what he has to say is of interest to the counselor. If a youngster is speaking, he should not be interrupted until he has exhausted his train of thought. Often he will begin to pose alternative solutions to his problems as he talks about them, and occasionally will arrive at a solution of his own without ever soliciting advice from his counselor. Any comments made by the counselor should be in the form of suggestions, and can be phrased as questions rather than absolute statements. The concept behind such an approach is to let the student make decisions for himself by merely directing his thinking so that the solution evolved comes from the student rather than the counselor. Youngsters have to learn to make decisions for themselves sooner or later, and counselors who encourage such practice should be commended. If a student discovers that he can consistently acquire tailor-made decisions from his counselor he will never learn to solve problems for himself. As the counselor listens to the counselee he may pose various alternative solutions to problems, but the ultimate selection of a solution should be structured so that the student feels he has made the decision. Proposed solutions to students' problems can be made only after extremely careful evaluation predicated upon an accurate assessment of the facts presented. An accurate assessment of facts is contigent upon attentive *listening*, not just the courtesy of the counselor keeping quiet while his student speaks. The counselor should always concentrate upon what the student says, not upon what he desires to hear. Listening, as well as speaking, can be biased to the extent that facts or opinions become completely distorted and therefore any subsequent evaluation or assessment would also be biased. If the counselor is doubtful about what is being said, he should ask for clarification and not be content with what he *thinks* is said. Students come to teachers and counselors because they believe that such people are interested in their problems; and such interest often needs to be fortified by reassurance in the form of inquiry by the counselor.

Much of our communication is not really two-way communication at all. Educators, politicians, businessmen, clergymen, and others in public service, want to have their views heard but few are willing to attentively listen to others. Many educators feign a willingness to listen to young people but few really hear what is being said because they are more interested in immediate rebuttal than in absorbing facts and assessing information. Students in class may *appear* to be listening but are later exposed by test results. It is not enough to be polite and just sit quietly while another individual is speaking. A sincere listener must follow the thoughts of the speaker by taking notes, asking questions, and seeking to have various aspects of the speaker's thoughts clarified. Listening skills require practice if they are to be learned and therefore should be utilized during any interview with a student, either formally or informally.

Listening to a student does not imply that the teacher must agree with everything being said. On the contrary, the teacher or counselor may disagree vigorously with a youngster, but must base his arguments for disagreement upon logic to refute what the student has stated. Unless a counselor thoroughly understands what has *actually* been said, he cannot effectively devise a counter argument. Young people, like others in our society, are poor listeners. Many of the young radicals have blatantly stated that *no one* is willing to listen to them, and this unfortunately is partially true. What they are really saying, however, is that everyone is not willing to listen and *immediately agree* with the pronouncements made. We cannot hope for improvement in the area of human relations until such time *all* people learn to listen as well as to speak. Many debates have been lost by contestants who, upon finishing one speech, immediately began preparing for their next without listening attentively to their adversary. If teachers and counselors would become as effective at listening as they are at speaking, they would accomplish more in the field of teacher-student relations as well as in counseling.

WHERE ANGELS FEAR TO TREAD

Fools do occasionally walk in where angels fear to tread, and some of these fools are psuedopractitioners who have just enough training in psychology to be dangerous. Teacher-training programs include course-work in general psychology, human growth and development, and frequently a course or two in adolescent psychology or similar elective subject matter. The brief exposure to psychology which is included in many teacher-training programs, or even in a specialization of counseling and guidance, does not qualify an individual to be practicing psychiatry. Psychiatry is an exacting form of medical science that demands years of study and preparation. Conscientious teachers and counselors naturally have a fervent desire to aid youngsters in solving their problems, but there are many psychological difficulties that can be resolved only through competent psychiatric treatment. The partially trained person who attempts to psychoanalyze an individual who has a deeply seated neurosis or psychosis is just as guilty of practicing medicine without a license as is one who indiscriminately prescribes medicines for a communicable disease.

Teachers who counsel youngsters have a responsibility for keeping notes and observing the behavior of students who might need psychiatric assistance, and if necessary aiding such students by referring them to a psychiatrist through the proper channels. If a teacher notices a youngster who demonstrates erratic behavior and seems to have a serious psychological problem, he should of course be concerned. The youngster must be counseled in an attempt to more closely observe his behavior and get his reactions to his school life, but not to effect an analysis and cure. The teacher should refer any deeply troubled student to the counselor after having apprised the counselor of the situation. In turn when the counselor believes the student is in need of psychiatric assistance, he should contact the parents and if necessary make arrangements for proper care. Thus the major role of either the teacher or counselor becomes one of identifying troubled youngsters, not curing them.

Most students will become troubled at some time, but most overcome their difficulties in a day or two and return to their normal behavioral pattern. Teachers with students in class who seem to have an established pattern or extraordinary behavior should observe them more closely. When such cases are brought to the attention of the school counselors and administration, it might be their desire to take further steps in assisting the student and the teacher may be called upon for further reports. Behavioral reports from teachers are often used by psychiatrists in their attempt to analyze and evaluate student behavior. By conscientious observation and reporting a teacher can do much to aid a disturbed youngster, but to attempt the role of psychiatrist would only lead to disaster. The diagnosis and treatment of mental disease is predicated upon logic and inductive reasoning which in turn is based upon years of training and past experience with similar cases. Therefore, the diagnosis and treatment of psychological disorders must remain in the hands of those who are competent in their field, not minimally trained "amateurs."

Many teachers have worked in other occupations, either during their college years or in the summer months. Students will often ask teachers about opportunities in various trades and professions. If the teacher has a thorough knowledge of a particular trade he can counsel the student effectively; if not, he can refer the student to a particular tradesman within the community or to the school counselor who should have vocational information of value. Vocational counseling is a necessary component of the guidance function, perhaps one of the most important. Every student has aspirations to succeed in some form of enterprise where he can earn his living, and should begin to formulate his choices early in life. These choices are often influenced by teachers and counselors who take an active interest in the lives and ambitions of their students and are willing to exert efforts to assist them. A substantial number of students attend college, but those who don't are infrequently counseled in relation to job opportunities and technical school programs. Most high schools emphasize their college preparatory programs and not vocational training. As a result, many teachers and counselors assume that most youngsters will attend college and direct their guidance efforts toward those students. Teachers should become more aware of the technical skills and building trades, and then would be more receptive toward youths who are interested in these methods of earning a livelihood.

Teachers of secretarial sciences, the school nurse, industrial arts personnel, and teachers of agricultural classes should make every attempt to gather information relative to those fields which they represent. By the same token biologists, chemists, and physicists should avail themselves of literature that relates to the sciences and the healing arts. Physical educators ought to compile a file of information about community recreation, industrial recreation, physical therapy, occupational therapy, and teaching opportunities in public and private schools and state institutions such as reformatories, prisons, and mental hospitals. If all materials were cataloged and made available to students a wealth of information would be disseminated and could complement the vocational counseling accomplished by both counselors and teachers. Libraries could shelve vocational information and make it more available to students than if filed in the counselor's office. However, it would be prudent to publish a list of teachers who could be contacted about various fields of specialization. This would place the teacher in the role of a resource person and enable him to counsel many students that could not be reached by the regular school counselor due to time considerations.

Some school districts have frowned upon teachers acting as counselors because of unsatisfactory experiences which have occurred. In order to have teachers successful as counselors and recognized as resource people, a planned program should be initiated by school districts so that students would know whom to contact in their search for vocational information. Such a program should be coordinated by the regular school counselors to avoid confusion and duplication. The school counselors should welcome such a program because even though they are competent and well trained the ratio of students to counselors prohibits them from functioning as effectively as they might. When youngsters repeatedly go to the counselor's office for information and find that he or she is too busy, they become discouraged and leave. By spreading general counseling tasks, especially those related to vocational guidance, among the general faculty, many youngsters could be reached who might otherwise remain in ignorance. To delegate *all* forms of counseling only to those who have the proper credentials is blatantly unfair to the students. In the first place, a student is forced into confiding to someone in whom he may not have any confidence, and in the second place, time and the large student-counselor ratio does not permit such a policy.

In formulating policies to control the guidance function, school boards and administrators should always be cognizant of what is best for the students, not what is administratively expedient. If an in-service program must be implemented in order to effect proper counseling and guidance techniques by teachers, it should be held. The school counselors probably would welcome suggestions from the general faculty and could discover that their student load would be lightened and at the same time the guidance function enhanced. Such an in-service training program would be valuable in structuring a functional guidance program and would afford an opportunity to explore the areas in which teachers and counselors could be the most effective. It would also provide an opportunity for clinical psychologists and psychiatrists to apprise counselors and teachers of the personal problems which youngsters have and need referral and what data might be of value to them.

Students need and indeed seek guidance from their teachers. They are unsure of their futures and respect the experience and training of adults, whether they are willing to admit it or not. People who counsel must be sympathetic and understanding but must not patronize or vacillate. When a student asks for an opinion, it should be based upon sound logic and, if necessary, research. No teacher or counselor should come forth with ready-made answers to any question unless he is relatively sure of his information and sources. Nothing can more quickly lead to distrust than assumptions and answers which are given to a student and are later found to be erroneous. Truth sometimes does hurt, but it is far better to cope with facts than to deal with glittering hopes that are soon smashed.

Physical educators and athletic coaches frequently find the level of aspiration of certain students far exceeds their ability to perform a certain skill or play a particular position on a team. It is wise for the counselor to inform such a youngster that he should always endeavor to perform as best he can but he must not expect to exceed his ability. This word of caution should not imply that the student's performance is poor, but it does allow him to progress as far as he can with the realization of possibly never achieving a level of performance which is beyond his level of motor ability. The truth may be a bitter pill to swallow at the time it becomes known, but at least it is an honest appraisal.

ADVISEMENT VERSUS GUIDANCE

Advisement is the act of telling a student what is known to be factual and therefore places the adviser in a position of having to be knowledgable about the subject or subject area in which he is advising. Physical educators, as other teachers, should be competent in advising youngsters either directly or indirectly. Direct advisement consists of providing firsthand factual information, and indirect advisement would consist of referring a student to someone known to be competent in his field. Many students desire information about college life and courses of study. However the regular counselors do not have the time to independently advise each student who seeks such knowledge. Most high school seniors, although visited by college representatives, have little knowledge of various courses of study, credit hours, graduation requirements, and other pertinent factors. Teachers, by virtue of their own college experience and their periodic return to summer school, can provide a valuable service in advising those who are preparing to enter college. A central file of college catalogs could be compiled by the school library, but to many high school students a catalog is meaningless unless it is properly interpreted by a person with experience as a student.

Competent physical educators should constantly be searching for bright young students who show an interest in physical education and the teaching profession. Such youngsters seldom realize what type of preparation is needed to become a physical educator. They fail to understand the need for the basic sciences or other facets of professional coursework, and usually have no knowledge of general education, major and minor subject areas, sequence courses, admission procedures for professional programs, grade point averages, and similar areas of concern. The secondary teachers could render a valuable service to higher education if they would undertake a program of individual advisement to prepare students *before* they actually enroll in college.

Preprofessional organizations have been established in some public schools and have advised students on a group basis. Obviously, not all students are interested in attending the same college or university, therefore a variety of physical programs must be investigated to afford the student the opportunity of choosing the college or university of his choice. Sponsors of Future Teachers of America have performed a commendable service in advising students about education in general, but many such sponsors do not have the background to render advice about specific courses of study. College and university departments of physical education usually provide a valuable source of information, much of which is not necessarily found in the general college catalog. A departmental library should contain brochures from a number of colleges and universities as well as their general catalogs and should be updated at least every three years. Most students attend college in their home state, and state institutions are willing to provide catalogs and brochures for purposes of advisement. If a student is interested in a particular school but no information is available, a postcard or letter requesting such information could be sent to the registrar or Division of Student Services at the school in question. The adviser should be sure that the institution is fully accredited prior to recommending it to any student. After a few years an adequate supply of information will be gathered for the future use of many students.

Group advisement consumes less time than individual conferences and stimulates students to ask questions and compare programs. No student should select a college or university before he has an opportunity to compare the programs or advantages and disadvantages of several colleges and universities. Youngsters who desire to enroll in community colleges need advice relative to transfer programs from two-year institutions to the four-year schools. Many junior colleges now have transfer guides which they are willing to provide for precollege advisement. Many college students select a particular institution for rather superficial reasons and later regret their choice. Transferring from one institution to another can be expensive because of incompatible programs that will not laterally transfer hours from one course of study to another. Physical educators who stay abreast of the trends in their discipline can render a valuable service to high school students who are desirous of entering the profession and have no knowledge of what is involved. If the physical educator is one who has not apprised himself of current trends and literature in his field, his advice could be of little value other than in very general terms.

A physical educator, biologist, mathematician, home economist, librarian, sociologist, or commercial teacher may be asked for advice about a business or profession with which he is not fully acquainted. In some instances, the teacher should be willing to seek out someone who is knowledgable and willing to discuss his field with the student. The student then can contact the recommended person and gain the advice he needs. It is not enough for a teacher to merely tell a student to "ask someone who knows"; the youngster might not know anyone to contact and therefore would never acquire the information he needs. School counselors should have a list of people in the community to whom they can refer youngsters and this list should be available for staff members to consult so that they in turn can properly advise students. Indirect advisement of this kind is vitally needed if students are to be provided adequate direction. Such programs require extensive community contacts and cooperation but are a necessary part of the counseling function.

To clearly differentiate between guidance and advisement would be difficult indeed. The term guidance usually implies that alternative solutions to problems are selected by the student and the guidance counselor assists the youngster in directing his approach. Guidance is the act of directing the thinking of a student rather than advising or telling him what should be done. Students need to know how to analyze and solve problems, and therefore guidance serves a very worthwhile function. However, occasionally advice is needed and indeed solicited by students. Every classroom teacher should take a course in counseling and guidance so he has a knowledge of the proper techniques that should be used.

Counseling and guidance is a field which has become a very significant aspect of education in recent years. The educational process has become more complicated as the American life style has changed. There are more occupations than ever before that demand technicians and specialists; more high school graduates are attending college and the junior college movement has grown immensely. As a result students need information in greater quantities than they ever have in the history of our country. Many high school students are concerned about their futures not only as workers but as citizens. Boys seek information about military life as well as about their careers, and girls are now as concerned about careers as they once were about marriage and family life. Our economy demands specialists in business as well as in the professions and trades. The age of computers has precipitated an entirely new industry and these machines have also added new dimensions to existing enterprises. The present variety of job opportunities has created a multitude of choices for young people and have been found to be frustrating by some. Counseling and guidance services must assist students in making proper selections so that their lives become less frustrated, however there are not enough counselors to accomplish the task nor the money to pay them. As a result of the impossible task assigned to trained counselors, teachers are having to assume a greater responsibility in the role of guidance counselors and physical educators are no exception.

Guidance demands patience and understanding. It is easy to advise or tell a youngster something but it is much more difficult to direct a student's actions by assisting him in the selection of his alternatives and then to hope he will make a correct decision. Every youngster deserves to succeed in the decision-making process; however there is also some merit in electing the wrong course of action and occasionally failing. When a youngster does elect an unsatisfactory procedure he should be further counseled so that he has an opportunity to reflect and determine why he failed and what steps he might have taken to avert failure.

Not all teachers have the temperament to counsel effectively and should not be expected to do so. Those who discover that students are seeking them as counselors should feel flattered that they are held in such high esteem, but should never engage in a personality contest in the attempt to "solicit business." Students who voluntarily seek counseling will benefit from it. Those who are *told* to consult a teacher or counselor are often resentful and will not respond well to either advice or guidance.

A full-time counselor should never have to serve as the school disciplinarian even though some schools have employed people for such a role. The teacher, by the very nature of his position, has no alternative but to discipline students when the need arises. His counseling duties however are placed upon him by students who seek his assistance, and those who have been disciplined by him may elect to consult with another person. Therefore, no conflict of interest should arise because the initiation of the guidance function lies with the student who is free to consult the counselor of his choice.

Counseling can be rewarding as well as interesting. However it can also be disappointing if the results are negative rather than positive. The teacher who counsels must be prepared for successes and failures and every conceivable type of behavior from his counselees. Some young-sters will be sullen and profane, others will cry, and still others will be elated and joyful. A teacher not prepared to be confronted by the emotions of his students should not attempt to guide and advise them. If he does discover that he is serving as a part-time counselor he should be serious in his purpose and professional in his attitude at all times, and must always remember that he is dealing with a fellow human being who has entrusted him with his most cherished possession—himself.

QUESTIONS FOR DISCUSSION

1. Who should be involved in the counseling function and why?
2. What are the characteristics of a competent counselor?
3. Are *all* teachers suited to the counseling function? If so, why? If not, why?
4. What are the characteristics of a good listener and why are they important?
5. What are the sources of information a counselor must utilize and of what importance are they?

6. Why are the terms counseling and psychoanalysis not compatible? Why should school counselors refer certain students to psychiatrists?
7. What is vocational counseling? Who should be engaged in vocational counseling and why?
8. Why should the administration assign any counseling duties to teachers? Why not let the professional counselors handle *all* of the counseling and guidance work?
9. How does advisement differ from counseling?
10. What is "group counseling"? What values would such a process have?
11. What is meant by a violation of confidence? Of what importance is *confidence* in the relationship between counselor and counselee?
12. Of what value are records to a counselor and when should they be used?

CASE STUDIES

MISS PARRISH

Miss Parrish had taught physical education at Jefferson High for many years and had the distinction of being a teacher who was sought after for counseling and guidance by a great many girls. Miss Parrish was an extremely professionally minded individual and very much a lady. She had a fine educational background and was respected by all who knew her. She enjoyed her informal counseling and regarded such sessions as a privilege rather than a duty.

Susan Holcombe was a bright student who aspired to being a lawyer. She was led to believe that law schools frowned upon female students and therefore did not provide them with the same opportunities extended to the men. She contacted Miss Parrish for advice only because she believed Miss Parrish had always been honest with her in previous encounters, not because of her knowledge of the legal profession. Miss Parrish realized, after discussing the matter with Susan, that the girl was reluctant to consult one of the local attorneys about her chances of becoming a lawyer and volunteered to assist Susan in gathering the information she desired.

Miss Parrish encouraged Susan to write a letter to the dean of the law school at the state university and explain her desires to him. She informed Susan that a direct approach would be best and she should request clarification of any controversial issues. Susan wrote the letter, and together she and Miss Parrish edited it to be sure it was grammatically correct. The letter contained all of the pertinent questions that Susan wanted answered and also inquired as to the rumors she had heard regarding discriminatory practices between the sexes.

Susan not only received a voluminous letter in response to her inquiry, but also was contacted by telephone and further questions were answered. Susan subsequently enrolled at the university in a prelaw curriculum and has since completed law school and is a successful practicing attorney.

Miss Parrish assisted many girls with similar problems, some of major proportions and others of lesser consequence. She never undertook a problem she felt unqualified to handle and frequently referred students to others for help. Her greatest strength was her willingness to listen to any and all youngsters who contacted her and to help them in any manner of which she was capable.

QUESTIONS

1. Why do you suppose that Susan Holcombe contacted Miss Parrish for advice about the legal profession rather than the regular counselor? What do you think of Miss Parrish's method of solving the problem?

MR. RENTON

Mr. Renton was an art instructor who desired to enter some aspect of administration. He decided that counseling and guidance was a challenging field and therefore took enough college coursework in the area to be certified. He was later appointed to a position which was untenable at best, that of both counselor and disciplinarian.

Renton was long on advice and short on guidance. He could hardly wait for a student to explain a problem before he in turn offered a solution. He was not at all gentle in his approach and frequently barked solutions as though they were orders to be followed strictly by the book. Many students voiced the opinion that they believed Renton to be frustrated in some way and refused to consult him about anything. When asked for vocational advice or counseling, Renton referred them to a stack of literature on whatever subject they happened to be interested in. Those who sought advice about college programs were similarly issued a catalog.

Mr. Renton's position as school disciplinarian involved the assignment of detention hours, recommendation for suspension or expulsion, and many minor forms of reprimand. He meticulously cataloged various offenses and devised a formula for the punishment of each. When a student would enter his office with a rather dubious excuse for absence or tardiness, Renton would classify it, usually sign it unexcused, and assign the punishment on the spot. Very seldom did the youngster have an opportunity to explain his side of the story; needless to say, the students had very little respect for Mr. Renton's abilities and most of them avoided him like the plague.

One of Renton's other tasks was to assist youngsters with their high school curriculum. He evaluated their cumulative folders and informed them whether or not they should follow a general course, a commercial course, or a college preparatory curriculum. Marcia Evans, a sophomore student, entered Renton's office one morning after just transferring to the school from an adjacent district. Her grades were very good but upon evaluating her folder Renton discovered that she had an I.Q. of only 81. He thereupon informed her that she should pursue a general course of study and she would have to be very diligent in her studies in order to obtain passing grades in "his school." Marcia balked at the idea of a general program because she staunchly maintained that she wished to attend college. Renton countered that she was mentally unfit for college, whereupon the girl began to cry and left the office. The next morning Marcia's parents came to see Mr. Renton and demanded that she be enrolled in a college preparatory program. He stated that in his professional judgment the girl would never be able to handle the coursework and cited her I.Q. as his basic source of evidence. Mrs. Evans asked Renton to contact the school district from which Marcia had transferred and inquire about her ability as a student there. Renton reluctantly placed a telephone call and discovered that the I.Q. cited in the cumulative folder was the result of the only intelligence test the child had ever had. The counselor also remembered that Marcia had been ill the day the test was administered and suggested that before Renton scheduled the girl he administer another mental maturity test. The test was administered the following morning and mysteriously Marcia's I.Q. rose from 80 to 130. Renton informed the parents that Marcia could enroll in the college prep program but also told them they should seek out the counselor in the other school district and scold him for entering a "phony score" on Marcia's cumulative folder.

QUESTIONS

1. How would you evaluate Mr. Renton as a professional? How would you evaluate him as a person?
2. Do you believe that Mr. Renton ever seriously gained anything from the formal coursework he took in counseling and guidance? Support your contention.
3. What do you think of combining the function of disciplinarian with that of a

guidance counselor? Why? Do you suppose this had anything to do with the manner in which Renton behaved?

4. What does the Renton case tell you about evaluating records? Be thorough in your answer.

MR. SCHEFFORD

Mr. Schefford was the Dean of Instruction at a small liberal arts college. As such he dealt with a great many department heads and faculty members who had problems to solve and who sought his guidance and advice. Schefford was deaf in one ear and therefore turned his good ear toward the speaker in order to hear better. He had developed a fine attitude toward listening because of his handicap and employed the art to the fullest degree.

Schefford discovered that faculty members would usually talk for some time and then begin to pose solutions to their problems without any guidance from him other than an occasional nod of the head or word of agreement or disapproval. Frequently Schefford would never utter a word during the entire session of "counseling." The counselee would pose a few alternatives to his problem, decide upon which course of action he would take and then rise to leave, thanking Schefford profusely for his time and assistance without realizing that he alone had been responsible for solving his own difficulty. Even more remarkable was the fact that faculty members openly mentioned how helpful Schefford had been and how attentive he was to their needs.

QUESTIONS

1. Do you believe that Mr. Schefford was perceptive, lazy, or just not able to cope with the problems presented to him? What was his strong point and do you consider it of value to others?

MR. HARSHFIELD

Mr. Harshfield accepted a position at a small high school as a physical education teacher and football coach. He was the type of person who related well to youngsters, was a good disciplinarian, and had a very diversified academic background. Harshfield spent many long hours planning his curriculum, served on some of the more important school committees, and was generally accepted as a teacher of some merit.

During the second year of Mr. Harshfield's tenure he was called into the principal's office and asked if he would be willing to serve as the school's counselor. Harshfield replied that he did not feel qualified since he did not possess the academic background for the position and knew that he could not be certified as a counselor. The principal informed Harshfield that he knew of no other faculty member on his staff who related as well to students or had any more background; therefore the district could probably have him certified on a restricted basis.

Harshfield took the matter under advisement and finally condescended to accept the position temporarily until the district was in a financial position to hire a full-time qualified guidance expert. After taking the job Harshfield contacted the county school superintendent's office and requested information which would provide him with a list of individuals to whom he could refer students if he believed them to have problems that he was either unqualified or unable to cope with. He secured a reference list of professional personnel and proceeded with his duties.

Most of the youngsters Mr. Harshfield encountered were interested in vocational guidance or college opportunities. He built up quite a file of vocational information and college cataloges and worked diligently with the students in making their selections. He discovered that information not available in his literature could be readily obtained in most cases by mail or by telephone. The youngsters were appreciative of his efforts and the time he was allocated for counseling was completely filled with appointments. Harshfield had relatively few students to counsel with personal problems and most of those were of a minor nature which the youngster usually worked out by himself. Problems which seemed serious were immediately referred to the county clinic inasmuch as Harshfield believed that he was definitely not qualified to administer psychiatric assistance. After working for two years as the school's only counselor, Harshfield was relieved of his responsibilities and replaced by a trained practitioner. He has since returned to his physical education and coaching duties on a full-time basis but discovered that his "after hours" counseling load is still fairly heavy.

QUESTIONS

1. Should Mr. Harshfield have accepted the job of counselor without the proper training? What would you have done if you had been placed in similar circumstances?
2. How did Harshfield handle the situation in your estimation? What other measures might he have taken?

MR. TINDELL

Mr. Tindell, principal of Glenwood High School, was rather concerned about the lack of opportunities for his students in relationship to career guidance. Two full-time counselors had been hired for boys and girls, but the school was in such an isolated area Tindell didn't believe the youngsters were receiving enough exposure to businesses and professions that were not present in the community. The high school was consolidated and therefore served a wide geographic area, but was not readily accessible to a metropolitan environment where opportunities would present themselves.

Tindell called a general faculty meeting and asked for suggestions that might solve his dilemma. Some of the faculty members proposed that one day a year be set aside as a career day on which speakers would be brought into the school to represent various businesses and professions. It was further proposed that in order to avoid annual duplication a three-year plan be drafted and only a few speakers be brought in each year and their areas be explored in depth.

Teachers from the several disciplines were charged with the responsibility of contacting members of the various businesses and professions represented within the county and in the nearest metropolitan area. The school board agreed to provide an automobile for those speakers who would have to come to the school from some distance away and the Chamber of Commerce made arrangements to house such persons at one of the local motels.

The initial planning of the event was a laborious task but the enthusiasm of students and teachers alike made it a more enjoyable task. A list of speakers was drafted and a three-year calendar of areas to be discussed was presented to the general faculty. After some deliberation and adjustment the program was adopted and invitations were sent to the speakers. The invitations were mailed well in advance of the time that the program was scheduled and the response was most satisfactory.

After the speakers arrived on campus they were given the opportunity to deliver their addresses and were then placed in individual rooms large enough to accommodate students who were interested in investigating the area in depth. Four "buzz" sessions were held for each speaker so that youngsters who were interested in more than one occupation would have the opportunity to explore each area. After the sessions were concluded an evaluation period was held and students could comment on factors they felt should be included in the program for the following year.

Many youngsters discovered interests that had not really occurred to them before and others became disenchanted with occupations they had previously considered. The counseling and guidance personnel made some excellent contacts as did individual teachers. In virtually every respect the program was believed to be successful and has been held annually for many years since.

QUESTIONS

1. What do you think of Glenwood High School's "career day"? Are you acquainted with similar projects?
2. What type of speakers might have been brought in by people in the physical education department? Do you think that these speakers would have any answers the teachers themselves could not have provided?
3. What determines the success or failure of such a venture as that initiated at Glenwood High School?

SUGGESTED RELATED READING

Kemp, Clarence Gratton, *Intangibles in Counselling.* Boston: Houghton Mifflin, 1967.

Nichols, Ralph G., and Thomas Lewis, *Listening and Speaking.* Dubuque, Iowa: Wm. C. Brown, 1954. A guide to effective oral communications.

Strang, Ruth, *Counseling Technics in College and Secondary School.* New York: Harper, 1949.

Strang, Ruth, *The Role of the Teacher in Personnel Work.* 4th ed. rev. New York: Teacher's College, Columbia University, 1953.

Strang, Ruth, and Glyn Morris, *Guidance in the Classroom.* New York: MacMillan, 1967.

Tyler, Leona E., *The Psychology of Human Differences.* 2nd ed. New York: Appleton-Century-Crofts, 1956.

13
EDUCATION OR TRAINING—
THERE IS
A DIFFERENCE

SPECIALIZATION AT THE EXPENSE
OF ENVIRONMENTAL APPRECIATION

Education is the process whereby human beings become aware of man's past and present surroundings in an attempt to apply such knowledge to the solution of current and future problems. A truly educated person must possess a broad base of information in a variety of disciplines if he is to attempt to understand the world around him and thus appreciate his own environment. To be educated implies that one has profited from his learning experiences and is therefore more perceptive than he was before. Education is not characterized by mere class attendance; it must encompass a meaningful experience which in some way will alter future behavior. The mere absorbtion of facts, without a subsequent attempt to utilize such facts, is of no value. If one is to consider himself educated, he must be prepared to capitalize upon the information to which he has been exposed and thereby improve himself and those with whom he comes into contact.

The term "general education" has been used in conjunction with programs in teacher education for many years. Few students have really considered the implications of their general education other than to rebel at the thought of taking courses in which they profess little interest or aptitude. Students who major in physical education, as well as those specializing in other disciplines, fail to recognize the value of a broad spectrum of *required* general education courses which they often consider irrelevant to their particular area of concentration. The failure to communicate the value of general education courses to students preparing to become physical education teachers lies with those who are involved in programs of professional preparation. Some college professors have never taught in the public schools and others have not taken the time to explain general education as it relates to the teaching profession.

All people, and especially educators, should be aware of man's past and present accomplishments, and must be willing to impart this knowledge to the students who comprise the new generation. Teachers and students alike cannot hope to function effectively in our present complex society unless they have an awareness of the world in which they live. This awareness can come only through diligent study of the humanities, sciences, mathematics, and the social and behavioral sciences. To eliminate these areas from the course of study for future teachers would indeed be fallacious.

Flexibility in curriculum is currently being demanded on more and more college and university campuses. Students frequently desire to take only those subjects in which they are interested and in many instances the demands of students are indulged, if for no other reason than to avoid confrontation. Scholars for many years have labored to devise curricula which would afford an opportunity for the student to explore many areas and at the same time be demanding enough to instill self-discipline and proper study habits. In their haste to accommodate the demands of a few vocal students, some colleges and universities have made their general education programs so flexible that they have actually provided additional specialization. Such specialization has come about by stipulating that the student may elect to take a large number of credit hours from each of three or four major areas such as the liberal arts, science and mathematics, social science, or some similar combination. By proper manipulation, a student could conceivably fulfill his requirement by taking nothing in humanities other than ceramics, or similarly he could elect all natural science courses in the science-mathematics block. He might also elect only anthropology courses to fulfill his social science requirement and never be exposed to economics, history or government classes. In effect, the intended flexibility of the liberalized general education curriculum results in providing the student with a very narrow background of subject matter and certainly does nothing to enhance his knowledge as a truly educated person.

School children look upon teachers as sources of wisdom and knowledge because they are the first group of people the youngster has encountered that represents the formal educative process. They expect teachers, regardless of their particular discipline, to possess the information necessary to answer many questions perhaps left unanswered at home. They realize the function of teaching is to impart knowledge and they are eager to approach their favorite teacher regarding any subject that may be of interest to them at a particular time. Physical educators must be able to communicate with students and should therefore be conversant in many fields; they must possess a basic knowledge themselves, and must further be able to refer students to the proper sources of information relative to questions that involve a depth of study. Many times a teacher can reach a student by evidencing some knowledge in a field of interest to the student but not necessarily directly related to the subject presently under discussion. Students, like all other human beings, are drawn closer to people who show an interest in things that are of interest to them. Such interest does not have to be characterized by expertise in the field, but should at least demonstrate basic knowledge and an ability to ask pertinent questions and respond in an intelligent manner to queries by the student. A physical education teacher who refuses to discuss any area, other than his own discipline, should not expect the same positive response from his students as one who is versed in other disciplines and who is skilled in communicating such knowledge to his students.

Physical educators work with students in a rather informal setting and therefore have an opportunity to discuss many problems with them. Coaches who travel with their athletes find an even greater opportunity to discuss various subjects with students on athletic trips, and soon discover that athletes do not confine their discussions to game procedures and strategy. Teachers and coaches who have a variety of interests and an ability to communicate those interests command greater respect than those who do not. Many youngsters are interested in world affairs, scientific discoveries, human behavior, art, literature, and other related subjects. No rational teacher or coach should expect students to confine their thoughts to football, basketball, wrestling, baseball, track, or similar motor activities. Naturally the teacher should relate first to his particular subject, but more importantly he should learn to relate to his students.

The faculty room at any public school is more than just a place in which lesson plans are made and coffee or soft drinks are dispensed; it is a forum for the problems of the day and the problems of the school. Faculty room discussions involve every subject from politics to philosophy and for a teacher to divorce himself from such discussions, due to ignorance or lack of self-confidence, is tantamount to committing professional suicide. The entire school community centers around the faculty room and any teacher who desires to become a member of that community should be ready to assume an active role in the deliberations that take place in faculty discussions.

There is nothing more indicative of a person's intelligence and knowledge than his ability to rationally discuss a variety of subjects. Likewise there is nothing quite as damning to the intellectual character of an individual as the lack of ability to discuss anything other than his own field of endeavor. Coaches and physical educators who insist upon directing their conversations exclusively toward athletic contests and the prowess of their "boys" are indeed to be pitied. Even though they may be well versed in other fields, they must demonstrate such knowledge to their fellow teachers. The teacher of any subject who dwells upon his particular discipline and shows no interest in the problems of others will find that he is often gently but firmly excluded from general discussions, and moreover that his actions may serve to alienate him from others when he attempts to enlist their aid to assist in projects for which he is responsible.

A sound general education does not cease upon graduation from college. The teacher, more than any other professional, must keep abreast of current knowledge in a variety of fields. One way by which this can be accomplished is through use of the school library. There is usually some time during the week a teacher can avail himself of library facilities even though it may be before or after school. If a teacher does not desire to use school library facilities, he may elect to spend some regularly scheduled time at the public library. A teacher using neither school nor public library facilities should subscribe to various publications that will enable him to broaden his knowledge. Such publications should include not only professional journals but also periodicals which relate to a variety of subject fields outside the realm of professional education. There are many weekly and monthly publications which are well written and serve as a source of enlightenment for the busy person. Unfortunately, many people rely upon the television screen as their source of information and neglect to read extensively. Many worthwhile documentaries and newscasts are presented on television as well as certain entertainment features, some well executed and others of questionable value. However, to become addicted to the television set at the expense of reading and research is unfortunate for any teacher. Professional preparation for teaching does not cease at the college classroom door, nor does it conclude with the completion of the bachelor's degree or the doctorate for that matter. Teachers, like medical practitioners, must continually upgrade themselves. If they allow themselves to lapse into a sedentary professional life, they soon discover that teaching has lost its luster and they have become drones rather than efficient producers of knowledge.

As previously mentioned, physical educators and coaches have for many years been stereotyped as individuals possessed of brawn but lacking in mentality. Cartoon caricatures frequently depict the physical educator or coach as a rather rotund individual clothed in a baggy sweatshirt, ball cap, and ill-fitting trousers. He often has a blank look on his face and, if captioned, the utterance is laced with poor grammar and inane remarks. Recent television productions have also portrayed physical educators as something other than scholarly even though such productions are supposedly researched. Perhaps the writers, during their research, have discovered that scholarly physical educators and coaches are not truly representative of the profession and indeed are portraying characters which are composites of examples they have observed. If this is true, the professional image of the physical educator has certainly suffered and needs to be revamped.

The leaders in the field of physical education have been found to be highly articulate individuals and as such should strive to instill those whom they prepare for the profession with scholarly traits and interests. If physical education is to be recognized as an integral and important aspect of public education, the practitioners of the discipline are going to have to exert every effort to overcome the image which has been established by the entertainment media. It is one thing to be ridiculed occasionally, but another to be consistently made fun of. One of the primary reasons our image has been so poor is that we have not made a concerted effort by both communication and deed to eradicate such an image. Physical educators must therefore be constantly alerted to the fact that their actions, words, and attitudes are not only a reflection of themselves, but also of their profession.

Frequently physical educators and coaches are asked to speak at various functions. A public speaker is confronted with the task of pleasing the audience, holding their interest, and selling his product. The product being sold could be a particular philosophy or a program such as physical education or athletics. However, the speaker, male or female, discovers that in order to sell a product the salesman himself must first be sold to his audience. Any representative of a product or firm in the business of retail selling knows that in order to survive the personnel as well as the product must have public appeal. People frequently buy from salesmen because they like the demeanor of the person, and place such evaluation above that of the product. If products and programs sold themselves, there would be no need for sales representatives in the first place. A merchant could simply list the various qualities of his merchandise and let the public flock to his doors. Most people who are in the market for a product have a certain amount of sales resistance. It is this resistance that must be broken down by the salesman if he wishes to consummate a deal. Some salesmen use pressure tactics and others use a soft approach; however, none are merely content to stand idly by while the customer inspects the merchandise. As teachers of physical education, we must also use a sales approach by first selling ourselves as articulate, learned individuals, and later by demonstrating our product through action and communication. There is no place in the profession of physical education for the inarticulate dolt who is, in all probability, as lazy and ill equipped in his teaching assignment as he is in academics. Such people tend to detract from the profession and constitute the poorest form of advertising that is imaginable.

If schools and colleges are called upon to provide speakers they should make every attempt to furnish the most knowledgable and articulate personnel available, and should insist that such speakers be adequately prepared for the task at hand. Some individuals are accomplished speakers and others are not; therefore unless a competent speaker can be furnished upon request the invitation should be declined. Furthermore, no speaker should ever accept an engagement unless he knows just what type of material is desired, how long his speech should be, and by what type of audience he will be confronted. Not all speakers are humorists and those without a natural flair for humor should not attempt it. Nothing detracts more from a well-delivered speech than a poorly related anecdote or a joke told in poor taste. Needless to say, dirty stories add nothing to a speech and only tend to brand their author as one so hampered in the use of the language that he must resort to very base stratagems. Such stories also constitute an affront to anyone in the audience who resents such antics and may well insult their intelligence.

Training, as differentiated from *education*, commonly means preparation in a particular skill. Therefore, training implies a rather narrow and explicit form of indoctrination which in general is associated with a technical endeavor. Training is usually associated with the program of instruction administered in a particular discipline that provides the "tools" with which the individual practitioner will function. In this context, the training of a physical educator would involve coursework in the professional activities, scientific bases, and methods of teaching. It is then possible to *train* a person to teach a particular skill without having *educated* him relative to the appreciation of things other than his particular endeavor.

Teachers cannot afford the luxury of a training program in which they must master only their own limited subject matter because they are constantly dealing with youngsters who have varied interests. Assuredly a master teacher must be extremely competent in his area of instruction, but he must extend himself beyond the limitations of such functions into the world around him. Again this is simply due to the fact that teachers teach *students* not subject matter. Some would argue that subject matter is of paramount importance. It is extremely important, but the consideration of what effect the subject matter has on the student is even more important. Therefore, a competent teacher must be extremely well versed in his subject field as well as in the area of human relationships. In addition he must be able to relate to the interests of others who are not involved in his subject area and through such relationships he may be more able to enlist the support of others for his program.

An auto mechanic may be well trained to repair a car, an electrician may be skilled in his trade, and a plumber in his. However, these individuals work primarily with *objects* not people; they deal with inanimates, not with emotions. This is not to imply that tradesmen should not be educated as well as trained; however, it does imply that the *education* of a teacher is equally as important as his *training* because of the very nature of his work in dealing with human beings. Certainly all people in all trades and professions should be well educated, but such an education may not be as critical to their immediate task as it would be to the teacher. Education to the teacher is a matter of proficient functioning *along with* his training in a particular discipline, and the two cannot be divorced if teaching is to be considered effectual.

YOU ARE NOT THE ONLY FROG

The beginning teacher must realize that he is not the only frog in the educational pond; that his is not the only discipline to be taught; and that in order for him to assume an effective professional posture he must communicate with his colleagues. Communication with others of varied interests requires one to have broad interests himself. Relationships between people can best be stimulated through intelligent discussions related to common subjects. Once rapport has been established between faculty members, mutual respect is founded which subsequently should lead to mutual cooperation. The prudent physical educator should search for common interest bonds between himself and his colleagues and should wholeheartedly support their interests and programs as part of the school program. Merely being a casual observer of activities other than those sponsored by the physical education department is not enough. Active participation in and support of all school activities are the keys to success for any teacher. Education must be a cooperative venture if it is to be successful. Faculty members who function as separate entities bent only on forwarding their own personal interests serve to create unnecessary administrative problems and dissension among students and fellow faculty members alike. Students and faculty who perceive that physical education teachers are interested in factors other than motor skills should have a greater respect for the physical educator as a sensitive human being, not just a builder of muscle tissue. Such students and faculty will become more interested in assisting with activities sponsored by the physical education department. Schools that have broken the barriers of communication by cooperative endeavor are generally more advanced in their educational procedures than are schools that allow self-interest groups to dominate the scene.

Youngsters who are interested in many different fields enroll in physical education classes. Some of these students have only a speaking acquaintance with such fields as science, drama, speech, industrial arts, political science, and other similar disciplines. Many such students would pursue these interests further if only encouraged by a person who was knowledgeable in the field. The physical educator should, by virtue of his general education, possess more knowledge in a wide variety of fields than his students and could well serve to motivate them toward their particular interest. Students need encouragement to take part in school activities; some are unsure of themselves and need reassurance from teachers. Athletes in particular should be encouraged to take part in activities other than athletics. Many athletes possess natural qualities of leadership and should be directed toward school government. Others have strong voices and intelligence which would serve them well in forensics or drama. Still other students enjoy singing or related musical pursuits and need a boost from interested faculty members. The physical educator or coach is usually an individual with whom students closely relate and he or she may exert a powerful influence over the lives of students.

The influence exerted by any teacher over a student should be positive. Therefore it follows that male students should emulate *gentlemen* who are well read and possessed of a wide range of interests, and female students should emulate *ladies* who evidence similar qualities of educational background. The physical educator who strives to epitomize the image of a well-educated human being and manifests the best qualities of both mental and physical development will soon discover that both his professional and private lives will be enhanced tremendously.

People teaching in any discipline are provided with a sound general education but are further trained in a specialty. No teacher can spend his entire life dedicated only to his field of specialization at the expense of his private life. Teachers, no matter how dedicated, soon discover that their families demand some attention and they themselves need a certain amount of diversion from their daily tasks. Family outings and hobbies should be undertaken in order to escape the demands of teaching and school problems. Activities which constitute a hobby for one individual may well be a "busman's" holiday for another. Physical educators frequently engage in hobbies that are completely removed from physical activity. One notable in the profession is an accomplished bird watcher as well as an avid amateur historian. Other physical educators dabble in the arts, some being accomplished sculptors and painters. No matter what the hobby, it should not necessarily assume the character of one's daily work. Frequently, musicians and artists engage in tennis or golf as a hobby and physical education teachers involve themselves in music or art. As an avenue toward better communication between faculty members, the physical educator should pursue a reciprocal agreement for instruction between himself and his fellow teachers. To exchange tennis or golf lessons for instruction in music, art, or information relative to raising tropical fish would indeed be a proper means toward better intrafaculty relationships and could be profitable to all parties concerned. For a specialist in any teaching discipline to isolate himself and channel his entire life toward his specialization is fallacious and only leads to shallowness and boredom.

ERUDITION VERSUS PSEUDO-INTELLECTUALISM

The erudite person is one who is widely knowledgeable and possesses a thirst for learning new things—he is indeed a true scholar. As a scholar, the erudite individual engages in a constant search for truth by employing logic and perception in his quest for knowledge. He maintains an open mind and is willing to studiously investigate both sides of any controversy before arriving at his conclusions. The scholar has learned that listening rather than talking is often beneficial to him as a vehicle to gather information and that he must reserve judgment relative to what has been said until he has thoroughly evaluated the data.

The pseudo-intellectual is a person who has gleaned a few facts, failed to study a subject in depth, and does not really know the difference between *saying something* and *having something to say.* Such people have a habit of displaying their ideas and ignorance to any group that will listen. They are often boorish and somewhat forceful in trying to foist their ideas upon others. The pseudo-intellect often closes his mind to the thoughts of others and never really listens to the other side of any argument. He is usually so busy trying to formulate his next speech that he does not pay strict attention to what is being said by others. Faculty meetings are frequently dominated by shallow thinkers whose major contribution is confusion rather than logical thought.

The new teacher should enter into faculty discussions only when he sincerely believes his contribution is worthwhile. He should patiently listen to others and attempt to sift factual and relevant material from mere diatribe. Moreover, he should always be receptive to constructive suggestions and maintain an open mind at all times. He should not hesitate to make suggestions of his own after carefully weighing facts and evidence, but he should also be willing to defer to the experience and the counsel of others.

The mind of the erudite human is like a sponge; it absorbs information, catalogs those things factual and logical, and then expels the extrinsic material which is of no value. Such a person is vitally concerned with the issues at hand, more so than with himself. The pseudo-intellectual, on the other hand, is genuinely interested in himself and how well he can manipulate others to his side of an argument. He is unwilling to study a problem in depth and alter his presuppositions even if he discovers evidence which would refute his original arguments. Many such people espouse solutions to problems without ever thoroughly understanding the problem itself, much less the solution. The pseudo-intellectual's favorite game is to attack his adversaries with a barrage of words and phrases, many of which are trite and meaningless, in an attempt to overwhelm his opponents with weighty verbosity usually devoid of logic. Any individual who must work cooperatively with a group, such as a teacher, can ill afford a pseudo-intellectual approach to school problems. If he does attempt such a guise he will shortly be discovered and branded as the true phony that he is. Conversely, the erudite teacher who demonstrates the characteristics of a deep and rational thinker willing to formulate his opinions carefully and pose his solutions with tact will be welcomed as a "fellow" in his school community.

Convictions should be held by all teachers, but they should be convictions based on acceptable quantitative and/or qualitative evidence. Physical educators must have sincere convictions about the programs they offer and such convictions should be founded upon research, empirical evidence, and sound philosophic constructs. However, some convictions may necessarily have to be altered should research or other evidence prove previous thoughts to be erroneous. Professional positions or convictions have been changed in many disciplines because of new information. The scholar not only keeps abreast of new developments so that he may progressively change if need be, but he welcomes such change as a benefit to his field of study. Only those who are professionally shallow and bullheaded refute positive and progressive alteration of patterns in their disciplines.

THE WORLD IS YOUR OYSTER—NOW WHAT?

The newly certified physical educator who is confronted by his first teaching position is beset with many problems and questions. He must recognize that he will be working with other experienced professionals and must be patient in the attempt to invoke his own ideas and methodology. Successful freshman legislators in the Congress of the United States soon learn that in order to be effective they must listen attentively to others and use discretion in initiating legislation. Beginning teachers frequently defeat their own purposes by forcing their ideas, no matter how valuable they might be, upon an administration which is prone to discount the impetuousness of youth. The more prudent neophyte should content himself with listening and learning during the initial months of his employment until he is accepted by his administration and colleagues. He will also discover suggestion serves better than criticism and demand. In any deliberations of curriculum or school policies the first-year teacher should feel free to state his convictions, but should always use the utmost discretion and be willing to defer to logic when obviously superior to his own. He should question, but his questions should be sincere attempts to learn, and he should never attack a policy unless he has absolute evidence to illustrate how and why the policy is questionable.

Many exemplary contributions have been made to physical education by those who approach their professional tasks with an intelligent and quiet approach rather than with bluster and bombast. The quiet approach may not be the most rapid, and the conscientious professional may discover that he must lose a few "political" battles in order to win the war of reform in his discipline. The new teacher cannot afford to criticize the efforts of colleagues who have lapsed into a sedentary professional life but must set the example by sound teaching methodology and educational excellence. He should seek counsel where needed and give his advice only when it is solicited. By following such precepts the new and enthusiastic teacher may inject vitality into a lagging program without also engendering the enmity of his associates.

Words have never substituted for action, nor rhetoric for worthy accomplishments. Students are quick to discern the difference between one who talks a good game and one who involves them in a true learning experience. The teacher who is well organized and demonstrates a mastery of his subject matter will ultimately endear himself to his students without engaging in a personality contest to do so. Each day of instruction should be accepted by the teacher as a challenge to his intellect and capabilities. Some days will be more educationally productive than others, but one should never become discouraged and lose faith in his own ability. Perseverance and tenacity of purpose are the characteristics that usually separate the successful practitioners from the unsuccessful in any endeavor. Teachers must learn that when class interest lags they in turn must display more enthusiasm than ever. Occasionally the teacher must even resort to theatrics in order to make a point. Those who are accomplished teachers are frequently people who involve themselves in "method acting" as a teaching device.

Physical educators who are young and enthusiastic occasionally find that their ideas and suggestions are not as readily accepted by others as they might desire. It is a natural instinct to become angry when confronted by seemingly endless red tape and opposition. However, anger is often the wind that blows out the lamp of the mind, and should not be substituted for a rational approach of waiting for a more propitious moment to arise for implementing new concepts. Teachers who become angry when their ideas are refuted only tend to alienate themselves further and frequently inflict a mortal wound upon their cause.

There will be many instances when the young teacher finds that obstacles of one sort or another hinder his professional progress. Instead of becoming emotionally upset at such inconveniences, the prudent individual should take cognizance of himself to determine whether he himself is responsible for his problems, and if not, what he can do to overcome his difficulty. It is much easier to blame others for curricular problems, improper maintenance, insufficient equipment, and related difficulties than it is to render assistance in the solution of such problems. Such teachers become so antagonistic over difficulties that they themselves become part of the problem and contribute absolutely nothing to its solution.

Changes in curricular offerings, revisions in facilities, and additions of equipment require decisions on the administrative level that are often compounded by budgetary difficulties and cannot be resolved within a short period of time. The beginning teacher should be aware of the financial condition of his school district and never expect that just because an idea or concept is good it can be funded immediately. Some administrators have served long enough to realize that certain expensive program alterations have never been followed through, and the financial outlay for such programs has been wasted. Therefore, administrators learned to evaluate the performance of new teachers very carefully prior to allocating funds for every new idea that comes along, no matter how beneficial it may sound.

Teachers who maintain equipment and budget wisely may ultimately discover such practices are looked upon with favor by both administration and school board members. Once it has become apparent a teacher is concerned with the expenditure of tax dollars, and strives to exact the greatest value from funds expended, his future projects may receive more serious consideration. No teacher should ever budget so closely that he or she causes the program to suffer unnecessarily. However, *all* teachers should be aware they are spending other people's money and should never be wasteful. The finances of the public schools are critical and are certainly the subject of public scrutiny. Each teacher should therefore exert his best efforts to obtain the greatest amount of instruction possible for each dollar spent.

Intelligence, outstanding educational background, and professional training are not enough for the beginning physical educator to rely upon if he desires success in his field. Personal demeanor is of primary importance to a teacher and cannot be stressed too strongly. Good manners are the essence of proper professional conduct. Many people of lesser ability advance far more rapidly in their chosen professions because of good manners than those who are inconsiderate and boorish in their attitudes toward others. Research shows there is no significant relationship between a college grade-point average and on-the-job performance in the teaching profession. Personality and consideration for others are potent forces used by successful physical educators. Teachers should always treat both students and fellow faculty members as they themselves would like to be treated. It should also be noted that discourteous behavior on the part of others should not prompt discourteous attitudes on the part of one's self. To be known as a friendly and courteous colleague, who is willing and ready to assist students and fellow faculty members, is indeed the key which may well unlock many doors to professional accomplishment.

Physical education is rapidly changing from the traditional regimented approach to one of a conceptual nature. Some of the more experienced teachers in the field have not stayed abreast of such changes and the young physical educators are actually better prepared to implement conceptual approaches to teaching. Every physical education teacher should chart his own course but should use common sense and judgment in implementing the new approaches so sorely needed. Many students who have previously been exposed to traditional approaches will tend to reject conceptual instruction simply because it is human nature to challenge any change that seems to be vastly different than what has gone before. Such changes in curriculum and methodology may not be received with enthusiasm by some administrators, parents, students, or school board members and must therefore be explained logically. Physical education faces the same challenge that confronted those who led the way in implementing the "new math." Education of the publics served by the school becomes vital to the success of physical education and should therefore be included in the plans of any physical educator who hopes to achieve success in altering patterns of the past.

Physical education classes are taught by some individuals who are completely against regimentation of any kind and by others who regiment their classes to the extent that they resemble the most orderly of military organizations. These teachers could be classified as radicals—either overly permissive or completely militaristic. Another group of teachers are those who are lazy and have no professional pride whatever; these are the drones. The competent teacher is one who, through logical analysis, is willing to borrow from the old, implement the best of the new, and by diligence and study dedicate himself to the art of teaching. Success breeds greater success and those who dedicate themselves will discover that working with youngsters can be a most exhilarating experience. School boards and administrators *usually* are quick to recognize teaching excellence. However, some administrators in large districts do not have the time to assess individual teachers and must depend upon supervisors who are subordinate to them. Both supervisors and executive level administrators get *feedback* from students, and such people tend to place credence in what they hear. Therefore the individual who justifiably deserves optimum performance from teachers is the student. The student is not only the focal point of the educational enterprise, but his satisfaction may also be the major key to personal professional success.

Those who are entering the profession of physical education should hold their heads high and be proud of what they are. They should never be ashamed of the fact that they do not teach what is commonly called an academic subject. What they should concern themselves about is whether their particular discipline is so structured as to exert a profound effect upon the lives of their students. The value of any discipline can only be measured by its impact upon students, not upon its recognition as being academic or nonacademic. Many youngsters have profited from courses in motor activities. Their life styles have been completely altered by their exposure to physical education and athletics and they may well look upon these experiences as the most rewarding of their entire school career.

After completing undergraduate studies, physical education teachers should return to graduate school to further prepare themselves for their chosen profession. Graduate school should be more meaningful to those who have taught for a few years than to those who pursue an advanced degree immediately after receiving the baccalaureate. There is no substitute for experience in any field, and the experience one gains in education can only be substantive if it relates directly to working with students, fellow faculty, staff members and all of the attendant problems. Student teaching cannot offer the kind of background found while functioning as a full-fledged physical educator. Until a teacher is really on his own and has been confronted by the types of decisions one must make as a professional individual, he will not have a full appreciation of his discipline.

Graduate students actively engaged in the teaching process can readily relate to on-the-job problems that are foreign to the average classroom student. Relationships with the administration, community, and colleagues, plus problems dealing with facilities, equipment, maintenance, and fiscal matters, are factors that make graduate classes interesting and meaningful because they are real rather than hypothetical. The sincere graduate student and physical educator is one who enrolls to gain new ideas but at the same time is interested in finding some solutions to the problems he already has.

The potential graduate student should use care in selecting the school he desires to attend. He should first ensure that the institution's graduate program is accredited and that it will provide him with the coursework he needs. Graduate studies should not be a mere matter of expediency, but should be carefully planned by both the student and his adviser working together as a team. Graduate studies usually involve some degree of specialization, either in the scientific bases, administration, correctives, or perhaps movement education. The student should select the program most closely tailored toward his interests and then seek an institution offering a quality program in that area of the discipline.

The curriculum one undertakes during graduate work is of course most important; however the people one encounters at graduate school can be of extreme value. People who have common problems can share their ideas and discuss mutual interests. Fellow graduate students, especially those pursuing the doctorate, are often aware of job opportunities and in fact are frequently potential employers themselves. Therefore, the contacts made while pursuing graduate studies are second only to the coursework itself and the conscientious graduate student would do well to avail himself of all the acquaintances he can make while attending school. Ideas for new teaching approaches are often spawned on college campuses and research facilities are usually available for the pursuit of individual problem analysis. All graduate students should become aware of the facilities and programs available to them and utilize these to the fullest extent.

Unfortunately there are some graduate students who become

members of the army of "course takers" who have no definite aim other than to amass credit hours for pay purposes. These are usually the same students who were marginal performers as undergraduates and who are drones as teachers. Such people have no place in the profession and should be eliminated. Hopefully, with the supply of physical educators far exceeding the demand, teacher-training institutions and school districts alike will be more selective in choosing those for the privilege of teaching children. Our youngsters are entitled to excellence, and hopefully through the dedicated efforts of all truly professional physical educators, they shall have it.

QUESTIONS FOR DISCUSSION

1. What are the values of general education to the individual teacher? How may he utilize these values in his daily work?
2. How does education differ from training?
3. What are some of the disadvantages of building extreme flexibility into a general education curriculum for teachers?
4. Why would a sound general education be of as much value to a physical educator as it would to an academician?
5. How can professional physical educators effect a change in their image as envisioned by the lay public?
6. What effect does the demeanor and physical image of a teacher have upon students? Why is a positive image of importance to our profession?
7. What positive steps should be taken by physical educators to relate to other teachers in the school community and why?
8. How does the pseudo-intellectual teacher adversely affect the teaching profession?
9. Is there such a thing as professional protocol in the field of education? If so, why is it important for young beginning teachers to observe protocol? If not, why?
10. What are some of the benefits of graduate school that cannot be gained only through classroom experiences?
11. Why should graduate study be pursued *after* one has taught for a year or so? Of what advantage would it be to attend graduate school immediately after receiving the bachelor's degree?

CASE STUDIES

MR. MITCHELL

Harry Mitchell had been graduated from college with an expanded major of concentration in physical education. In addition to the regular requirements Mitchell had completed every coaching course available but had taken almost no elective coursework outside his area of immediate interest. His knowledge of the humanities, political science, social and physical sciences was very limited. He was a likable fellow who worked diligently in his classes and on the court and field.

Mitchell was an excellent coach. He was a good disciplinarian, possessed a thorough knowledge of fundamentals in football and basketball, and got along well with his athletes. In athletics he was innovative and many of his creative ideas were adopted by other coaches in the league in which his teams played. Coach Mitchell attended numerous coaching clinics and was quite active in the state coaches association.

Some people are natural conversationalists. Harry Mitchell was such a person as long as the topic related to athletics, but when the conversation drifted into some other phase of human endeavor Coach Mitchell immediately became relatively silent. Obviously he was uncomfortable in the presence of others who were unwilling to devote an entire discussion to athletic statistics, anecdotes related to athletic performance, or the future possibilities of athletic training procedures.

As a result of his all-encompassing interest in athletics, Mitchell's teams were quite successful but never received the full support of many faculty members who did not know Harry Mitchell as a person. Many of these people believed the coach was a rather self-centered individual who was either so ignorant of his surroundings that he should never have entered education, or he was an absolute egotist who cared nothing about interests other than his own.

One of Coach Mitchell's assistants became rather concerned about various comments he had heard regarding Harry's conversational demeanor and realized the athletic program was suffering because of Mitchell's inadvertant ignorance. The assistant, Mr. Martin, knew Harry extremely well and engaged him in a discussion of the matter. He tactfully suggested that Harry was such a dedicated person he had perhaps not realized how his public image had become somewhat tarnished by his obsession with only one line of communication. He further explained to Harry that someday in the future Mitchell might desire to leave coaching and should begin now to prepare himself for such an eventuality.

Mitchell listened to Martin and became more ill at ease as the conversation progressed. He was visibly upset, but being an intelligent person began to realize his shortcomings and asked Coach Martin for advice. Martin discreetly advised Harry that his first chore would be to become a good listener. Then he should discuss athletics only when others initiated the subject in conversation and should try to contribute occasionally when the discussion moved to another topic.

It was difficult for Mitchell to remedy a habit that had been a part of him for so long, but he approached the task with the zeal characteristic of his coaching. It took a number of years for Harry Mitchell to alter his behavioral pattern but through concerted psychological effort, diligent reading, and attentively listening to others, Coach Mitchell came to be accepted by his colleagues as a much more astute individual and a true member of the school community.

QUESTIONS

1. How would you evaluate Harry Mitchell's general education background in terms of his being able to relate to areas other than his own specialization? Do you believe that Coach Mitchell was possibly handicapped by his background?
2. Does the Mitchell case provide you with any insight into your own general education? If you have misgivings, what could you do to alleviate them? Should Mitchell be blamed for his shortcomings? If so, why? If not, why?

MR. CANNON

Bill Cannon was a very unusual man. He was a mathematics teacher well liked by his students and extremely well accepted by his fellow faculty members. Also he was an accomplished musician, photographer, marksman, and amateur political scientist. In addition he was involved in many community affairs including local government and church work. His awareness of his surroundings and other people indeed made him a delightful fellow to be with.

Cannon was not a monopolist in conversation and discussion, but was a formidable contributor of knowledge. Never did he seem to be opinionated to the extent that he would not defer to logic which was better than his own and he had a wonderful facility for having something to say, rather than merely saying something in order to be heard. Young teachers came to look upon Cannon as a man to seek for advice. He was always ready to assist others when he believed he had something of value to offer, but was quick to refer people to a more competent source if necessary. When confronted by a question for which he had no background, he was humble enough to plead ignorance.

Mr. Cannon taught for many years at the same high school and was loved by some but respected by all. He was the quiet type of individual who performed an exceptional service to education and to his community, and would long be remembered by his students and colleagues as a man who was possibly a genius in his own right, both socially and intellectually. When Bill Cannon sponsored a project, he didn't have to enlist assistance, people just naturally volunteered. They believed that anything Cannon was doing must be worthwhile, and moreover they simply felt obligated to the man because of his intelligence and personal charm. Bill Cannon was not an extrovert in any way, he just had a knack of quietly getting things done in an efficient manner that was never offensive to anyone. No one ever really thought *about* Bill Cannon, they thought with him.

QUESTIONS

1. What were Bill Cannon's strong points? Why do you suppose he was so well liked by his fellow faculty members and students?
2. Do you believe that Cannon's educational background was as much a factor in his development as perhaps his overall environment? How would you rank Mr. Cannon as a "well-rounded individual"? Why?

MR. SPIEGEL

Mr. Spiegel had entered Marcus High School as teacher from another part of the country. He had been an "all-American" football player and an Olympic boxing contender, and was assigned to teach physical education and coach both football and basketball. His teams in the eastern part of the nation had been extremely successful, but he and his family were forced to move to a warmer climate due to Spiegel's poor health. A warmer dry climate was beneficial to him because he was suffering from asthma.

Coach Spiegel instituted a comprehensive physical education program and worked diligently to ensure its success. A much more "wide open" offense was instituted and the defenses were superior to any that had previously been taught. His boys were exposed to new playing techniques and adapted exceptionally well. During his first season the football team won nine games and lost but one.

Spiegel was a taskmaster who demanded a 100 percent effort on the part of his boys. Always gentle but firm, he never let a mistake go unnoticed. A very comprehensive unit in combatives was employed in his physical education classes but he was also a firm believer in coeducational physical education and cooperated fully with the women's department. He insisted that his students and athletes behave as gentlemen and chastised anyone severely who uttered any foul language in his presence.

Coach Spiegel's undergraduate studies had been in physical education and his masters degree had been awarded in political science. He was an avid reader and possessed a broad range of subject matter interest which he conveyed to his students, both after class and on athletic trips. His students were encouraged to take part in school plays and other activities which he believed to be of value in rouding out their educational background. Civic organizations called on him to speak on various subjects because he was not only well versed, but because he had a wonderful facility for putting his subject across. Some of his colleagues were jealous of Spiegel and made no atempt to conceal their emotions. This was indeed unfortunate as it served only to alienate such people from the students and Spiegel's faculty friends who held him in such high esteem. Due to his interest in other activities, however, Spiegel was supported by most of the general faculty and townspeople

Mr. Mundt, the principal of Marcus High, had never participated in athletics or combatives and was vigorously opposed to such activities because of their "dehumanizing" effect upon youngsters. He aligned himself with faculty members who were jealous of Spiegel and proceeded to do everything possible to thwart Spiegel's program. The principal made fun of the coach at every opportunity and insinuated that he was a grossly ignorant individual capitalizing upon the abilities of his boys to further his own "questionable career." Mr. Spiegel never reacted to the castigations and innuendo put forth by Mundt, and indeed went out of his way to be considerate of the man and his position. Other faculty members tried to intercede with Mundt on behalf of Spiegel but were always met with rebuke.

It became apparent to Mr. Spiegel that he could not get along with Mundt and believed in the interest of harmony he should perhaps seek another job. The students and many faculty members implored Spiegel to stay at Marcus but he accepted a position elsewhere. The school which employed Spiegel made excellent use of the man's talents and he rapidly became one of the most revered men on the faculty, respected not only for his coaching ability but also for his intelligence and his contributions to the school and community at large.

QUESTIONS

1. What factors in Mr. Spiegel's background do you believe contributed to his being disliked by some of his colleagues? Do you believe that Spiegel engaged in dehumanizing tactics?

2. How would you defend yourself against attacks such as those made by Mr. Mundt? Do you think that Spiegel should have pressed the issue? Why or why not?

3. How would you evaluate Mr. Mundt as a principal? Do you believe that Mr. Spiegel should have received more backing from the faculty? Why, in your estimation, was such backing not forthcoming?

MR. RAMIREZ AND MR. BELLOWS

Mr. Ramirez was a professor of English at a junior college and had completed his graduate studies at an Ivy League university as the recipient of a Phi Beta Kappa key. Mr. Bellows taught in the same department and had been graduated from a local state university as an honor student in the masters program.

Ramirez was an extremely intelligent fellow who had personally initiated many campus symposia and other intellectual exercises. He was a deep thinker who had written and published many professional works, and also had taken an active part on campus committees and related activities. Students taking classes from Ramirez found him to be an excellent teacher, demanding but fair. His material was presented in a common sense manner and every facet of each lesson was patiently explained. Ramirez encouraged initiative and extra credit assignments from his students but regarded such assignments as work done beyond that normally expected, never as a substitute for the prescribed load.

The contributions that Mr. Ramirez made to his school were inestimable; however, many times he was never extended proper credit for his efforts. A well-rounded, no-nonsense person who believed in the education of the whole person, he sought to develop himself physically as well as mentally. For physical activity Ramirez followed a strenuous exercise and sports program, and his mental prowess was sharpened by prodigious study and perception. He was always energetic toward any physical challenge and his appetite for intellectual fulfillment seemed boundless.

Mr. Bellows regarded himself as an extreme intellect. Usually he was contemplating some sort of monumental project which would somehow catapult him into the ranks of the true intelligentsia of his field—unfortunately, none of his ideas ever reached fruition. Bellows would sit in committee meetings and periodically contribute as if on a schedule. He would frequently make remarks unrelated to the subject being discussed but always carefully colored such remarks with as many polysyllabic words as possible, and usually with an obviously feigned accent.

Bellow's students commented frequently about not being able to understand assignments or explanations because of a language barrier. When students personally confronted the man with this charge, they were told that college freshmen should be expected to know such words and he could not hlep it if they had "chosen to bask in ignorance." In no instance did Bellows offer to assist students with vocabulary building even when it was apparent that this was one of their most prevalent needs. Bellows continually informed students of their mediocrity and decried the fact that the public schools were doing such a poor job of preparing people for college.

Physically, Bellows was about 50 pounds overweight, and when asked by Ramirez why he didn't engage in an exercise program, replied that he didn't believe in such "animalistic practices" and was on a rigid diet to control his obesity. The "rigid" diet was possibly attempted at home but certainly didn't deter Bellows from frequenting the student center and ingesting huge portions of cake or pie. If asked about the violation of his diet, Bellows usually replied that he needed the additional sustenance in order to overcome fatigue and get through a trying day.

QUESTIONS

1. Which man would you regard as a true intellect, Mr. Ramirez or Mr. Bellows? Why?
2. What were the factors distinguishing Mr. Ramirez as a teacher?
3. What do you think of Bellow's approach to the inadequacy of his students? What approach would you have taken in a similar situation?
4. Do you feel that somewhere in his education Mr. Bellows was "short-changed"? How could this happen to an honor student?

MR. SHULL

Mr. Shull was a high school athletic director. He succeeded a gentleman who moved into an administrative position at another institution but prior to leaving had initiated a new but marginal athletic budget.

Shull realized his budget was small and therefore called his coaches together for an assessment of the situation. The coaches evaluated their respective budgets carefully and decided they needed additional funds if they were to purchase quality equipment that would be suitable for their needs. Shull asked each coach to inventory all items used for his particular sport and report to him the needs for the following year. After receiving the reports, Shull asked the district office for a figure which would indicate the projected high school enrollment for the following year and from that figure computed the increase in the number of boys who would possibly take part in athletics.

Shull, in agreement with his coaches, decided they should attempt to purchase only first quality equipment with the intention of obtaining more years of use from such items than could be expected from inferior goods. The superintendent concurred with the idea of quality purchase but stated he would like to see the athletic department order a small number of less expensive items of the same type in order to implement "cost-use" study. Shull agreed, but with the stipulation that only *nonprotective* equipment be of an inferior type; the superintendent agreed.

The athletes were apprised of the fact that some "inferior" goods of a nonprotective nature would be issued and periodically they would be passed from one player to the next so that no single person would be penalized by having poor equipment. Each item ordered was dated as to time of purchase and marked accordingly. All equipment was placed on inventory with the name of the manufacturer and the price and date of purchase duly recorded.

After each season of play all equipment used for that particular sport was cleaned, repaired if necessary, and properly stored. Records were kept of repair costs and were entered on the equipment inventory cards. At the conclusion of a three-year period it was found that most of the less expensive clothing items were completely worn out and the quality goods were still serviceable for additional use. As these items wore out Shull computed a prorated annual cost and discovered that the more expensive items were actually less costly in the long run than the inferior goods. A report was sent to the school board of the results of Shull's study and was received with enthusiasm by all members.

Shull and his coaches never "padded" a budget and compared merchandise thoroughly before buying anything. They established a reputation in their league of having exceptionally fine equipment, and especially so in view of the small budget that they were forced to work with. No student was ever turned away for lack of equipment and all were issued the best gear available.

The styles used in game suits were such that in the event an item became damaged beyond repair, it could easily be replaced. Even though the suits were simple in design they were always outstanding because of their obvious quality and fit, and the athletes were proud to wear them. In no case, however, did Shull hesitate to purchase the latest and most improved quality of protective devices such as football pads, headgear, and baseball batting caps. These items were believed to be strictly functional and cost was considered as secondary to safety.

QUESTIONS

1. How would you evaluate Mr. Shull's approach to budgeting for athletics? Do you believe that his system is, or should be, widely used?
2. Do you believe that Shull's approach had any educational values? If so, what were they?
3. Would you like to work for a man like Shull? Why or why not?

MISS TREADWAY AND MISS ALBERT

Miss Treadway received her education at a small liberal arts college that had an excellent reputation for its teacher-training program. Miss Albert had attended a major university where women's physical education programs had gained national prominence. Both teachers were currently teaching in a public high school and each had taught for approximately the same number of years.

Miss Albert was a demanding but skillful teacher. She was always well prepared for her classes, assumed her extracurricular duties and carried them out with dispatch, and related well with other faculty members. Her life out of school was devoted to bowling leagues, women's softball, the Business and Professional Women's Association, and a directorship on the community recreation board. She did not become involved in any church activities and declined to serve on professional education committees either at the local or state level.

Miss Treadway was meticulous in her planning of units and lessons, worked diligently on school committees, served as an officer in the Association of American University Women, sang in her church choir, and was an active member of her professional association.

Miss Albert loved to "talk shop" but seemed to be able to discuss little else when confronted by people who were not particularly interested in athletics. She therefore did not mix socially and, even though friendly with her fellow faculty members, shied away from discussions of an academic nature which were not related to her field.

Miss Treadway attended many social gatherings and was frequently called upon for lectures and consultation in regard to her field of specialization and other areas as well. She was eager to engage in conversation with fellow faculty members about school life, world affairs, politics, and general contemporary subjects which were not remotely connected with her discipline. Not only was she accepted in such discussions, but her opinion was highly respected.

Although Miss Treadway and Miss Albert shared an office at school they did not associate with each other in community affairs.

They apparently got along well together as professionals but otherwise went their separate ways. After teaching for approximately five years, Miss Treadway was invited to accept a position on a college faculty and therefore resigned her public school position. Upon Miss Treadway's leaving, Miss Albert wished her the best of luck and remarked, "I certainly wish someone would give me a break like that someday." Miss Treadway smiled and replied that she also hoped Miss Albert would get a similar "break."

QUESTIONS

1. Do you believe that the educational background of Miss Treadway and Miss Albert had anything to do with their demeanor and the conduct of their lives? What factors might have differed in their college lives?
2. Which person would you rather have on your staff, Miss Treadway or Miss Albert? Why? (They were both good teachers.)
3. Why did Miss Treadway get such a "break" as to be invited to teach on a college faculty? Who makes such "breaks"?

SUGGESTED RELATED READING

Adler, Mortimer Jerome, *How to Read a Book*. New York: Simon and Schuster, 1940. The art of getting a liberal education.

Adler, Mortimer Jerome, *The Time of Our Lives*. New York: Holt, Rinehart & Winston, 1970. The ethics of common sense.

Conant, James B., *The Education of American Teachers*. New York: McGraw-Hill, 1964.

Hutchins, Robert M., *Some Observations on American Education*. Cambridge, England: University Press, 1956.

INDEX

ABCDEFGH798765432